T3-BOV-887

Japan and the United States Today: Exchange Rates, Macroeconomic Policies, and Financial Market Innovations

Hugh T. Patrick
Ryuichiro Tachi

Editors

CARNEGIE LIBRARY
LIVINGSTONE COLLEGE
SALISBURY, N. C. 28144

Center on Japanese Economy and Business
Columbia University

NEW YORK, 1986

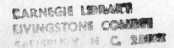
CARNEGIE LIBRARY
LIVINGSTONE COLLEGE
SALISBURY, N. C. 28144

120952

Japan and the United States today.

  Bibliography: p.
  Papers presented at a conference held at the Essex House, New York, June 4–5, 1986.
  1. Foreign exchange problem—United States—Congresses. 2. Foreign exchange problem—
Japan—Congresses. 3. United States—Economic policy—1981- —Congresses. 4. Japan—
Economic policy—1945- —Congresses. 5. United States—Foreign economic relations—
Japan—Congresses. 6. Japan—Foreign economic relations—United States—Congresses.
I. Patrick, Hugh T. II. Tachi, Ryūichirō, 1921-   HG3903.J35 1986 332′.042′0952   86-
32640   ISBN 0-231-06575-2

Copyright © 1987 by the Center on Japanese Economy and Business
All rights reserved
Printed by Capital City Press, Montpelier, Vermont

Contents

Sponsors

THE CENTER ON JAPANESE ECONOMY AND BUSINESS
Graduate School of Business, Columbia University

The Center on Japanese Economy and Business was established in 1986 under the directorship of Hugh T. Patrick, R. D. Calkins Professor of International Business at the Columbia Business School, and a noted authority on the economy of Japan.

The Center is responsive to the need for greater understanding of Japan in American business, professional, and government sectors. Drawing on the University's extensive resources, the Center plans an active program of research and training. Its initial focus will include U.S.-Japan economic relations, comparative financial markets, macroeconomic policies, and the dynamics of Japanese business behavior.

The Center on Japanese Economy and Business
522 Uris Hall, Columbia University, New York, New York 10027
Telephone: (212) 280–3976

THE INSTITUTE OF FISCAL AND MONETARY POLICY
Ministry of Finance, The Japanese Government

The Institute of Fiscal and Monetary Policy was founded in May 1985 as a research organization in the Ministry of Finance. Its President is Ryuichiro Tachi, Professor Emeritus of the University of Tokyo.

The Institute's purpose is to study the implications for economic policy of structural changes in the Japanese economy and growing interdependence among nations. Goals include consolidating research efforts, developing an information system, and training personnel to deal with these issues. Sponsorship of conferences and a Visiting Scholar program reflects the Institute's emphasis on an exchange of views with scholars from abroad.

The Institute of Fiscal and Monetary Policy
3-1-1 Kasumigaseki Chiyoda-ku, Tokyo 100 Japan
Telephone: (03) 581-4111 Ext. 5221 or 5226

THE FOUNDATION FOR ADVANCED INFORMATION AND RESEARCH, JAPAN

The Foundation for Advanced Information and Research, Japan was established in November 1985 as a private, non-profit organization. FAIR's President is Taroichi Yoshida, former President of the Asian Development Bank and currently an advisor to the Industrial Bank of Japan.

FAIR's purpose is to promote international understanding and cooperation in the development of the Pacific Basin area. The Board of Governors and Partners of FAIR consists of representatives from major Japanese companies. Prominent figures from government as well as private organizations serve as Advisors and Councilors, while many leading scholars from abroad are Associate Members.

The Foundation for Advanced Information and Research, Japan
Toranomon Central Building, 1-7-1 Nishi-Shimbashi, Minato-ku, Tokyo 105 Japan
Telephone: (03) 503-0231/3

Preface

In RESPONSE to the need for greater understanding of Japan, the Center on Japanese Economy and Business plans a regular series of conferences, seminars, and publications. The first conference was held in New York on June 4–5, 1986. It brought together American and Japanese decision makers in finance, business, and government as well as academic specialists on each country's economic policy. The papers, speeches, and discussion produced by the conference have been edited and collected in this volume.

The views expressed herein are those of the participants and do not necessarily reflect the views of any organizations with which they may be associated. The conference was jointly sponsored by the Center on Japanese Economy and Business at the Graduate School of Business, Columbia University, and the Institute of Fiscal and Monetary Policy of the Japanese Ministry of Finance, together with the Foundation for Advanced Information and Research, Japan. Financial support for the conference was also provided by IBM World Trade Americas/Far East Corporation and by Sumitomo Corporation of America.

HUGH T. PATRICK
Director, Center on Japanese Economy and Business

December 1986

Introduction

Hugh T. Patrick

Director, Center on Japanese Economy and Business, Columbia University

Ryuichiro Tachi

President, Institute of Fiscal and Monetary Policy, Japan Ministry of Finance

THREE TYPES of major change have occurred in the international financial and economic environment from early 1985 through the first half of 1986. They are having profound impacts, both short-run and longer-run, on the American and the Japanese economies. The most important has been the dramatic drop in three major world prices: the price of oil, the price of the dollar in terms of major foreign currencies, and the levels of market interest rates. Second has been the U.S. government's decision to join its major economic partners to intervene in the foreign-exchange markets to drive down the overvalued dollar, reflected in the Group of Five (G-5) Plaza Agreement announced September 22, 1985. The third has been the huge increase in Japanese capital flows into New York financial markets, notably Japanese purchases of U.S. Treasury bills and government bonds.

In order to evaluate and examine the implications of these changes, the Center on Japanese Economy and Business at Columbia University and the Institute of Fiscal and Monetary Policy of Japan's Ministry of Finance held a policy-oriented conference on "Japan and the United States Today: Exchange Rates, Macroeconomic Policies, and Financial Market Innovations" at the Essex House, New York City on June 4–5, 1986. The speakers, panel members, and participants in the audience comprised a distinguished group of American and Japanese members of the private financial and business, government, and academic communities. Total participation was limited to 150 persons, approximately 60 percent from American institutions and 40 percent from Japanese institutions. This volume presents the edited papers and discussion of the conference. We believe it provides relevant and useful, up-to-date information and analyses on the macroeconomic, exchange rate, and financial market conditions and policy issues in both the United States and Japan.

While the conference focused on the United States and Japan today, discussion was naturally set in a broader context. First, it was well recognized that because the United States and Japan are the world's largest and second-largest market economies, the issues are global rather than narrowly bilateral. U.S.

and Japanese economic growth, exchange rates, trade, and account balances are deeply intertwined with what goes on in the rest of the world as well. In some respects the United States and Japan are extreme cases in the global economy, even though both currently have very low inflation rates, large government budget deficits, and relatively high real interest rates. The United States has the world's largest trade and current account deficit, spending more than it saves at home, and still high though declining rates of unemployment. Japan has the world's largest trade and current account surplus, saving considerably more than it spends at home, and very low though rising rates of unemployment. U.S. policies have been key in bringing about a reduction in nominal interest rates throughout the world since dollar-denominated financial claims are an overwhelmingly large share of world finance. The sharp drop in oil prices within the past year has directly benefited Japan the most among the industrial nations.

While the emphasis was on the present and the future, it reflected a historical context well understood by all. When Professor Richard Cooper published his book *Economic Policy in an Interdependent World* some eighteen years ago, few foresaw just how interdependent with other economies the United States would become, and no one predicted the size, scope, and degree of interdependence which characterizes the relationship between Japan and the United States today. After all, both nations have sharply different historical and cultural backgrounds, even as they share fundamental beliefs in democracy and in a free market economic system. Both nations possess basically strong economies, and support the system of free trade. While the United States has grown absolutely, its relative economic position in the world has declined. Over the same period, Japan has risen to prominence as a major participant in world production, trade, and finance, and indeed as a major competitor for many American companies.

Even more dramatic than changes in trade have been the changes in finance—domestically within each country, bilaterally, and globally. In the late 1970s, under the pressure of inflation the United States moved rapidly to deregulate further what was already a quite market-oriented financial system. As a consequence, there has been a burgeoning of American financial markets, a spate of financial innovations, mergers and acquisitions among financial institutions, and the waxing and waning of the fortunes of individual institutions. Japan too has been engaging in dramatic financial deregulation and liberalization—though more cautiously and from a much higher initial level of control. The changes in structure and innovations in instruments and mechanisms in both countries have provided the basis for a virtual explosion of international financial flows, including importantly those between Japan and the United States. Many forces have been at work: volatile exchange rates; large interest rate differentials; a burgeoning U.S. global current-account deficit and, concomitantly, a Japanese global surplus; the vigorous and now huge expansion of Japanese financial institutions into U.S. and other financial markets; and the strong efforts of American institutions to enter Japanese markets.

The U.S.-Japan economic relationship has not merely grown to immense size; it has expanded in an increasingly multifaceted and two-way set of flows — a widening range of goods and services, financial instruments, technology, and direct investment. Even between such close partners as Japan and the United States, it is probably inevitable that a deepening interdependence in trade and capital would give rise to friction. These frictions, furthermore, have spread from such industries as textiles, steel, and autos, to high technologies and service sectors importantly including finance, from economics to politics, society and culture. Moreover, from the early 1980s, the much-overvalued dollar exacerbated these frictions, augmenting the trade and current-account deficits of the U.S. balance of payments and reducing American industrial competitiveness. Fortunately, the degree of overvaluation has decreased substantially from February 1985 to the present, reinforced by the specter and reality of joint governmental intervention since September 1985.

The formal presentations of papers and speeches provide a great deal of information and insight, and contain pointed, stimulating, and at times controversial or provocative appraisals of specific issues. The informal discussion in each session was of exceptional quality. Probing questions were raised, and dissenting views were expressed. They served to enhance the focus on major issues. We do not attempt to provide a summary here of the formal presentations and the more informal give-and-take between the panel members and those in the audience. Rather we briefly delineate some of the major substantive themes of policy concern and provide our perspective on the flow of the discussion of them.

Our discussion proceeded at several different levels, often simultaneously. The participants shared a set of assumptions, explicit or implicit, regarding fundamental objectives, and indeed, by and large, regarding more immediate goals as well. There was somewhat less consensus as to where we are going: forecasts of economic growth, exchange rates, financial market and financial institution performance, and the like. Accordingly, there was also less consensus regarding further policy actions which should be taken, and the likelihood they actually would be taken.

Underlying the entire discussion was the imperative to maintain an open, market-oriented, free trading system and an open, market-oriented free system of international financial and capital flows. The major concern was that, unless the U.S. economy grows well and its balance of payments current account improves, the Congress will successfully enact strongly protectionist legislation. A further concern was that Japan should take a greater leadership role to maintain the international economic system, mainly by continuing to open its financial and goods markets. Wojnilower expressed concern that we cannot have both: free capital flows will be at the expense not only of stable exchange rates but, more importantly, of free trade.

Indeed, a second fundamental objective, though less explicitly treated, was to achieve a set of equilibrium exchange rates among the major currencies and world traders; and even to achieve a system of relatively stable exchange-rate relationships. It was well recognized that equilibrium rates are conditional; they depend on oil prices, government budgets, and balance of payments targets among other factors. Most regarded it premature to think seriously of a system of stable exchange rates given the difficulty in achieving the required harmonization of macroeconomic policies among the major industrial nations.

On the other hand, there was consensus on the importance of achieving and maintaining reasonably good economic growth in the United States, in Japan, and, indeed, in the world economy. Without such growth, reduction in the U.S. current-account deficit becomes more difficult and the required amount of further devaluation of the dollar increases; the likelihood of U.S. protectionism increases; and the potential dangers of the overhang of Third World debt become more ominous.

At the forefront of our discussions were more immediate objectives, and the appropriate policies to achieve them. On some topics there was close to unanimous agreement; on others there were differences of opinion, mostly of degree and nuance, though on a few matters the differences were considerable. These differences in part reflected the universal human traits of wanting the other party to solve the problem, and of pursuing one's own economic self-interest.

Virtually everyone agreed with Bergsten and Yoshitomi, among other speakers, that reduction of the U.S. global trade and current-account deficit is the key issue; and that the U.S. government budget deficit is the proximate cause of the problem. Wojnilower, however, attacked these basic premises in his luncheon speech. Mishkin interestingly argued that, even so, the source of high real interest rates lies in the changes in U.S. monetary regime instituted in October 1979. Everyone agreed that solving the budget problem is the sole responsibility of the United States. However, there was divergence on the issue of responsibility for resolution of the U.S. balance of payments problem. Some Japanese felt this is essentially an American problem to be solved by appropriate American policies. Most Americans felt that, while it is mainly an American responsibility, in this interdependent world some responsibility also lies with Japan and the other major industrial powers, and its successful reduction is in their own self-interest. The comment on Yoshitomi's paper by Marris, distributed at the conference, particularly argues this position.

The large Japanese current-account surplus, projected to rise further in 1986 and possibly even in 1987 as projected by Ueda among others, was also a source both of concern and of divergent views. Many Americans felt the surplus should be decreased by further policy steps, for international political as well as economic reasons. Most Japanese were more sanguine. They pointed out that the further rise is temporary due to J-curve price effects; that the surplus will inevitably decrease as the effects of the sharp yen appreciation work their way through the domestic economy; and that the world is short of savings so it is good that the Japanese save so much and are willing to lend it abroad. There seemed general agreement that Japan's structural current-account surplus is on the order of 1–2 percent of GNP, and that this is tolerable.

A closely related theme was that of Japan's growth performance over the next year or two. Views diverged on projections of the Japanese growth rate, and hence on the international implications and on the need for policy action. Japanese policymakers held to the view that the OECD and the Japan Economic Planning Agency growth projections of about 4 percent real growth in domestic demand and 3 percent growth in GNP are reasonable. Most participants were skeptical, expecting slower growth. Accordingly, American participants urged Japan to undertake more expansive fiscal and monetary policies to attain these growth rates. The argument was couched mainly in terms of the beneficial effects on the U.S. balance of payments and, to our mind more importantly, on the world economy. Reduction of the U.S. trade deficit requires an increase in the U.S. share of world exports and/or decrease in its share of world imports; the net reduction in demand for foreign products will tend to slow world growth. From the American perspective, more rapid Japanese growth and concomitant decrease in its trade balance is a needed stimulative offset for the world economy. From the Japanese perspective, Japan alone cannot offset the impact of U.S. actions, and anyway the matter of growth and the appropriate macroeconomic policies are essentially domestic economic and political matters. Interestingly, there was little discussion of U.S. growth prospects – in part perhaps because the U.S. economy at the time seemed more or less on course.

Also closely related are the issues of the international role of the yen and of the yen-dollar exchange rate. Gyooten cogently traced the seemingly inevitable rise of the yen as a reserve currency and as a transactions currency, and well raised a number of concerns implied by a multi-reserve currency system. Johnson and Loopesko provided a comprehensive and careful analysis of the determinants of the yen-dollar exchange rate, and the relationship of the exchange-rate and current-account balances. Komiya effectively explained why the G -5 intervention of September 1985 was so effective, and why it is so difficult to obtain consensus in favor of joint intervention now.

Naturally, prospective future movements of the yen-dollar rate were of great interest to all participants. Most Japanese practitioners felt that at 160 the yen had appreciated far enough at least for a while; time is needed for the economy to adjust. On the other hand, most Americans felt that the decrease in the dollar had been sufficient only to halt the trend toward a further worsening of the U.S. current-account deficit, not to bring about a significant decrease in that deficit. In this view, the dollar will and should decline further, primarily through market forces and influenced by interest-rate, budget, and growth policies in both countries. How far the dollar will have to decline depends on a variety of factors, most notably the targeted position of the U.S. current account, the rate of world growth (and hence U.S. exports), and the price of oil.

It is, of course, inappropriate to focus solely on the yen-dollar rate as de Vries points out, since the yen has appreciated more than the currencies of other industrial countries, while Canadian, newly industrializing countries (NICs), and other developing country currencies have not appreciated much, if at all, against the dollar. On a trade-weighted basis, the depreciation of the dollar has been far less, and the yen appreciation somewhat less, than the bilateral rate. A global rather than purely bilateral perspective is called for.

It was well recognized that the domestic and international financial markets in New York and Tokyo are not just important in themselves, but also involved intimately in the interplay between economic performance, balance of payments, and exchange rates. Financial markets are the place through which exchange rates are determined. As Gyooten and Suzuki pointed out, the increasingly varied menu of financial instruments, particularly denominated in dollars but also in yen, has made international capital flows more attractive. And capital flows have had an increasingly important effect on exchange rate determination. Chino, Kusukawa, Whittemore, and Suzuki trace these changes and suggestively evaluate their implications. One key issue currently debated is whether lending and underwriting activities should continue to be separated, under the Glass-Steagall Act in the United States and under Article 65 of the Securities and Exchange Law in Japan, or whether commercial banks should be allowed to engage in investment-banking activities. Not surprisingly, opinion on this issue was divided, not between Japanese and Americans, but pitting investment bankers and securities companies against commercial bankers.

Edwards raised a different regulatory issue, observing that deregulation has resulted in increased commercial-bank risk taking, the cost of which is subsidized by *de facto* governmental guarantees of large banks at least. He argued that this is potentially dangerous for the U.S. financial system, and that new methods of insurance should be devised so that banks bear their full costs of risk taking. While others felt this was not an immediate issue, we believe it should be of longer-run concern for both the United States and Japan.

An issue of immediate interest to all participants, because of their financial-market implications among other reasons, was the near-term prospects for more expansive monetary policies and central bank discount rate cuts in the United States and/or Japan. Quite appropriately, the respective central bank representatives (Johnson and Suzuki) were careful not to suggest changes in their own policies. At the same time there was some urging that the other country provide greater monetary stimulus. As it happened, the Federal Reserve discount rate was cut on June 11 from 6.5 percent to 6.0 percent; the Bank of Japan did not follow suit.

While the frictions in the U.S.-Japan economic relationship were not a central theme of the conference, we believed it important to use the final session to examine some of the broader political as well as economic implications of our discussions on macroeconomic policies, exchange rates, and financial markets. Indeed concern about the problems and the points of friction underlay many of the formal presentations and much of the informal discussion throughout the conference. Frictions arise out of differences in economic performance, both macro and micro; and performance depends upon economic behavior, public and private policies, and the institutional framework.

While much of our discussion focused on behavior and policy, Nakatani directly addressed implications of differences in institutions, in particular the respective tax systems of the two countries. The Japanese tax system is pro-saving, anti-investment; the American the opposite. This promotes the flow of capital from Japan to the U.S., a weaker yen, and a larger trade surplus. While greater harmonization of tax systems is desirable, it runs into the desire to protect natural sovereignty.

Curtis examined the political implications for the management of the U.S.-Japan economic relationship in light of the conference discussions and saw the relationship becoming worse, and soon, if the policies discussed at the conference persist. Politically, the bilateral trade imbalance is the key variable, despite our focus on global imbalances. Curtis saw high risk in Japan continuing to handle the trade imbalance solely by yen appreciation while continuing fiscal conservatism, yet made a compelling argument as to why increased Japanese government spending is politically so difficult. Patrick, in his concluding remarks, was more optimistic in that he, like some others, projected a decrease in the bilateral trade imbalance within one year. Both saw a new source of friction emanating not from the United States but from Japan, as Japanese criticized American policymakers for allowing the yen to appreciate so much, and for not jointly intervening in foreign exchange markets to stabilize the yen.

All these issues, and others, form the core of the material that follows, in both the formal presentations and in the discussions they engendered.

* * *

The genesis of this conference lay in discussions begun in fall 1985. We owe much throughout to the advice and inspiration of our colleague at the Ministry of Finance, Yuichiro Nagatomi. We also received excellent guidance and help from many other colleagues on both sides of the Pacific.

The conference would not have been possible without the financial and other support of our co-sponsor, the Foundation for Advanced Information and Research, Japan; Masato Nakamura of the FAIR staff deserves special mention. On the American side funding was generously provided by IBM World Trade Americas/Far East Corporation and Sumitomo Corporation of America. We express our deep appreciation to them all.

The organization and holding of the conference was skilled labor-intensive, as has been the editing of this volume. We thank the staff members of the Institute of Fiscal and Monetary Policy and the Center on Japanese Economy and Business, in particular Mariko Fujii and Motoo Kusakabe of the Institute, and Alicia Ralski, Kim Schoenholtz, Laurie Strachan, Elizabeth Tsunoda, and Robert Uriu of the Center. Catherine Davidson of the Columbia Business School excellently copy-edited as well as transcribed the papers and discussions.

Our deepest thanks goes to those who provided the intellectual substance for what proved to be an excellent and exciting two days: the panel speakers, moderators, luncheon speakers, and the participants in the audience. They not only made those days memorable; they produced the materials embodied in this volume.

The U.S.-Japan Economic Problem: Next Steps

C. Fred Bergsten
Director, Institute for International Economics

LET ME BEGIN by summarizing my seven major conclusions, to make sure that they get on the table, and then go through the analysis that underlies them.

First, the 25 percent decline of the trade-weighted dollar which has occurred over the last year, though a large exchange-rate change in absolute terms, is sufficient only to stabilize the global U.S. trade deficit at somewhere between $100 billion and $125 billion a year. That is because the U.S. position deteriorated so enormously with the massive rise of the dollar to early 1985, when it had become overvalued by at least 40 percent, and when the U.S. was on a path toward annual current-account deficits to $300 billion by the end of the decade.

Secondly, the currency changes to date, though large in absolute terms, have likewise not gone far enough to reduce Japan's global surplus. Indeed, Japan's surplus will rise substantially in 1986, probably to $75 billion or so. The ten top Japanese economic institutes, whose forecasts were recently reported in the *Nihon Keizai Shimbun*, expect the Japanese current-account surplus to remain above $50 billion for the rest of the decade even if the yen rises to 150 to the dollar (See Table 1).

Three, it is thus imperative that the currency adjustment continues a good deal further, since there is no other effective remedy for the huge trade and current-account imbalances in the short to medium run. The trade-weighted dollar needs to fall another 10–15 percent; the yen needs to rise back to at least 160, from its rates in the 170s in the last few weeks.

Four, to achieve and sustain this further currency change, the United States must reduce its budget deficit substantially, to avoid any renewed rise in interest rates, and preferably to reduce short-term interest rates further. Japan needs to speed the growth of domestic demand, and thus its economy, which now appears to be growing in real terms at only about 2–3 percent. The Group of Five needs to continue to jawbone and intervene to promote the further correction needed in these currencies, and certainly must avoid any inferences that it is satisfied with the current exchange-rate level. The United States and Japan should also be working together in the new Group of Seven and elsewhere to promote appreciation of some of the other key currencies, which have so far failed to contribute adequately to the international adjustment.

TABLE 1

Ten Leading Japanese
Forecasts of Japan's Economy in 1989

	Yen dollar exchange rate	Current account surplus (in billions of dollars)
Research Institute on the National Economy	150	51
Sumitomo Bank	150	65
Daiwa Research	150	25
Japan Economic Research Center	180	54
Industrial Bank of Japan	160	50
Long Term Credit Bank of Japan	150	40
Nomura Research	160	40
Marubeni Corp.	160	65
Mitsui & Co.	155	65
Mitsubishi Research	160	45
Average	159	51

Source: *Japan Economic Journal (Nihon Keizai Shimbun)*, April 19, 1986 p. 16.

Fifth, the outlook for underlying economic forces, such as relative productivity growth, inflation rates, international investment positions — with the U.S. now the world's largest debtor country, and Japan the world's largest creditor country, and both rising sharply — suggests that Japan's competitive position will continue to improve against the United States for at least the remainder of this decade. The yen will therefore need to continue to appreciate steadily, reaching somewhere between 120 and 130 to the dollar by the end of the decade.

Sixth, I am afraid that the alternative to this scenario is, at a minimum, further creeping protectionism here in the United States, directed primarily though not solely against Japan, and perhaps even a sharp outbreak of trade protection through legislation (or Administration action to head off legislation) which would cause major disruption to the entire international trading system and world economy.

In addition, if we cannot get orderly adjustment a disorderly collapse of the dollar would, at some point in the future, become inevitable if the United States sought to keep financing deficits of $100 billion or more indefinitely. So a failure to complete the adjustment effort launched by the Group of Five (G-5) in September 1985 would thus be likely to disrupt the entire international trading and financial system. More constructive adjustment measures are essential.

Finally, the rapid pace of the rise in the yen has clearly caused some dislocation in the Japanese economy and resultant political problems. This, it seems to me, represents primarily the cost of nearly five years of neglect of the trade and currency problems by both the United States and Japan. The further rises that I have suggested are required for the yen in the future could cause similar problems. So it seems to me that the United States and Japan have a major interest in stabilizing and smoothing the inevitable adjustment in exchange-rate relationships and should take the lead in reforming the international monetary system perhaps by constructing a system of target zones, or an effective regime of guided floats, per the outline agreed at the Tokyo summit in May 1986.

Those are my major conclusions. Let me trace the analysis that leads me there.

First, I would simply outline the problem. As all of you know, the U.S. trade deficit hit $150 billion last year, with imports calculated on a C.I.F. basis. In the fourth quarter of last year and the first quarter of this year, the U.S. trade deficit rose to an annual rate of about $175 billion. In at least two or three of those months, U.S. imports were almost twice as great as U.S. exports, a ratio that no other industrial country has even come close to in the postwar period.

About three-quarters of the rise in the U.S. trade deficit from the early 1980s can be attributed, in my view, to the rise in the exchange rate of the dollar, which, depending on your index, went up from 60 to 100 percent from 1980 to early 1985. America simply priced itself out of world markets through the enormous rise in the exchange rate. By late 1984 or early 1985, the dollar had become overvalued compared with the underlying competitive relationship between the U.S. and the rest of the world by about 40 percent. We did some simulations in the Institute for International Economics, published in Stephen Marris's study *Deficits and the Dollar*, late last year, which tried to suggest what would have happened to the U.S. external position if the dollar had remained at the level of late 1984–85. The model showed that the U.S. trade deficit would have risen above $200 billion by 1990. In addition, net interest payments on the borrowings from abroad needed to finance such trade deficits would have reached about $100 billion by the end of the decade. So the U.S. current account was headed toward an external imbalance of $300 billion by the end of this decade, with a net foreign debt well above $1 trillion had the exchange rate stayed at the level of a year ago. This is the analytical baseline against which, it seems to me, actual changes and proposed solutions should be compared. We can't simply compare results with the 1985 full-year deficit of $150 billion; we need to compare it with where things were going when the situation was as I state a year ago.

Fortunately, of course, the dollar began to decline in February 1985, and it was given a major push by the total reversal of U.S. policy and the G-5 initiative in September 1985. As of June 2, 1986, the dollar had fallen by about 25 percent on a trade-weighted basis from its peak.

There are several key effects of that change to date, and I think the models used by the International Monetary Fund (IMF), the Treasury Department, the Federal Reserve, and my own Institute for International Economics agree about these effects. First, the deterioration in the U.S. external position — that trend growth toward an external deficit of $300 billion by the end of the decade — has been arrested. We are no longer headed down that path.

Secondly, once we get through the J-curve timing effects, the trade and current-account deficits should decline substantially in nominal terms in the second half of this year, and certainly in 1987, from the peak levels of about $175 billion reached around the turn of last year. In addition, the bilateral U.S. deficit with Japan should fall considerably, perhaps by about $20–$25 billion, from the $50 billion level reached in 1985.

Third, in real price-adjusted terms, the U.S. external deficits should fall enough to add approximately one-half of one percentage point to U.S. economic growth in both 1986 and 1987, and thus in real terms give a modest positive push to our economy. This will reverse the adverse drag that the trade deterioration generated for our GNP over the last four years.

However, at the exchange rates of Monday, June 2 – the yen at 175, DM at 230, and so on – the global U.S. trade and current-account deficits in nominal terms will not fall by very much, if any, below the record full-year level of 1985. They would probably start rising again toward the end of the decade. Again, that is based not only on our own model but what comes out of the IMF and the official U.S. government analyses. All these suggest that, though there will be some gains from where we stand today, they still would leave the U.S. trade and current-account deficits at extremely high levels.

During the last six months, the U.S. external deficits were probably at their peak, unless the dollar were to go up again, with the trade imbalance, as I said earlier, hitting an annual rate of $175 billion. That is simply because the United States has been getting the worst of both worlds: the adverse lagged volume effects of the strong dollar through 1984, which had such a devastating effect on U.S. competitiveness, and the adverse price effects, the J-curve, of the sharp fall of the dollar during most of the last year. The bulk of the favorable volume effects of the more competitive dollar will take 12–18 months to show up in large scale in the trade data, and so should start to appear in the second half of this year and have full effect toward the latter part of 1987. These projections, incidentally, assume a price pass-through from exchange-rate changes to price changes of about 50 percent, which is the historical record, but one cannot be sure that it will, in fact, translate quite so proportionately this time, given the fact that the currency imbalance was twice as great as it has ever been in the past.

But even with optimistic assumptions on the effect of the exchange-rate corrections to date, the U.S. external deficit would, as I have suggested, remain at or above $100 billion with the dollar at its present level, and it would probably start rising again toward the end of the decade.

This situation is completely unsustainable for two reasons. First, there is an internal U.S. reason. The internal political system in the United States is most unlikely to accept continuing deficits of this magnitude, with the implied decimation of our export industries and our import-competing industries. A continuing steady escalation of import barriers for individual industries would be almost certain, as we are now seeing, and an across-the-board outbreak would be quite possible. In either case, the international trading system would be severely disrupted with enormous costs to all countries, especially Japan, but also, of course, to the United States itself.

The second reason for the current situation remaining unsustainable, in my view, is the external factor: it is implausible that the rest of the world will continue indefinitely to finance U.S. deficits of more than $100 billion per year. To date the decline of the dollar has been completely orderly. There has been no adverse effect on American inflation or interest rates, and foreign investment, particularly Japanese investment, has continued to pour into the dollar. Indeed, some of my friends from Japan have said that the capital inflow from Japan to the United States in April reached all-time record levels, as the dollar was hitting its all time low point against the yen at about 160. Apparently, a lot of Japanese investors thought that 160 was a fire-sale price, and were eager to buy dollar assets at that point, so the money continued to flow in. The landing so far has been completely soft, despite the occasional protestations to the contrary by Paul Volcker, Gerald Corrigan and others. But foreign demand for dollars will clearly reach a saturation level at some point, and could then, of course have severe adverse effects on the U.S. economy, pushing inflation and interest rates up sharply, and therefore, perhaps, pushing the U.S. economy into a sharp recession.

It is, then, critically important that the dollar adjust by the additional 15 percent needed to move the external position at least into some reasonable equilibrium. In my view, that continued adjustment should occur as quickly as possible, to take advantage of favorable current conditions — low inflation, low interest rates, the continuing capital inflow — thereby minimizing the risk of a hard landing. If adjustment occurs quickly enough it might have a significant possibility of heading off this protectionist creep, which could, literally within the next few months, break out into an enormous disruption of the world trading system. I will have some specific suggestions on how to complete that correction after saying a few words about the Japanese dimension of the problem.

Japan's external surplus reached about $50 billion last year, and, as I mentioned, will rise sharply this year for two reasons: first, the sharp decline in the price of oil which will have an enormous favorable effect on the Japanese trade balance, and, second, the absence of any significant rise in the exchange rate of the yen against currencies other than the dollar and those tied to the dollar. The yen has not risen much if any against the European currencies, so the trade-weighted yen has not appreciated anything like its exchange rate against the dollar. As I already mentioned, virtually all Japanese forecasters expect Japan's global surplus to remain above $50 billion for the remainder of this decade even if the yen rises to 150 against the dollar.

That Japanese consensus view seems to have two major implications: first, Japanese industry will remain highly competitive even with a considerably stronger yen. These Japanese economists believe that these surpluses will be internationally sustainable for at least several more years.

I agree with the first conclusion, that Japanese industry will continue competitive even with a sharply stronger yen. I sharply disagree with the second conclusion, that the world will sustain external surpluses on the part of Japan on the order of $50 billion or so for the rest of the decade.

Japan's huge global surplus, without further changes in exchange rates and other policies, will continue to place enormous pressure on the world trading system. Coupled with the protectionist pressure in the United States, the prospects for maintaining an open world trading system would not be good. Therefore, Japan would seem to have a vital national interest in promoting further adjustment of the continuing imbalances as rapidly as possible.

I recognize that the rapid pace of yen appreciation, although it is still inadequate to achieve the full adjustment needed, has caused some dislocation to the Japanese economy. Much of that dislocation, I would submit, however, has affected small and medium-sized Japanese firms which probably were exporting in the first place only because the yen became so weak back in 1983 and 1984, and probably represent a misallocation of resources within the Japanese economy. In other words, surplus countries as well as deficit countries experience resource misallocation and are caused difficulties by currency imbalances.

With the yen at 150 or even 165 to the dollar, however,it is clear that many Japanese industries would experience at least a temporary decline, or at least a sharp slowdown in output. Again, there is a table from the *Nihon Keizai Shimbun* in May 1986 that indicates that on an industry-by-industry basis. (See Table 2.) Obviously, these economic results are having political implications in Japan, particularly in the run-up to a major national election.

It seems to me, however, that this adjustment problem within Japan should carry a major lesson for all of us: it reflects the inevitable impact of ignoring the build-up of such huge international imbalances for four to five years. Much of the blame for that neglect falls on the United States, of course. But Japan

TABLE 2

Projections of Japan's Economy
After Tokyo Summit

(Fiscal 1986, percent changes from previous year)		
	At 165:1	At 150:1
Real economic growth	2.3	1.5
Consumer price increase	1.0	0.4
Trade surplus ($ billion)	81.8	82.5
Current account surplus ($ billion)	74.8	73.4
Decline in company profits due to strong yen (trillion yen)	−3.05	−3.69
Changes in industrial output:		
Textiles	−0.3	−1.1
Chemicals	−0.1	−1.3
Iron and steel	−1.8	−3.8
Non-ferrous metals	−2.2	−4.8
Non-electrical machinery	+1.5	−6.1
Electronics	+2.8	+0.7
Shipbuilding	−2.6	−5.4
Autos	+1.0	−1.0
Precision machines	+2.1	−0.2
Services	+3.4	+3.2

Source: NEEDS forecast, *Japan Economic Journal* (*Nihon Keizai Shimbun*), May 24, 1986.

also did very little to avert the onset of its large surplus. It seems to me that the need to avoid an international trade breakdown now is so acute that both countries need to make every effort to complete the needed correction as soon as possible.

How can this be done? Let me, in my final remarks, give a few thoughts on that array of questions.

The underlying causes of the American deficit and the Japanese surplus, and the currency misalignment which transmits them are, relatively simple.

From the American standpoint, we are simply spending more than we can produce, and investing more than we can save. The clear cause of both phenomena is the sharp rise in the budget deficit by over 3 percent of GNP from the early 1980s until now. Both private savings and private investment have remained near traditional levels. These two gaps — spending more than we produce, investing more than we can save — are made up from abroad. The trade gap fulfills our excess demand for goods, and the corresponding capital inflow fills our savings gap.

I'm fond of saying that we now have learned the miracle of supply-side economics: the miracle is that foreigners supply most of the goods and foreigners supply all of the money. That enabled the United States to experience its recovery without crowding out, and without renewed inflation, but at the cost of building up these external imbalances that I mentioned. It was our external sector that was crowded out, not our domestic private investment.

The Japanese case is, of course, the opposite. Japan saves more than it can invest at home, hence its capital flows abroad; the real transfer is accomplished by a huge trade surplus. Japan's savings rate has fallen considerably in the past fifteen years, but its domestic investment has fallen even faster: private investment, due to the slowdown in economic growth since 1973, government investment (or dissaving), because of the sharp fall in the budget deficit since 1980, also by more than 3 percent of GNP.

Fundamental solutions to these problems could require structural change in both economies. The U.S. needs a substantial increase in private savings; Japan needs to restore a higher level of private investment. But prospects for such changes are highly uncertain, and at best, will take many years to achieve.

Fortunately, more immediate remedies are available. As noted, a central cause of the huge international imbalances in the 1980s has been the opposite thrust of fiscal policy in the two countries: the sharp increase in the U.S. budget deficit, the sharp decrease in Japan's budget deficit. Thus, America's major contribution to the needed correction is to achieve a sharp reduction in our fiscal excess to less than 2 percent of GNP by the end of the decade.

Japan's correct course is a bit more complicated, but symmetrical on the other side of the equation and should be aimed at boosting the growth of domestic demand in Japan. To that end, Japan could do three things: undertake supply-side tax cuts to increase private investment; make some increased one-shot government spending on public infrastructure; and begin to undertake structural reforms to promote a housing boom, particularly by improving the

efficiency of land utilization by realistic appraisals of the bases of property taxation and by deregulation of housing codes.

New measures are needed by both countries, which might, by themselves,
prompt the additional currency correction needed to achieve equilibrium in
their external accounts. But I would also argue that the G-5 initiative of September 1985 demonstrated that substantial currency adjustment is possible, at
least for a time, without major action on the fundamentals. Indeed, the success
of the G-5 effort to date reveals the pervasive extent to which psychology and
expectation of official intentions can dominate the exchange markets, at least
in the short to medium run. I would therefore argue that the G-5 should, at
a minimum, avoid any appearance of satisfaction with the extent of the currency correction to date, and indeed renew its effort to move both dollar and
yen to equilibrium levels, both by their public statements and by direct intervention.

It appears to me that a rate of 160 yen to the dollar would be approximately
correct for achieving global equilibrium for the U.S. and Japan at this time,
if all other currencies were to move proportionately — meaning the DM to about
2 to the dollar, from its current 2.30, with the associated European currencies
rising proportionately, and with the Canadian dollar, which accounts for about
20 percent of American trade, appreciating by, perhaps, another 10 percent.
Failing such movement on the part of other currencies, the yen might have to
rise a bit more.

Let me clarify, in conclusion, one element in the currency suggestions that
I have made. In the study that Bill Cline and I published on the U.S.-Japan
economic problem late in 1985, we suggested that the equilibrium yen-dollar
rate was about 190 to 1. In the Japanese language publication of that, which
came out in early May, just a month ago, that same number, of course, was
in place. The reason that I am now suggesting 160 to 1 is not because I have
a rolling target, that the yen should always be stronger than it is in today's market,
but rather because of the sharp fall in oil prices, which has a differentially
favorable effect on Japan's external position.

When we originally did our calculation that the yen-dollar rate should plane
off at 190 to 1, we had allowed for about a 15 percent *weakening* of the yen
because of the second oil-price shock. It seemed to us that, given the differentially *adverse* effect that had on Japan and the yen exchange rate, and the need
for Japan to run a stronger trade surplus in the rest of its accounts, that element
should have weakened the equilibrium yen rate by about 15 percent. Subsequent to our publication last fall came the sharp decline in oil prices, which,
at a minimum, has reversed the second upside oil shock of the late 1970s. Therefore, we have simply suggested that the rate needed now for yen equilibrium
in the world economy is about 160 to 1.

For the longer run, there are reasons to believe that Japan's competitive position will continue to strengthen, Japan's large and growing earnings on services
account, as the world's largest creditor country, suggests that its trade surplus
needs to be less large in the future. America's new position as the world's largest

debtor country suggests that our trade surplus will have to grow even more to finance our interest payments.

Therefore we must expect, over the rest of the decade, steady pressure toward Japanese surpluses and American deficits which, in my view, can only be adjusted to constructively if the yen-dollar rate continues to rise, probably reaching a level somewhere on the order of 120 to 130 to 1 by the end of this decade.

In light of this outlook, and in light of the history of trade conflict between the two countries over the past 15 years, the United States and Japan must recognize that the current trade crisis between them reflects a deeper problem: the failure of the international monetary system to maintain a competitive relationship between their currencies. Each of the previous U.S.-Japan crisis periods — in 1970–72, 1976–78, and recently — occurred when the dollar became substantially overvalued and the yen substantially undervalued. The first two of these crises were relieved, to a large extent, when the currencies were realigned. The United States and Japan thus have a major interest in promoting the adoption of a more efficient international monetary system.

This could be done by moving to "target zones," where the major countries agreed on currency ranges (perhaps 15–20 percent at the outset) which would accurately reflect the underlying competitive relationships between their currencies. (The ranges would change over time as these relationships changed.) Rates would then fluctuate freely during most periods, but national authorities would intervene and make policy changes as necessary to keep their currencies from deviating substantially from their competitive levels.

Another approach to the same objective would be serious implementation of the "enhanced multilateral surveillance" system adopted at the Tokyo summit. Participating countries would submit national forecasts of all their key economic variables, and efforts — presumably led by the IMF — would then be made to assure the international compatibility of these "objective indicators." When a country deviated from its targets, the group could call it to the table and seek policy modifications. This system could, in fact, work out to be very similar to "target zones," and Secretary Baker has testified to the Congress that exchange rates and current-account positions would be the most important of the indicators. As Secretary Baker also testified, however, the "proof will be in the pudding"—whether the countries implement this agreement any more seriously than the somewhat similar agreements on surveillance that have emanated from previous summits.

Growth Gaps, Exchange Rates and Asymmetry:
Is it Possible to Unwind Current-Account Imbalances Without Fiscal Expansion in Japan?

Masaru Yoshitomi

Director, Economics and Statistics Department, Organization for Economic Cooperation and Development

Introduction

THE FOLLOWING BELIEF is widespread among economists as well as government officials: since both the continued overvaluation of the dollar and strong domestic demand in the U.S. were responsible for the emergence of huge current-account imbalances from 1982 to 1985, unwinding such imbalances will require not only the correction of the overvalued dollar, but also a strong domestic demand in non-U.S. major economies. In particular, since the emergence of such international imbalances was associated with fiscal asymmetry, between the U.S. and other major countries over the same period, it is also believed that unwinding international imbalances will require unwinding fiscal asymmetry (i.e., fiscal deflation in the U.S. and fiscal reflation in the non-U.S. major economies, particularly in Japan and Germany). In general, it is said that the exchange rate alone cannot rectify large external imbalances so that the reversal of the growth gap (i.e., the growth differential in favor of non-U.S. major economies) should play an important complementary role. This paper will examine these propositions so as to highlight what appropriate policies should be pursued by major countries in the present context.

This paper will also touch on the assessment of risks associated with huge international imbalances. Until recently, what brought an end to a cycle of economic expansion was, in general, an acceleration of price inflation. In the present "disinflation" period, it is often argued that what would put an end to the current economic expansion would not necessarily be an accelerated inflation but risks to the world economy arising from large international imbalances. Two kinds of risks are frequently cited: protectionism and the collapse of the dollar.

The Group of Five (G-5) meeting of September 1985 was aimed at alleviating

TABLE 1

Exchange Rates of Selected Currencies
14–18 April 1986 Percentage Changes Since:

	G5 (A)	Dollar Peak (B)	End-1984 (C)	Aver. 1984	Aver. 1980
Dollar-Effective	− 15.89	− 22.75	− 18.18	− 13.25	12.50
Vis-à-vis Yen	− 26.80	− 32.07	− 28.84	− 25.36	− 20.03
Vis-à-vis DM	− 21.59	− 33.16	− 27.70	− 20.10	25.15
Yen-Effective	27.21	29.49	28.53	27.39	55.30
Vis-à-vis $	36.62	47.22	40.54	33.98	25.04
Vis-à-vis DM	7.12	− 1.59	1.60	7.05	56.49
DM-Effective	6.26	9.77	10.44	8.79	17.17
Vis-à-vis $	27.53	49.60	38.32	25.16	− 20.09
Vis-à-vis Yen	− 6.65	1.62	− 1.58	− 6.58	− 36.10

(A) 16th–20th September, 1985.
(B) 4th–8th March, 1985.
(C) Last week of the year.

protectionism through correcting grossly misaligned exchange rates. From the G-5 meeting to mid-April 1986, the dollar depreciated by 15.9 percent effectively, by 26.8 percent against the yen and by 21.6 percent vis-à-vis the DM. The dollar's decline in effective terms reversed more than two-thirds of its rise from 1980 to the peak of April 1985. However, vis-à-vis the yen, the dollar was now 20 percent weaker than the average in 1980, when the dollar started to rise, whereas the dollar still remained higher by 25.2 percent against the DM. These exchange-rate relationships are all expressed in nominal terms. In real terms using unit labor costs, at mid-April 1986 the dollar was still 33 percent stronger against the DM than in 1980, while the dollar was 8 percent weaker against the yen. (See Table 1 and Figures 1 and 2.)

And yet current-account imbalances are projected to expand in 1986–87 compared with 1985. Under the assumptions of the mid-April exchange-rate relationships (Y 180 to the dollar, and DM 2.3 to the dollar), and $15 per barrel of oil, the OECD projects the U.S. deficits at $132 and $125 billion in 1986 and 1987 respectively, compared with $118 in 1985. The Japanese surplus is projected at $77 billion and $71 billion in 1986 and 1987 respectively, as against $49 billion in 1985. (See Table 2.) This aggravation of international payment imbalances is attributable entirely to J-curve effects and lower oil prices. Will these aggravated international imbalances increase the risks of protectionism and a free fall of the U.S. dollar? This is a key issue that the present paper also plans to examine.

I. Asymmetries of fiscal impact between the U.S. and Japan

Is unwinding fiscal asymmetry desirable? Unwinding fiscal asymmetry in the present context means fiscal consolidation in the U.S. on the one hand and

FIGURE 1

EXCHANGE RATES OF THE DOLLAR VIS A VIS SELECTED CURRENCIES (1)

NOMINAL

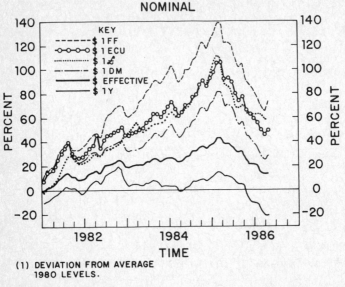

TIME

(1) DEVIATION FROM AVERAGE 1980 LEVELS.

SOURCE: OECD, ECONOMIC OUTLOOK, NO. 39 (JUNE 1986)

fiscal reflation in Japan and Germany on the other. This policy recommendation will be subject to the following set of criticisms. Fiscal reflation today will require fiscal consolidation tomorrow. If Japan and Germany adopted a Reaganomics approach, featuring supply-side tax cuts but also larger structural budget deficits, these countries would need to adopt a Gramm-Rudman-Hollings act a few years later. This suggests that expansionary fiscal policies in the short term would not help to stimulate domestic demand over the medium run (five to six years) on a sustainable basis. On the one hand, expansionary macro policies should play a counter-cyclical role in the short run (if we believe it is effective), while on the other, unwinding the present international imbalances is bound to be a medium-term policy objective, since the huge imbalances could not be corrected in the short run without undermining other policy objectives (e.g., to avoid serious acceleration of inflation in surplus countries and/or to prevent a serious recession in deficit countries as well as in the world economy). Hence, the short-run expansionary macro policies would not be helpful in fulfilling the medium-term policy objective, unless we unrealistically believed that the short-run expansionary macro policies could increase domestic demand on a sustained basis even after such once-and-for-all injection had to be withdrawn in order to correct larger structural deficits. In addition, such "go and

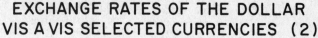

FIGURE 2

EXCHANGE RATES OF THE DOLLAR VIS A VIS SELECTED CURRENCIES (2)

REAL

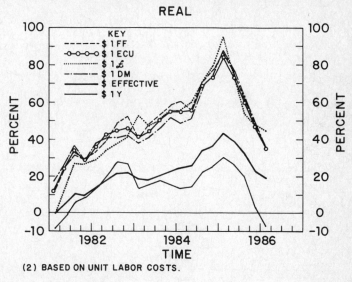

(2) BASED ON UNIT LABOR COSTS.

SOURCE: OECD, ECONOMIC
OUTLOOK, NO. 39 (JUNE 1986)

stop" fiscal policies would generate a very unstable macroeconomic framework, which tends to destabilize market expectations about the future course of economic development, and hence undermine sound productive investment based on long-run views on markets.

My general approach to fiscal policy is that once budget balances become broadly consistent with domestic investment-savings balances, fiscal policy should remain essentially neutral to effective demand; that is, budget imbalances should remain broadly unchanged in relation to nominal GNP. This broadly neutral stance should now be applied to fiscal policies in Japan and Germany, where restrictive fiscal policies can switch to neutral ones, since at the level of the general government the cyclically adjusted budget deficits have been cut down to the levels broadly consistent with investment-savings imbalances in both countries. Such a switch of fiscal policy itself would help to increase demand. In fact, German fiscal policy has become neutral in 1986, and is expected to remain so in the medium run. In contrast, it is much less controversial that fiscal consolidation is badly needed in the U.S. so that the U.S. budget deficits should be contained to a level compatible with sustainable investment-savings balances.

Is such a world-wide fiscal policy switch among major countries sufficient to unwind international imbalances? To some people who assume that the U.S.

TABLE 2

G-3: GNP, Domestic Demand and Current Account 1984–87

	1984	1985	1986	1987	1986 I	1986 II	1987 I	1987 II
	Seasonally adjusted at annual rates (a)							
	Percentage changes from previous period							
Real GNP								
United States	6.6	2.2	3	3 1/4	3 1/4	3 1/4	3 1/4	3 1/4
Japan	5.1	4.6	3 1/4	3	2 1/4	2 1/4	3	3 1/2
Germany	3.0	2.4	3 1/2	3	2 1/2	3 1/2	3	2 1/4
Real total domestic demand								
United States	8.5	2.8	3 1/4	3 1/2	2 1/4	3 1/4	3 1/2	3 1/2
Japan	3.8	3.7	4 1/4	4 1/4	4 1/4	4 1/4	4	4 1/2
Germany	2.0	1.4	4 1/4	4 1/4	3 1/2	5	4 1/4	3 1/4
	$ billion							
Current balance								
United States	− 107.4	− 117.7	− 132	− 125	− 136	− 128	− 126	− 123
Japan	35.0	49.3	77	71	74	79	73	68
Germany	6.3	13.1	29	22	29	28	23	20
	Percentage changes from previous period							
World trade (b)	8.7	3.1	3 1/2	4	4	3 1/4	3 1/4	4

a. Assumptions underlying the projections include:
   – no change in actual and announced policies;
   – unchanged exchange rates from 9th April 1986; in particular $1 = yen 180.2, DM 2.326.
   – Dollar price (OECD fob imports) for internationally traded oil of $20 per barrel for 1986 first half, and $15 thereafter.
b. Arithmetic average of the growth rates of the world import volume and the world export volume.

The cut-off date for information used in the compilation of the forecasts was 9th April 1986.

current-account deficits have been enlarged by fiscal restriction in Japan and Germany, a switch in fiscal policy from a restrictive to a neutral stance in these countries would not be enough to reduce the U.S. external deficits. However, such understanding is not correct, as I will discuss below. Full link simulation results obtained from various world models, including the OECD Interlink, indicate that a sustained reduction of U.S. government expenditure (non-wage) by 1 percent of GNP with a non-accommodating monetary policy will result in an improvement of the external account by 0.25 to 0.30 percent of GNP during several years under the fixed exchange-rate system. In the same simulation, Japan's current-account balance will be adversely affected by 0.20 to 0.25 percent of GNP in almost the same years. Germany's external balance will also be affected as much as Japan's. Thus, the U.S. fiscal action strongly affects not only its own current-account balance but also the Japanese and German external balances.

However, the reverse does not hold true. That is, either Japanese or German fiscal action can affect its own external account but neither of them strongly influences the U.S. current account. Indeed, Japan's fiscal action of 1 percent of GNP can affect its own current account by about 0.20 to 0.25 percent of GNP during several years under the fixed exchange-rate system. In the case of Germany, the adverse impact of expansionary fiscal policy on the current account will range from 0.25 to 0.35 percent of GNP, depending on the year.

How much can Japanese and German fiscal actions affect the U.S. external account? Very little. Full link simulation results show that sustained expansion of government expenditure in Japan by 1 percent of GNP starting with non-accommodating monetary policy will influence the foreign imbalance by only 0.02 to 0.03 percent of U.S. GNP. The influence of German fiscal action on the U.S. current account will be about the same. This is an important asymmetry in cross-influence of fiscal policy between the U.S. and any one of the other major countries. The size of this asymmetry is roughly a ratio of ten to one, as indicated by the above simulation results.

A very similar conclusion can also be drawn from the recent simulation exercise performed by H. J. Edison and R. Tryon who used the Federal Reserve Board Multi-Country Model. [1] Compared with the baseline, a U.S. fiscal contraction (with no monetary accommodation) which would reduce the government budget deficit by $115 billion by 1990 would reduce the U.S. current-account deficit by $93 billion (and trade deficit by $33 billion) in the same year, and would reduce Japan's current-account surplus by $27 billion (and trade surplus by $20 billion). The cross-impact of such a U.S. fiscal consolidation on the Japanese external account is found to be large. This is partly because of a 7 percent effective depreciation of the dollar by 1990 as against the baseline exchange-rate projection and a 7 percent effective appreciation of the yen. These exchange-rate changes induced by U.S. fiscal consolidation are, however, small compared with the aforementioned magnitude of the recent correction of misaligned exchange rates. Since the U.S. fiscal consolidation exerts deflationary effects on the Japanese and the German economies, a second simulation was performed in which Japan and Germany respond to the deflationary impact by easing monetary policy to hold their real exchange rates constant. A result of such easy monetary policy is a rise of Japanese real GNP in 1990 by 0.7 percent above the baseline as compared with a 2.8 percent decline in real GNP in the first simulation case of no monetary ease in Japan. This monetary ease will, therefore, improve real Japanese GNP by 3.5 percent. How much does this 3.5 percent improvement in Japanese real GNP help to correct the U.S. external deficit in 1990? The simulation shows that a reduction of the U.S. current account will remain largely unchanged at $94 billion as against the previously cited $92.7 billion with no monetary ease in Japan. Their paper, therefore, concludes: "What is striking about this policy response (monetary ease in Japan and Germany) is that it has essentially no effect on the U.S. economy: the path for incomes, prices, interest rates, and the current account are virtually identical in the two simulations" (page 20).

Although Edison and Tryon's method of performing simulations differs from mine in several respects, both simulations demonstrate that the cross-impact of U.S. income changes on Japanese (and German) external accounts is far larger than that of Japanese (and German) income changes on the U.S. external account. This asymmetry of the cross-impact can only be demonstrated by using world econometric models which explicitly incorporate world trade matrices, but not by using single-country models which lack such matrices, and hence treat world trade as an exogenous variable.

Two important policy conclusions can be drawn from the simulation exercise. First, as far as fiscal policies are concerned, only U.S. action can effectively influence its own current-account deficit; even joint expansionary fiscal action by Japan and Germany has little effect on the U.S. external account. This asymmetry stems from the sheer size of the U.S. economy, the high import elasticity of U.S. income, and the different composition of imports by commodity and region between the U.S. and Japan (and Germany). If we assume that the large U.S. current-account deficit is not sustainable, the most effective action to correct it is U.S. fiscal action, not Japanese or a German action. Hence, the approach of putting one's own house in order is still very valid for U.S. fiscal policies. Another important policy conclusion to be drawn from the simulation exercise is that not only will Japanese and German fiscal action be effective in reducing their own external surpluses but also U.S. fiscal consolidation will effectively influence the Japanese and German external accounts. In other words, an approach of putting one's own fiscal house in order in the U.S. is internationally fully compatible with the aim of fighting protectionism through simultaneously reducing international imbalances of the U.S., Japan, and Germany.

It can, therefore, be concluded that if the strengthened protectionist sentiment is associated with the U.S. current-account deficit, U.S. fiscal consolidation will be more effective in fighting it than Japanese or German fiscal expansion will be. Even in the case where protectionism is associated with the combined international imbalances of the U.S. deficit and Japanese surplus, the reduction of the U.S. budget deficits will be most effective in counteracting protectionism. Japanese fiscal action will not help much in reducing U.S. external deficits. Of course, the joint action of fiscal consolidation by the U.S. and fiscal expansion by Japan would certainly be effective in correcting imbalances of their respective countries, but as discussed earlier, Japanese fiscal expansion would entail its fiscal consolidation sooner or later. The reversal of the so-called growth gap between the U.S. on the one hand and Japan and Germany on the other sounds very attractive in correcting U.S. external deficits, but the cross-impact of Japanese or German fiscal expansions on the U.S. deficits is just very small. It is indeed true that the U.S. fiscal expansion during 1982–85 caused a substantial increase of both the U.S. external deficit and the Japanese and German surpluses, but it does not mean that higher domestic demand supported by fiscal expansion in Japan and Germany can substantially reduce the U.S. external deficit, let alone their own external surpluses. The cross-impact of fiscal actions on other countries' external accounts is asymmetric between the U.S. on the one hand and Japan and Germany on the other.

II. The Impact of Exchange-Rate Changes and Monetary Policies

However, an important question still remains unanswered. Would the above-mentioned international fiscal policy switch (which distinguishes itself from unwinding the hitherto-observed fiscal asymmetry as explained above) be sufficient to unwind huge international imbalances? My answer is no. We need exchange-rate policies. Furthermore, we may need structural adjustment policies for the U.S. and Japan. And equally important, we need a better-defined concept of unsustainability of international imbalances and hence a well-defined medium-run "goal" or perspective for the development of international imbalances. Lastly, we will have to define how Japanese economic management should react to the deflationary impact of the U.S. fiscal consolidation and the yen appreciation, both of which are needed for unwinding present international imbalances. This paper will examine the impact of exchange-rate changes and the policy measures Japan could adopt to take care of the deflationary impact.

A full link simulation exercise indicates the following: a 10 percent depreciation of the U.S. dollar against all non-U.S. major currencies (which turns out to be a 6.2 percent depreciation of the effective exchange rate of the U.S. dollar) will not only improve the U.S. foreign account by 0.26 to 0.27 percent of GNP from the third year, but also reduce the Japanese current-account surplus by 0.7 to 0.8 percent of GNP through an effective exchange-rate appreciation of the yen by 7 percent and the German surplus by around 0.9 percent of GNP through an appreciation of the effective exchange rate of the DM by 6.6 percent.

From the peak of the dollar in early March 1985 to mid-April 1986, the effective exchange rate of the U.S. dollar depreciated by nearly 23 percent, the yen appreciated vis-à-vis the dollar by 47 percent (the effective exchange rate of the yen by 29.5 percent) and the DM appreciated against the dollar by nearly 50 percent (the effective exchange rate of the DM by less than 10 percent). Applying a linearity and using effective exchange rates, the current account in proportion to GNP will change in the third year and thereafter for the U.S. by about 1 percent, for Japan by 3 percent, and for Germany by 1.4 percent.

Monetary policies under the floating regime are perceived as beggar-thy-neighbour policies (i.e., raising GNP of an initiating country through improving its external account at the cost of its neighbours; or controlling inflation of an initiating country through the appreciation of its currency at the cost of inflation of its neighbours' economies). However, these Mundell-Fleming effects of monetary policy in the small open economy under the floating exchange rates do not hold true for monetary policies in large major countries. This is because such beggar-thy-neighbour effects would be usually offset by income effects of monetary policies in initiating large countries. For example, expansionary monetary policy will tend to offset the deflationary impact of its currency depreciation on foreign economies through higher domestic demand in the initiating country, and vice versa.

III. Summing Up the Impact of Macro Policy and Exchange-Rate Changes on the Present International Imbalances

In sum, the following policy mix in G-3 countries can unwind international imbalances. First, the decrease of the U.S. structural fiscal deficit by 3 percent of GNP would reduce the U.S. current-account deficit by nearly 1 percent of GNP. Second, the cross-impact of such U.S. fiscal action would reduce the Japanese external surplus by around 0.7 percent of Japanese GNP, and the German surplus by about the same percent of German GNP. Third, if the switch of fiscal policies from a restrictive to a neutral stance suggests an increase in government expenditure by about 0.5 percent of GNP compared with the baseline assumption, such a switch would reduce the Japanese current-account surplus by 0.1 percent of GNP and the German surplus by 0.2 percent of GNP. The cross-impact on the U.S. external account of fiscal policies in the two countries is very small at any rate. Fourth, the correction of misaligned exchange rates realized over the past year (from early March 1985 to mid-April 1986) would contribute significantly to unwinding international imbalances: for the U.S. by 1 percent of GNP, for Japan by 3 percent of GNP, and for Germany by 1.4 percent. Fifth, monetary policies through lowering the hitherto high interest rates would increase domestic demand without generating beggar-thy-neighbour policies.

If the policy mixes summarized here are pursued, they will be consistent not only with the OECD medium-term financial strategy and stronger domestic demand, but also with unwinding present international imbalances in the medium term. The U.S. external deficit will decline by nearly 2 percent of GNP (compared with the 1985 deficit of 3 percent of GNP); the Japanese surplus will decline by nearly 4 percent of GNP (compared with the 1985 surplus of 3.6 percent of GNP); and the German surplus will decline by about 2.5 percent of GNP (compared with 3 percent of GNP in 1985). It goes without saying that these numbers just indicate the broad order of magnitude but they are very illustrative.

However, what will happen to world demand if the U.S. budget deficit is cut? It would be very deflationary, some people say. Indeed, the rest of the OECD economies will be hit adversely, but such deflationary impact will be less than one-quarter of a percent of real GNP in correspondence to a sustained reduction of non-wage government expenditures by 1 percent of GNP in the U.S. Japan's GNP will be hit most adversely, by around 0.34 percent, followed by Germany at around 0.2 percent of GNP. This is not negligible, but not alarming either.

IV. How to Deal with the Deflationary Impact on Japan

The impact of the cut of the U.S. budget deficit and the depreciation of the dollar, both of which are required for unwinding international imbalances, has a deflationary effect on the Japanese economy, at least in the short run. However, lower oil prices will largely offset such deflationary impact. In fact, the

OECD has recently made projections based on the assumptions of Y180 to the dollar, $20 per barrel in the first half of 1986 and $15 per barrel thereafter, and the reduction of the structural budget deficit of the U.S. by 0.4 percent of GNP in 1987. The projections show that real domestic demand in Japan will grow by 4 to 4.25 percent per year, and real GNP by 3 to 3.25 percent per year in 1986 and 1987 (Table 2). In other words, Japanese net exports are projected to contribute negatively to the growth of real GNP, and such negative contributions will amount to 0.9 percent of GNP in each year. The J-curve effects and lower oil prices, however, are projected to increase the nominal current-account surplus of Japan in 1986 and 1987 compared with that in 1985, but the continued decline in real net exports will be increasingly dominant in the course of 1987, so that even a nominal current-account surplus will decline from the projected peak of $79 billion (on an annual basis) in the second half of 1986 to $68 billion in the second half of 1987, as shown in Table 2. A decline of $11 billion in a year is significant. Despite such a sharp decline in net real exports, the growth rate of real GNP is projected to hold at the level of 3 to 3.25 percent.

What are the international and domestic implications of such a combination of domestic demand and GNP growth in Japan? In order to answer this question, we should distinguish among various policy objectives. First, if our policy objective is to reduce the present international imbalances, the significant negative contribution of real net exports to GNP growth should be positively appreciated, since it will contribute to achieving this objective. Second, if our policy objective is to maintain high-employment GNP in Japan, the growth of GNP should matter to Japan and the Japanese authorities, but not necessarily to the rest of the world. The issue of whether a 3 to 3.25 percent growth of real GNP is too low for Japan to meet domestic objectives should be an essentially domestic concern, including the issue of whether a fine-tuning policy should be undertaken or not. Third, if our policy objective is to maintain world demand as high as possible in order to help, say, heavily indebted developing countries, the growth rate of Japan's demand for imports and hence of domestic absorption will be an international concern. In that case, an issue of whether or not the 4.25 percent growth of domestic demand in Japan is too low should be discussed. In many policy discussions, these different policy objectives are so mixed up that policy messages do not emerge clearly. If the policy objective is to unwind international imbalances, the U.S. fiscal consolidation and the hitherto-realized depreciation of the dollar should attain the objective, as discussed above. In the case of the U.S. economy, the deflationary impact of the budget deficit cut will be largely offset by the dollar depreciation and lower interest rates. A major remaining question should, therefore, be how to cope with the deflationary impact on Japan of the reduction of the U.S. budget deficit and the appreciation of the yen.

For the short run, three policy measures can be suggested. First, it is desirable for policy to encourage full pass-through of lower import prices to the domestic price level so as to provide the greatest support for domestic demand. Second, a further reduction of interest rates seems possible in view of virtually flat domestic price levels and the higher yen. Lower interest rates should not only help to increase domestic demand but also contribute to preventing the yen from rising too sharply. Given the near-zero rate of inflation, the term-structure of interest rates could be 2 to 4 percent. Third, fiscal policy at the level of the general government can now become neutral, as mentioned earlier. Even if the central government wants to continue its own budgetary consolidation aimed at eliminating new issues of "deficit financing" national bonds by fiscal year 1990, it can still make flexible use of "construction" bonds, bearing in mind that interest payments on additional construction bonds have to be made through the current account of the central government's budget. Furthermore, local governments can be encouraged to issue their bonds to finance larger public-works expenditures.

In the medium run, the Japanese tax system could appropriately be made nearly neutral with respect to personal savings. The resulting higher revenue could enable a reduction of corporate and personal income tax. However, it appears that a real problem is not Japanese "over-savings" but American "under-savings." Therefore, the effect of such a Japanese tax reform on international payments imbalances could be strengthened if at the same time the tax system in the U.S. were changed to increase incentives to save and reduce incentives for household borrowing, including for housing. Japan may be investing too little compared with its necessary savings. Deregulation and tax changes should help to increase expenditure on housing in such a way that price increases of residential land will not be provoked.

An interesting question can also be asked. The current-account surplus is, after all, a reflection of domestic I/S imbalances in Japan, at least in exports. Even if it is assumed that Japan is now a net capital exporter based on chronic current-account surplus accounting for, say, 1.5 percent of GNP, Japanese I/S imbalances will have to be narrowed down by about 2.5 percent of GNP (compared with the surplus of 1985 accounting for about 4 percent of GNP). Is this large reduction of the excess of domestic savings over investment really possible without expanding the structural budget deficit by 2.5 percent of GNP? This question appears relevant particularly because the structural budget deficit of the general government declined in Japan from 4 percent to about 1.5 percent of GNP between 1980 and 1985. I think that it will not be impossible for a neutral fiscal stance to be consistent with the correction of the Japanese external surplus over the medium run (five to six years); the ratio of domestic investment to GNP can be raised by 1.25 percent of GNP by the three policy measures I mentioned, while the domestic savings ratio to GNP may decline by 1.25 percent of GNP due to the rapid aging of the population and the tax reform I touched on above.

V. Conclusions

It has recently been claimed that there is no way for Japan and Germany to evade the choice between reflationary policies and further revaluations of their currency against the dollar if the present large current-account imbalances are to be unwound. It has also been claimed that if Japan and Germany do not adopt timely reflationary policies, the process of unwinding the imbalances will take place through the collapse of the dollar (i.e., a hard landing scenario) accompanied by the tightening of monetary policy in the U.S., and hence renewed worldwide recession. This paper challenges these propositions which have become widespread among professional economists and government officials.

It is indeed true that strong currencies tend to force the Japanese and German authorities to undertake reflationary policies because of their deflationary impact on their own output (i.e., GNP). After all, the combination of expenditure-switching policies through stronger currencies with expenditure-increasing policies through reflationary policies is needed both for rectifying their external surpluses and for maintaining their own high-employment GNP. However, it is a dangerous illusion that stronger growth in Japan and Germany can effectively contribute to reducing the U.S. external deficits, and hence to preventing the dollar from collapsing. This paper concludes, based on preliminary results of full link simulation of a world model, that the reduction of the U.S. budget deficit amounting to 3 percent of GNP in the medium run and the hitherto realized exchange-rate changes after the dollar peak of early March 1985 would be sufficient to largely correct not only the U.S. current-account deficit but also the Japanese and German surpluses. It will, therefore, be possible to unwind the present international imbalances without fiscal expansion (i.e., increasing structural budget deficits) in Japan. The cross-impact of U.S. fiscal action on the Japanese and German external account is very large, whereas that of the latter countries' fiscal action on the U.S. international payments balance is negligible — an important asymmetry of the cross-impact of fiscal action in one country on the current accounts of its trading partners. This asymmetry, therefore, indicates that higher growth in Japan and Germany will not help much in reducing the U.S. current-account deficit or in preventing the strengthening of protectionism and/or the collapse of the dollar, both of which are allegedly associated with the U.S.'s large external deficit. So far, a sharp fall of the dollar has not been accompanied by higher interest rates, or by the tightening of monetary policy in the U.S., so that the sharp fall has not been turned into a collapse or free fall of the dollar, thanks to stable domestic inflation and lower oil prices. A key to preventing the collapse of the dollar is the maintenance of low, stable inflation rates through well-controlled monetary aggregates in the U.S.

NOTES

1. H.J. Edison and R. Tryon, "An Empirical Analysis of Policy Coordination in the U.S., Japan, and Europe." March 14, 1986.

Comments on Mr. Yoshitomi's Paper— "Growth Gaps, Exchange Rates and Asymmetry"

Stephen Marris

Senior Fellow, Institute for International Economics

SINCE MR. YOSHITOMI's interesting paper purports to refute some of the main analytical findings and policy recommendations in my book *Deficits and the Dollar: the World Economy at Risk*,[1] some comments would seem to be in order.

Fiscal asymmetry

Much of the reasoning rests on simulation results from the OECD's Inter-link model showing that while fiscal contraction in the United States significantly improves the U.S. current balance, fiscal expansion in Japan and Germany has a negligible effect on the U.S. current balance. There appear to be two main reasons for this result:

(i) The properties of the OECD model are such that the positive benefits to the U.S. current balance from faster growth in Japan and Germany resulting from fiscal expansion are almost completely offset by a depreciation of their currencies against the dollar which, according to the OECD model, will also be a consequence of fiscal expansion. For the United States, however, the properties of the model are such that fiscal contraction improves the current balance both through slower growth *and* a depreciation of the dollar.

(ii) The second reason, only touched on in the paper, is that under present circumstances, there are good reasons for expecting that one percent higher *growth* in the rest of the world — whether resulting from fiscal expansion or in any other way — will benefit the U.S. current balance less than one percent lower growth in the United States.

On the first point, the following comments are relevant. The "fiscal asymmetry" in the OECD model arises from its properties with respect to two of the most controversial and empirically elusive relationships in modern economics: the relation between budget deficits and interest rates, and between interest rates and exchange rates. It is, therefore, hardly surprising that different models produce different results, and that the properties of the OECD model in this respect have changed significantly over time. In broad terms, the record of the last few years is ambiguous. Fiscal expansion in the United States was, indeed, accompanied by currency appreciation. But fiscal contraction in Japan and Europe was accompanied by currency *depreciation*, whereas according to the fiscal asymmetry paradigm it should have been associated with currency appreciation.

The main explanation given for this fiscal asymmetry in the paper is "the sheer size of the U.S. economy." But the GNP of the rest of the OECD area is 50 percent greater than that of the United States. And the empirical work discussed in my book shows that, in general over the postwar years, the dollar has tended to depreciate (or, under fixed rates, the U.S. balance on official settlements has gone into deficit) whenever domestic demand was increasing faster in the rest of the OECD area *as a whole* than in the United States, and vice versa. In other words, *concerted* fiscal expansion in the rest of the OECD area is likely to be associated with currency *appreciation*, not depreciation.

Given the above, there must be reservations about making major policy recommendations on the basis of simulations of models in which exchange rates are treated endogenously, especially since such models have very largely failed to track the actual behavior of exchange rates in the recent past (and particularly over the last twelve months).

There are, however, some more solid analytical reasons for expecting an asymmetry in the impact of changes in *growth rates* in the United States and the rest of the world on the U.S. current balance.

The first is that in most models the income elasticity of demand for U.S. imports is higher than the income elasticity of demand for U.S. exports. It should perhaps be noted that empirical estimates of this "elasticity gap" have been declining over the last 20 years, and that there are identification problems in separating out income and price effects. It nevertheless seems wise to base policy recommendations on the assumption that the U.S. has a somewhat higher income elasticity than other countries. (In the D&D model used in my book the elasticities used are 1.8 and 1.5 respectively.)

More important, in the present context, are the consequences of the fact that U.S. imports are currently so much higher than U.S. exports. Taking goods and non-factor services together, U.S. exports in 1985 were about 70 percent of U.S. imports. For this reason alone, therefore, one percent faster growth in the rest of the world would, *under present circumstances*, benefit the U.S. current balance by 30 percent less than one percent less growth in the United States. And, combined with the higher U.S. income elasticity this means that in the D&D model, one percent more growth in the rest of the world benefits the U.S. current balance 42 percent less than one percent less growth in the United States.

This phenomenon calls for several comments. First, it means that the benefits from faster growth in the rest of the world are very much less for the "first mile" of U.S. adjustment, when there is a very large gap between imports and exports, than for the last mile when this gap is just about closed. From the policy point of view, therefore, we should be looking at simulations of the complete adjustment and not just a marginal first step. In the simulations reported in Mr. Yoshitomi's paper, for example, where the benefits to the U.S. current balance from faster growth in Japan and Germany are almost completely offset by a depreciation of the yen and the deutsche mark, the adjustment process never gets beyond the "first mile."

A second important point, mentioned in passing in the paper, is that adjustment coming from faster growth in Japan and Germany will take place at a higher level of world trade than one coming through slower U.S. growth. It is not clear, however, how far the simulations reported by Mr. Yoshitomi take into account the full implications of this difference. In the D&D model, for example, using results obtained by William Cline,[2] growth in the developing countries is quite sensitive to growth in the OECD area. Thus faster growth in the OECD area outside the United States benefits the U.S. current balance by making possible faster growth in the developing countries.

Global interrelations of this kind may help to explain one of the oddities in the results reported by Mr. Yoshitomi. On the one hand, he shows that fiscal expansion has a significant adverse impact on the current balances of Japan and Germany themselves over the first two to three years. But, on the other hand, it has a quite negligible beneficial impact on the U.S. current balance. This clearly means that somebody *else's* current balance improves. But then what is assumed about the policy response of these other countries? If they simply accept the benefits to their current balances resulting from fiscal expansion in Japan and Germany it is hardly surprising that the benefits to the U.S. current balance are very small. If, on the other hand, it is assumed that the other OECD countries at least take enough expansionary action to prevent an *improvement* in their current account positions, then, clearly, there would be a one-for-one relation between the improvement in the U.S. position and the deterioration in that of Japan and Germany. Indeed, leaving aside the "fiscal asymmetry" oddity of the OECD model, it seems very possible this is the main reason for the very different results for the U.S. current balance reported in Mr. Yoshitomi's paper compared with the outcome of the "cooperative scenario" analyzed in *Deficits and the Dollar*, in which it is assumed that virtually all other OECD countries contribute to the adjustment process through a faster growth of domestic demand, and that the developing countries take advantage of increased exports to raise imports rather than to reduce their current-account deficit.

There is a further, equally fundamental point. Because one mechanism of adjustment (slower growth in the United States) is more "effective" than another (faster growth in the rest of the world), it does not follow that it is more desirable in welfare terms. Japan, for example, is in exactly the opposite position to the United States: its exports greatly exceed its imports (by about 50 percent). The most "effective" way of reducing the Japanese current-account surplus would thus be to slow down growth in the rest of the world rather than speed up growth in Japan, but it would be hardly surprising if the rest of the world demurred. Equally, it would be hardly surprising for the United States to prefer an adjustment process which involved little if any reduction in U.S. growth below its potential growth rate. This would surely also be preferable at the world level, for so long as there is no clear evidence of excess demand and inflationary dangers in the rest of the world—as is the case today.

Policy Implications

In Mr. Yoshitomi's view, fiscal expansion in Japan and Germany would not only be ineffective in terms of contributing to the U.S. external correction, but would also be undesirable because, in his view, "once budget balances become broadly consistent with domestic investment-savings balances, fiscal policy should remain essentially neutral. . . ." This categoric rejection of the use of fiscal policy for demand-management purposes calls for several comments.

The main reason put forward for taking this position is that discretionary ("go and stop") fiscal policy generates "a very unstable macroeconomic framework which tends to destabilize market expectations." As a general proposition, this view, that discretionary fiscal policy may destabilize rather than help to stabilize the private sector, has attracted increasing support over the last ten years. But as a practical matter it hardly seems applicable to the experience of Japan in the 1980s. In the first half of the decade the Japanese economy has experienced a positive shock from the (foreign) private sector equivalent to as much as 5 percent of GNP; and, according to figures given in Mr. Yoshitomi's paper, it is now going to experience a negative external shock of up to 4 percent of GNP over the rest of the decade. To suggest that errors of judgement in the implementation of discretionary fiscal policy could generate greater disturbances and uncertainties than these massive external shocks is hardly credible.[3] For so long as the economy is subject to shocks of this order of magnitude coming from the private sector, it would surely be more plausible to argue that knowledge that the government was prepared to follow a discretionary fiscal policy would help to *stabilize* rather than destabilize expectations.

A second consequence of taking this position on fiscal policy is that it leaves monetary policy as the sole instrument for demand management. This presumably explains why Mr. Yoshitomi argues in favor of bringing nominal interest rates down to 2 percent (short term) and 4 percent (long term). However admirable this ambitious objective may be, there must be serious doubts as to how soon it could be achieved without excessive money creation. As it is, the Bank of Japan is already concerned about the impact on asset values of the excessive liquidity in the economy. More generally, it would be unfortunate if doctrinaire views about not using fiscal policy for demand management purposes were to lead Japan and Europe to respond to a falling dollar by excessive rates of monetary expansion, which was precisely what happened when the dollar was weak in 1971–73.

Finally, there is the further question of the level at which the fiscal position should be "consolidated." In 1985 the actual budget deficit was equivalent to a bit over one percent of GNP. According to the analysis of the Japanese investment-savings balance in *Deficits and the Dollar*, the private sector, at present levels of capacity utilization, and the present growth path for the Japanese economy, is likely to generate excess savings equivalent to 5 percent of

GNP or more. For the present budget position to be "consistent with domestic investment-savings balances" Japan would thus have to run current-account surpluses equivalent to 4 percent of GNP indefinitely into the future. As of now, however, it is clear that this is more than the rest of the world is prepared to absorb.

In this sense, therefore, it is not really true to suggest that "whether a 3.25 percent growth of real GNP is too low for Japan . . . should be essentially a domestic concern." Unless and until effective action is taken to change the structural relation between savings and investment in the Japanese private sector, the rest of the world has a legitimate interest in seeing that the growth rate aimed at, in conjunction with the structural budget position, generates sufficient investment demand to absorb enough domestic savings at home to leave Japan with a current-account surplus which the rest of the world is able to absorb without generating intolerable protectionist pressures.

The negative impact of U.S. adjustment on the Japanese economy

The third main argument in the paper is that a fiscal stimulus is not in any case necessary because the growth of Japanese domestic demand is forecast by the OECD to accelerate to 4.25 percent in 1986 and 1987. This forecast is, however, open to doubt on several counts.

First, it is doubtful whether the forecast growth of domestic demand is consistent with the negative impact of declining net exports, which is put at the equivalent of 0.9 percent of GNP in both years. When I last inquired, the foreign trade multipliers in the OECD Interlink model were in the 2.0 to 2.5 range. Taking a 2.0 value, this would imply that, *ex ante*, the growth of Japanese domestic demand, which averaged 3 percent a year from 1982 to 1985, is expected to accelerate to over 5.15 percent in the following two years.

There are, moreover, good grounds for expecting a foreign-trade multiplier at the upper end of the range for Japan. According to various estimates, between 50 and 75 percent of the increase in investment in this recovery stemmed directly or indirectly from increased export demand, and the importance of this factor is being confirmed by the way investment demand has been weakening as export demand falls off. Equally, there is evidence that the pressure on profits from the rising yen has put downward pressure on nominal wage increases. *A priori*, therefore, it would be surprising to see *any* acceleration in Japanese domestic demand between a period when net exports were increasing at the equivalent of one percent of GNP, and one in which the reverse is expected to be the case.

The argument therefore apparently hangs on the expectation of a very strong boost to domestic demand from a combination of lower interest rates and lower oil prices.[4] The following comments are relevant:

    (i) In the judgment of most observers, lower interest rates in Japan are likely to give only a rather moderate stimulus to investment at a time when export demand is weak.

(ii) With profit margins heavily squeezed by the strong yen, it seems likely that to an important extent cost savings in the private sector from lower energy prices will be used to prop up profits rather than passed on to the consumer.

(iii) Oil-producing countries have lost as much as 50 percent, or $70-80 billion, of their export earnings. There is no way in which they will be able to finance an increase in their combined current-account deficit of this order of magnitude. In time, if oil prices stay at present levels, they will have to cut back their imports by a roughly equivalent amount. Japanese exports to OPEC countries (equivalent to about 1.5 percent of GNP) are of broadly the same order of magnitude as the gains accruing to Japan from lower oil prices (around $15 billion). Thus the loss of exports could in time offset up to half the potential boost to domestic demand, which in turn will be reduced to the extent that energy cost reductions are not passed on to consumers.

To sum up, the Japanese economy has yet to feel the full impact of either the correction of the U.S. current-account deficit or the loss of export markets in oil-producing countries, which will be building up in the remainder of 1986 and should reach full force in 1987. Given the importance of the foreign-trade multiplier in the Japanese economy, it would be surprising if GNP growth were to exceed 3 percent over the next two or three years (and could well be weaker), compared with a potential growth rate variously estimated at 4 to 5½ percent. This judgment tends to be confirmed by the successive downward revisions of private forecasts for the Japanese economy in recent months.

Mr. Yoshitomi's policy recommendations

Mr. Yoshitomi's recommendation that fiscal policy should at least become *neutral* is welcome, since as recently as May, 1986, the OECD Secretariat was forecasting a further shift to *restraint* equivalent to 0.8 percent of GNP in 1986. According to the analysis given above, however, this does not go nearly far enough.

To the non-Japanese observer, it is hard to follow the suggestion that it is all right for local governments to increase their borrowing, but that the central government should continue to reduce its borrowing. One would have thought that the most valid consideration is whether the types of public investment which should be stepped up are of a kind best administered by local or central government.[5]

It is also difficult for the non-Japanese observer to understand the difference between the issue of "deficit financing" as opposed to "construction" bonds. The distinction appears to relate back to the idea of distinguishing between the budget position on current and capital account ("above and below the line") which was common 20 or so years ago. But since then, it has generally become accepted that this has little meaning in terms of analyzing the impact of the budget on the economy. There may be a legitimate desire to decrease the share of current expenditure in total public expenditure. But a deficit is a deficit, and insofar as the concern is to prevent an excessive rise in public debt, it makes little difference what name is put on the bonds issued to finance it.

Finally, many would agree with the suggestion that the U.S. tax system should be changed to increase incentives to save and reduce incentives for household borrowing in the United States. They would also agree that Japan may be "underinvesting." But I would go on to argue that the single most effective way of correcting this would be to aim for a higher growth rate, in line with the higher potential growth rate which would be possible if more of Japanese private savings were used to finance domestic investment, rather than a very large current-account surplus.

NOTES

1. Institute for International Economics, December 1985. Japanese edition to be published by Tōyō Keizai, September 1986.
2. *International Debt: Systemic Risk and Policy Response*, Institute for International Economics, Washington, D.C., 1984.
3. In reality, of course, fiscal restraint during the first half of the decade, carried out in the name of fiscal consolidation, played an important demand-management role in preventing the massive external stimulus from driving the Japanese economy into an inflationary boom.
4. It is intriguing to note how fiscal consolidation is achieved in the OECD area during the 1980s in Mr. Yoshitomi's scenario. In the first half of the decade, fiscal consolidation is made possible in Japan and Germany because the negative impact on world demand is offset by fiscal deconsolidation in the United States. In the second half of the decade, fiscal consolidation in the United States is possible because the negative impact on world demand is offset by the drop in oil prices (implying massive fiscal deconsolidation by the oil-producing countries?). Obviously, the right way to achieve fiscal consolidation is to achieve growth sufficiently fast to raise investment to the point that the budget deficit can be cut back without an adverse impact on demand. The United States achieved this but did not cut back the budget deficit. Europe and Japan did not achieve the desired rise in investment, but did cut back their budget deficits, freeing up the savings needed to finance the U.S. budget deficit.
5. The experience of other countries, moreover, has often been that it is more difficult to implement a discretionary fiscal policy at the local level than by the central government. Once local authorities have been encouraged to spend more, it has often proved difficult to persuade them to cut back spending when this becomes appropriate.

U.S. Macroeconomic Policy and Performance in the 1980s: An Overview

Frederic S. Mishkin

Professor, Graduate School of Business, Columbia University

I
INTRODUCTION

THE UNITED STATES has the largest economy in the world and developments in the U.S. economy have a wide ranging impact on economic activity in all other countries. Indeed, Otmar Emminger, a past president of the German central bank, characterized other countries' economic relationship with the U.S. as "being in the same boat with an elephant."[1] Because the elephant's shifts in position grossly (pun intended) affect those who are sitting in the same boat, an understanding of recent macroeconomic policy and performance in the United States is valuable to anyone concerned with international economic relations.

This paper provides an overview of U.S. macroeconomic policy and performance in the 1980s by first outlining the behavior of key economic variables and then discussing the policies that have affected these variables. After gaining some insight into the interaction between these policies and macroeconomic performance, we can then go on to examine where macro policy and the U.S. economy may be heading in the next several years.

II
U.S. MACROECONOMIC PERFORMANCE IN THE 1980s

Real Economic Activity

Figures 1 and 2 provide an outline of developments in real economic activity from 1980 to 1985. In this period, the economy experienced two recessions leading to real GNP growth averaging 2.3 percent at an annual rate, substantially less than the postwar average of 3.4 percent.[2] The 1980s began with the unemployment rate at 6.3 percent, not far from the natural rate (full employment) level which most economists feel resides between five and six percent. The recession which started in January 1980 and ended in July 1980 was short but was also sharp. Real GNP declined at a 9 percent annual rate for only one quarter, 1980-II, when credit controls which restricted business and con-

FIGURE 1

REAL GNP GROWTH RATE: 1980-85

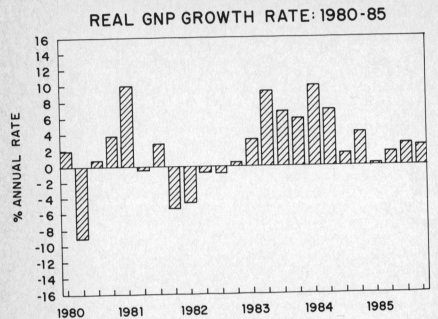

FIGURE 2

UNEMPLOYMENT RATE: 1980-85

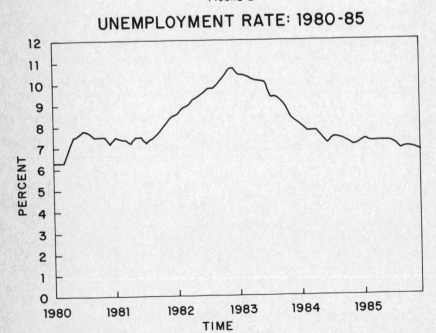

FIGURE 3

INFLATION RATE: 1970-86

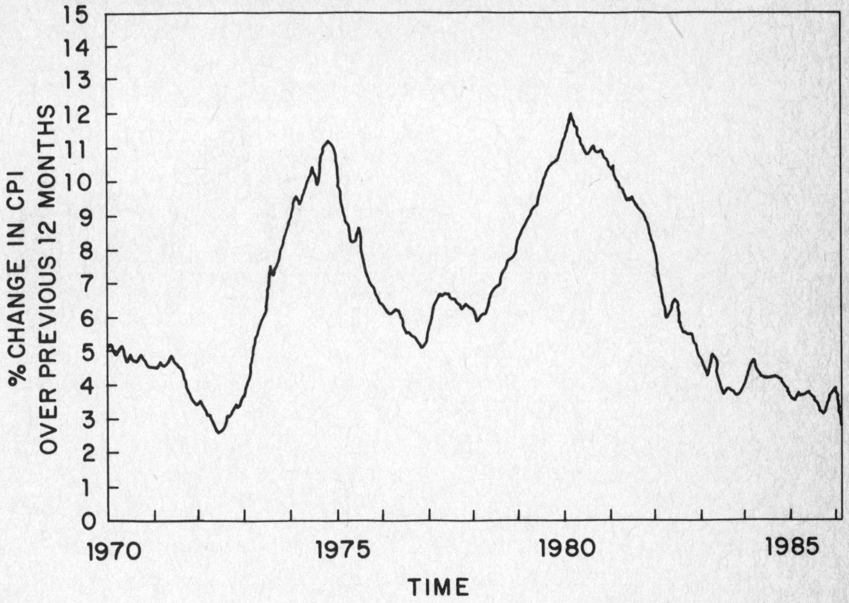

sumer loans were imposed on the economy. The result was that the unemployment rate climbed to 7.8 percent. The expansion following the trough in July 1980 after the credit controls were abandoned was the shortest in the postwar period, lasting only twelve months. A second recession began in July 1981 with output falling for four straight quarters, and the unemployment rate was driven to double-digit levels, peaking at 10.7 percent. The subsequent recovery starting in November 1982 has been in line with other postwar recoveries: real GNP growth has averaged 4.0 percent and unemployment declined to near the 7 percent level by early 1986.

Prices

The lackluster real GNP performance in the 1980s stemming from the two recessions is, however, associated with the most striking development in this period, a substantial improvement on the inflation front. At the start of the 1980s, the inflation rate (the percentage change in the Consumer Price Index (CPI) over the previous twelve months) exceeded 11 percent.[3] The high inflation rate was the result of a high core inflation rate due to high money growth in the 1970s and an upward impulse to the price level from the sharp increase of oil prices in the late 1970s associated with the fall of the Shah of Iran.[4] With the 1980 recession, the inflation rate began to fall, and during the 1981–82 recession the decline in inflation accelerated, leaving the inflation rate below the five

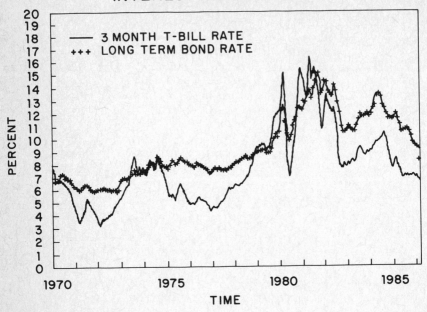

FIGURE 4

INTEREST RATES: 1970-86

percent level for the first time in ten years. In February and March of 1986, the CPI has actually declined for two months running, a feat last repeated over twenty years ago.

Financial Markets

Figure 4 depicts developments in the bond market. The 1980–82 period experienced not only high interest rates on short and long-term bonds, but also great volatility in these interest rates. In March 1980, interest rates on three-month U.S. Treasury bills peaked at over 15 percent, while those on 20-year U.S. Treasury bonds exceeded 12 percent. An extremely rapid fall in these rates then occurred, with three-month bill rates falling by half to 7 percent by June of 1980 while long-term rates fell below 10 percent. The rapid fall from March to June was then followed by an equally rapid climb in rates, leading to levels of both short and long-term interest rates above 15 percent in 1981. The period from 1980 to 1981 suffered not only from the highest interest rates on Treasury securities in all of U.S. history, but also from the most volatile rates as well. With the decline in inflation in 1982, interest rates finally began their fall from their unprecedentedly high levels. Currently, the Treasury bill rate is around the 6 percent level, while long-term government bonds are yielding less than 8 percent.

Although nominal interest rates have fallen to levels found in the 1970s, real

FIGURE 5

REAL INTEREST RATE
ON 3 MONTH T-BILL: 1970-86

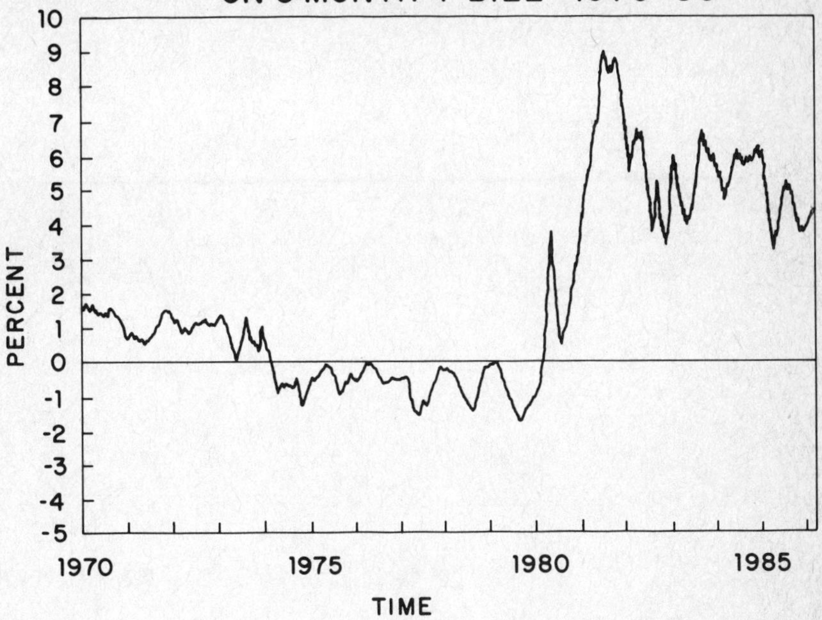

interest rates — that is interest rates adjusted for expected changes in the price level — have not. Figure 5 plots estimates of the real interest rate on three-month Treasury bills from 1970 to the beginning of 1986.[5] Despite the high level of nominal interest rates in the late 1970s, real interest rates were very low and were even negative for most of the 1970s. In the 1980s, we have quite a different story. Real interest rates climbed to levels that are unprecedented in the postwar period, reaching a peak of over 8 percent in 1981. By the mid 1980s, although nominal interest rates have fallen below levels found in the late 1970s, real interest rates have remained higher than at any time in the postwar period prior to 1979, continuing to exceed 4 percent. These high real interest rates have been of great concern to policymakers throughout the world, and explaining their unusual behavior is a puzzle that we will return to later.

The performance of equity markets in the 1980s has become a bright spot in the economy. As is seen in Figure 6, by the beginning of 1980, the real value of common stocks (as measured by the Standard & Poor's 500 index, deflated by the CPI) was substantially below the peak value reached in the beginning of 1973. Despite a relatively flat performance in nominal terms from 1980 to 1982, the increasing price level led to stock prices hitting a trough in real terms by mid 1982; their real value was less than half that at the peak in 1973. Subsequently one of the great postwar bull markets began. In real terms, stock prices

FIGURE 6

REAL STOCK PRICES: 1970-86

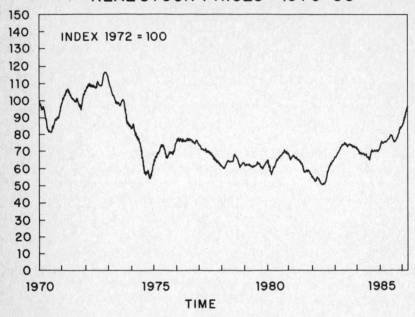

nearly doubled, leaving their current real value only slightly less than that reached at their peak. Just in the first three months of this year, 1986, stock prices have increased by over 10 percent. This strength in the value of American equities has been matched by equally strong performance in the equity markets throughout the world.

The Foreign-Exchange Market and the Current Account

The developments in the foreign-exchange market are illustrated by Figure 7 which shows the effective exchange-rate index for the U.S. dollar—that is, the value of the dollar in terms of a trade-weighted basket of foreign currencies. By the beginning of 1980, the dollar had declined 25 percent from its value during the fixed exchange-rate period before 1971. The subsequent rise in the dollar was both prolonged and substantial: the U.S. dollar reached record highs by early 1985, appreciating by over 80 percent relative to foreign currencies. The strong dollar in this period has been the subject of much concern both by American and foreign policymakers. One reason has been its effect on the balance of trade in goods and services between the U.S. and the rest of the world. The effect of the exchange rate on trade has long lags. Thus, the strengthening dollar which led to a weakening of U.S. competitiveness did not lead to substantial current-account deficits (Figure 8) until 1983, when the current-account deficit reached $40 billion. Since 1983, the current-account deficit has been on the order of $100 billion and the U.S. has been driven from being a net creditor

FIGURE 7

U.S. EFFECTIVE EXCHANGE RATE: 1970-85

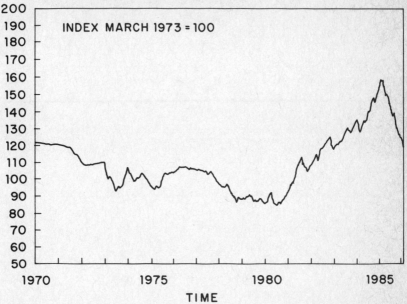

INDEX MARCH 1973 = 100

TIME

vis-à-vis the rest of the world to being a net debtor. Since early 1985, the U.S. dollar has declined sharply in value, giving up over half the gains achieved over the previous five years. The lower value of the dollar has increased American competitiveness and should lead to a decline in the current-account deficit. But because this takes time, we see no improvement in the current-account balance through the end of 1985.

Now that we have examined some of the main economic developments in the United States during the 1980s, we now need to turn to the conduct of macroeconomic policy in order to understand why these developments have occurred.

III

MACROECONOMIC POLICY

Probably the most important feature of economic performance in the 1980s has been a significant decline in the rate of price level increases. To first understand this phenomenon we must first look at how monetary policy was used to quell the inflationary fires in the early 1980s.

Monetary Policy in the Early 1980s and the Fight Against Inflation

Our discussion of monetary policy in the early 1980s must first begin with the appointment of Paul Volcker as the Chairman of the Board of Governors

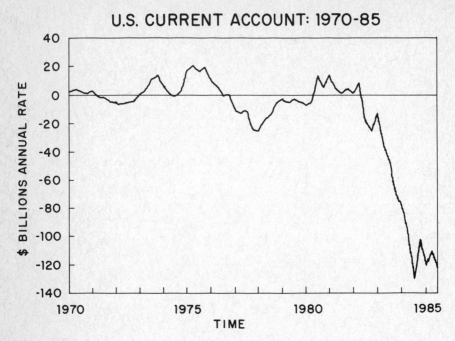

FIGURE 8

U.S. CURRENT ACCOUNT: 1970-85

of the Federal Reserve System in August 1979. Before Volcker's ascension to his post as Chairman, monetary policy had proved to be highly expansionary and inflationary. Thus when Volcker embarked on his new job, he was faced with a Federal Reserve that had little credibility as an agent of price stability and yet the inflation rate was climbing into double-digit territory and the U.S. dollar was weakening. To turn this situation around, Volcker embarked on a bold strategy to rid the American economy of inflation and strengthen the dollar by first announcing on October 6, 1979 a dramatic change in the operating procedures of the Fed.

Before the change in operating procedures, the Fed paid lip service to targeting monetary aggregates, but in actuality pursued a strategy of smoothing interest-rate fluctuations by giving precedence to targets on the federal-funds rate (the overnight, interbank loan rate) which were only allowed to move within a fairly tight band. The announced change in the Fed's operating procedures suggested that the Fed would now more aggressively pursue the targeting of monetary aggregates by abandonment of federal-funds rate targets. (Specifically, the target range for the federal-funds rate was widened by more than a factor of five, while the primary operating target became nonborrowed reserves.) Although a stated goal of the new operating procedures was more accurate control of money supply growth, a monetarist experiment of a gradual reduction in money supply growth was not carried out because the Fed was not very suc-

FIGURE 9

M1 GROWTH RATE: 1970-85

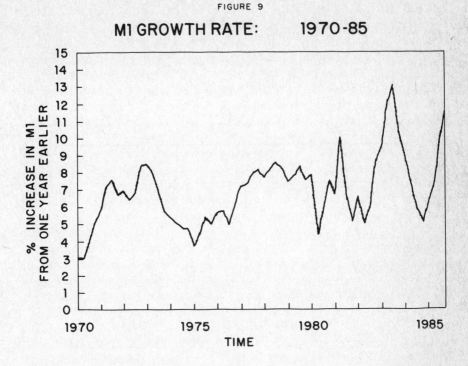

cessful in stabilizing monetary growth. Figure 9 which shows the growth rate of the M1 monetary aggregate (the percentage increase from one year earlier) indicates that after October 1979, the fluctuations in money supply growth *increased* rather than decreased as might have been expected from the Fed's statements. What went wrong?

There are several possible answers to this question. The first is that the economy was exposed to several shocks after October 1979 that made monetary control more difficult. Among these shocks was the acceleration of financial deregulation which added new categories of deposits such as NOW accounts to the measures of monetary aggregates. In addition, in March 1980 President Jimmy Carter, as part of his new anti-inflation program, authorized the Fed under the Credit Control Act to impose credit controls which restricted the growth of consumer and business loans. Money supply growth fell sharply immediately after these controls were imposed and then rose sharply again after the controls were abandoned in July 1980.

A second possible explanation is that effective monetary control was not possible using nonborrowed reserves targets under the then existing system of lagged reserve requirements in which required reserves for a given week were calculated on the basis of the level of deposits two weeks earlier.[6]

My preferred explanation for the failure of the Fed to accurately control money growth after October 1979, was that this was never really the intent of Volcker's policy shift. A view that has been confirmed by discussions with some former Fed officials is that despite Volcker's statements about the need to target monetary aggregates, he was not committed to these targets. Rather he was far more concerned with using interest rate movements to wring inflation out of the economy. Volcker's primary reason for changing the Fed's operating procedure was to free his hand to manipulate interest rates in order to fight inflation. Abandoning interest-rate targets was necessary if he were to be able to raise interest rates sharply when a slowdown in the economy was required to dampen inflation. This view of Volcker's strategy suggests that the Fed's announced attachment to monetary-aggregate targets may have been a smokescreen to keep the Fed from being blamed for the high interest rates that would result from the new policy.

A story consistent with this interpretation of Fed strategy can be gleaned from the interest-rate movements shown in Figure 4. After the October 6 announcement, short-term interest rates were raised by nearly five hundred basis points (five percentage points) until in March 1980 they exceeded 15 percent. With the imposition of credit controls in March 1980 and the rapid decline in real GNP in the second quarter of 1980, the Fed eased up on its policy and allowed interest rates to decline sharply. With the recovery starting in July 1980, inflation remained persistent, still exceeding a 10 percent rate (see Figure 3). Since the inflation fight was not yet won, the Fed tightened the screws again, sending short-term interest rates above the 15 percent level for a second time. Finally, with the 1981–82 recession that led to a large loss of output and high unemployment, inflation began to come down. With the inflationary psychology apparently broken, interest rates were now allowed to fall.

With the scenario outlined above, large fluctuations in money supply growth after October 1979 should not be particularly surprising. Many monetarists have criticized the Fed for the erratic money growth rates during this period, but there are good arguments supporting the view that the Fed was correct to pay little attention to monetary-aggregate targets in the early 1980s. Market forces, new computer technology and financial deregulation as a result of major bank legislation in 1980 and 1982 were making monetary aggregates less reliable as an indicator of monetary policy. For example the spread of NOW accounts after the Depository Institutions Deregulation and Monetary Control Act (DIDMCA) of 1980 and the increase of money market mutual fund assets made interpretation of the monetary aggregates extremely difficult after October 1979. Indeed, the Fed embarked on several redefinitions of the monetary aggregates in the early 1980s in an effort to obtain a more economically relevant definition of the money supply.

Another piece of evidence suggesting that monetary targeting was not appropriate during this period is the behavior of M1 velocity depicted in Figure 10. Beginning in the 1980s, M1 velocity began to undergo more substantial fluctuations as well as large deviations from the trend rate of growth established before October 1979. Particularly striking is the sharp decline in velocity that starts at the end of 1981 and ends in the first quarter of 1983. This decline

FIGURE 10

VELOCITY: 1970-85

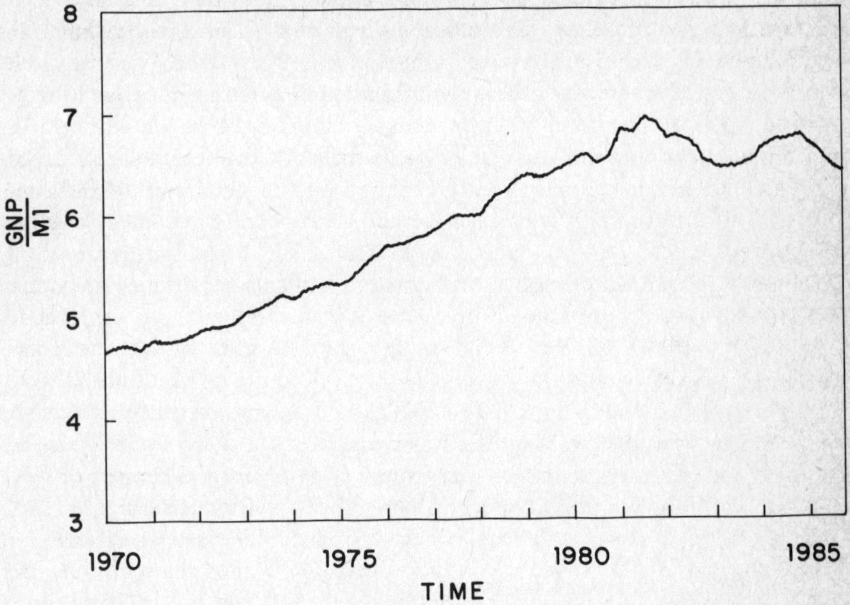

is then followed by another large swing up and down in velocity from 1983 to 1985. Looking at the velocity numbers in the 1980s does not increase one's confidence in the efficacy of a constant money growth rate rule during this period. Volcker's pragmatism and reluctance to adhere to monetarist prescriptions may thus have been called for in the unusual environment of the early 1980s.

Fiscal Policy: Were the Reagan Budget Deficits the Source of High Real Interest Rates?

The other major development in macroeconomic policy in the 1980s was the tremendous growth in the federal budget deficit resulting from the fiscal policies of the Reagan Administration. Despite the supply-siders' predictions that tax cuts would generate sufficient revenue to leave the federal budget in balance even if there was no shrinkage in government spending, the 1981 Reagan tax cut along with continuing growth in the government sector (mostly stemming from the military buildup) led to budget deficits in the $200 billion range. As is evident in Figure 11, the official budget deficit on a national income accounts basis jumped from around 2 percent of GNP in 1980 and 1981 to around 5 percent of GNP from 1982–85.

The shift in the behavior of budget deficits is even more striking if we are more careful in defining what an appropriate concept of a budget deficit should be. An economically relevant measure of a budget deficit should tell us whether the government is becoming more or less indebted *in real terms*, that is, in terms of real goods and services. Even if the federal government is increasing the *nominal* amount of its debt by running a deficit on an official basis, its *real* indebtedness can be falling if increases in the price level sufficiently shrink the real value of the debt that has been issued previously. An economically relevant measure of the budget deficit must thus be corrected for the effect of price level changes on the real value of previously issued debt (particularly during high inflation periods) and also on changes in the market value of the debt arising from changes in interest rates. Figure 11 shows an adjusted budget deficit measure as a percent of GNP which is based on corrections calculated by Robert Eisner.[7]

The adjusted budget numbers in Figure 11 indicate that the recent deficit experience is even more unusual than the official numbers suggest. In every year from 1970 to 1985, the official budget numbers indicate that the federal government was in deficit. However, the picture is quite different with the adjusted budget number: from 1970 to 1980, the budget was nearly as likely to be in surplus as in deficit. After the Reagan tax cuts, a sharp break in the behavior of the adjusted deficit occurs; from a level of only .6 percent of GNP in 1981, the deficit jumps to nearly 6 percent of GNP in 1982.

The jump in the budget deficits that we see particularly after 1981 in Figure

FIGURE 11

FEDERAL BUDGET DEFICIT
(−)AS% OF GNP: 1970-85

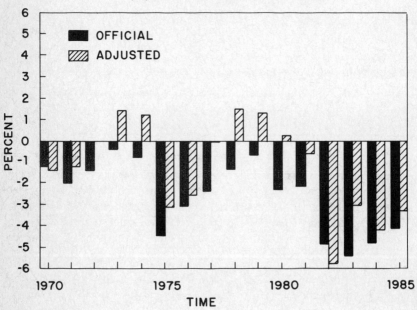

11 is often pointed to as the source of the current high real interest rates found in Figure 5. These high real interest rates are often cited as the cause of the strong dollar from 1981–84,[8] which, in turn, stimulated the huge current-account deficits from 1983 to 1985. Should the blame for the high real interest rates and the deterioration of the U.S. balance of trade be placed onto the budget deficit?

Recent research that I have conducted with John Huizinga sheds some light on this question.[9] Modern monetary theory suggests that regime changes have an important impact on the stochastic process of many economic variables. As we have seen, with the change in operating procedures in October 1979, the Fed changed the method of conducting monetary policy in order to reverse the inflationary monetary policy of the 1970s. Is this monetary regime change associated with a shift in the stochastic process of real interest rates which resulted in the high real interest rates in the 1980s?

The answer appears to be yes. When the Fed alters its behavior in October 1979, there is a statistically significant shift in the stochastic process of real interest rates. In addition, if one asks when the shift in the stochastic process of real rate actually occurs, statistical evidence indicates that it corresponds to the October 1979 change in the monetary policy regime. These results point the finger at Volcker's change in monetary policy regime as a major factor causing the current high level of real interest rates.

The research strategy in my work with Huizinga is one in which we look for a clearly definable historical event such as the October 1979 change in Fed operating procedures, and then see if there is a significant change in the behavior of a particular economic variable immediately afterwards. Suppose that we know the first event is *exogenous*, that is, it occurs as a result of an independent action that could not possibly be caused by the other economic variable. Then when a significant change in the economic variable follows the exogenous event, we have strong evidence that the first event is *causing* the change in behavior of the economic variable. In a sense then, we are treating the October 1979 change in the Fed operating procedures as an exogenous event—in other words, a controlled experiment—and when we see the shift in the behavior of the real interest rate, we are ascribing causation from the monetary regime shift to the change in real rate behavior.

One danger of such a historical-econometric analysis is that it runs the danger of fitting one historical episode with one tailor-made theory. Truly convincing evidence that the Fed's monetary policy regime change led to high real interest rates must involve examination of similar "controlled experiments" in other time periods. We thus focused on another episode of monetary regime shift that has many similarities to the October 1979 shift. At the beginning of 1920, the pursuit of a real bills doctrine by the Fed led to rapid monetary growth, a sustained high level of inflation similar to that of the late 1970s and a weak dollar. In January and June of 1920, the Fed decided to reverse its inflationary monetary policy by raising the discount rate sharply—by 1¼ percent in January and 1 percent in June. In the early years of the Fed, changing the discount rate was the main tool of monetary policy, and it was particularly potent at this time because the total amount of member-bank borrowing from the Fed exceeded the amount of nonborrowed reserves. The result of this policy was a rapid disinflation (in fact, a deflation). This disinflation is similar to what we have seen in recent years and thus we might expect to find parallels between the two periods.

The analysis of the period surrounding 1920 reveals a significant shift in the stochastic process of real interest rates which has many similarities to the recent experience. For example, the 1920 monetary-regime change and the subsequent disinflation is associated with a weakening of the correlation of expected inflation with nominal interest-rate movements and a shift to a sustained higher level of real interest rates. The striking correspondence between the impact of the monetary-regime shifts on real interest rates in 1920 and 1979 provides strong support for the view that the recent shift in real-rate behavior is a monetary phenomenon. Particularly important in this regard is that high budget deficits were not a feature of the 1920s,[10] thus suggesting that monetary factors are more important than budget deficits to the recent behavior of real interest rates.[11]

Monetary Policy After October 1982

On October 5, the Fed announced that it was deemphasizing monetary-aggregate targets, and, as is clear in Figure 5, the Fed was returning to its policy of smoothing short-term interest rates. In order to keep interest rates from rising in 1983, the Fed accommodated a bulge in money demand by allowing the money supply to grow at rates in excess of 10 percent (see Figure 9). The fact that the more rapid growth in the money supply in 1983 did not lead to a rise in inflationary expectations can be attributed to Volcker's success with his anti-inflation program and his hard won credibility as a serious inflation fighter who would not allow the inflationary fires to reignite.

By early 1985, the strength of the dollar and the current-account deficits in excess of $100 billion were leading to increasing protectionist pressure in the U.S. Congress. Statements from Federal Reserve officials indicated that they felt that the dollar was too high, and fear of growing protectionism was probably a factor in stimulating the Fed to pursue a more expansionary monetary policy to bring down the value of the dollar. The result has been growth rates of the money supply again in excess of 10 percent and a sharp fall in the dollar.

IV
WHERE ARE WE HEADING?

It is always difficult to predict the future, but the overview of past macro policy and performance may provide some clues as to where we are heading.

In recent months, there has been some debate over whether the sluggish economic growth over the past year requires the pursuit of a more expansionary monetary policy. This debate has been particularly acute at the Federal Reserve where it erupted over a decision to cut the discount rate, with the outcome that, at first, Chairman Volcker, who opposed the cut, was overruled by a vote of the Board of Governors, an extremely unusual occurrence.

There are several factors that will affect the economy's performance and the choice of macro policies. As we have seen, developments in the foreign-exchange market can affect the Federal Reserve's decisions about monetary policy. The overly strong dollar in early 1985 may have prompted the Fed to a more expansionary policy. The dramatic fall in the dollar since then may work in the opposite direction now. There currently seems to be a consensus at the Federal Reserve as well as at other central banks that the slide in the dollar has proceeded far enough. Indeed, one reason for Volcker's recent opposition to the discount-rate cut is that he felt it would weaken the dollar if it came before similar cuts by other central banks. Given that Volcker was eventually upheld by the Board and that his chief adversary, Preston Martin, the vice-chairman, resigned, it seems reasonable to expect a less expansionary monetary policy in 1986–1987.

The most dramatic economic development in 1986 has been OPEC's inability to prop up crude-oil prices with the result that they have fallen by over 50 percent. Despite slow growth in real GNP in 1985, we should recognize that the drop in oil prices is a very favorable supply shock that should greatly stimulate the economy.

We can put the analysis of the impact of the favorable supply shock into a standard textbook aggregate-demand-and-supply framework. A direct effect of the oil price shock is a decline in the price level since gasoline and other forms of energy are an important element of consumer expenditures. Indeed, the Consumer Price Index fell in both February and March 1986, while the Producer Price Index started falling in January. In addition, there are indirect effects on the price level because energy, which is a basic cost of production, has now become cheaper. One result of the favorable supply shock is then a fall in the aggregate supply curve, which leads to an expansionary effect on real output through traditional mechanisms such as a fall in interest rates.

We must also not forget that the favorable supply shock also has potential effects on the aggregate demand curve. Because the U.S. is a net importer of energy, a drop in the price of oil increases the wealth of Americans. Indeed, since the beginning of 1986, stock prices have increased by over 10 percent, increasing the value of equities by over $300 billion. This sizable increase in wealth will stimulate increased consumer spending and so will shift the aggregate demand curve out to the right.[12] This too will lead to increased real output.

The current outlook for the economy is thus a good one. In the near future, the inflation rate should be low as a result of the oil-price decline, while the economy should undergo further expansion. Does this mean that we should end our worries about a resurgence of inflation? Overconfidence on this score is unwarranted. We must remember that a halving of the price of oil produces a once-and-for-all lowering of the price level. However, the resulting, permanently lower price level does not imply that the inflation rate will be permanently reduced. If monetary policy continues to be expansionary, then the decline in oil prices will produce only a temporary decline in inflation. Once the oil-price shock has worked its way through the system, the inflation rate will begin to reflect the underlying monetary expansion. The rapid rates of money growth that we have been experiencing in the last year, if not reversed, thus present a potential danger to the economy which could lead to the undoing of the Fed's successful fight against inflation.

APPENDIX
SOURCES OF DATA FOR FIGURES 1–11

Figure 1: annualized rate of change of GNP in 1972$ from the previous quarter; obtained from the Citibase data bank with updates from the *Survey of Current Business.*

Figure 2: civilian unemployment rate from the Citibase data bank with updates from the *Survey of Current Business.*

Figure 3: percent change in CPI from the 12 months earlier; CPI series is on a rental equivalence basis and is described in Huizinga and Mishkin (1984).

Figure 4: 3-month Treasury-bill rate and the 20-year Treasury-bond rate are obtained from the Citibase data bank with updates from the *Federal Reserve Bulletin.*

Figure 5: calculated with procedure described in footnote 5.

Figure 6: Standard & Poor's 500 index deflated by the CPI series used in Figure 3.

Figure 7: effective exchange-rate index obtained from Citibase data bank with updates from the *Federal Reserve Bulletin.*

Figure 8: U.S. current-account balance obtained from Citibase data bank with updates from the *Survey of Current Business.*

Figure 9: percent increase in quarterly average M1 from one year earlier; M1 obtained from Citibase data bank with updates from the *Federal Reserve Bulletin.*

Figure 10: nominal GNP obtained from Citibase data bank divided by the M1 series used in Figure 9.

Figure 11: official and adjusted federal budget deficit obtained from Eisner (1986b), divided by the nominal GNP series used in Figure 10.

NOTES

1. Solomon, 1982, p. 180.
2. By "postwar" I mean after World War II.
3. The CPI series for the period before January 1983 used here is not the CPI-U index reported by the Bureau of Labor Statistics (BLS). Before 1983, the BLS's CPI-U index has serious distortions because of its treatment of housing prices. Specifically, it overstates the inflation rate when mortgage rates are rising as in 1980 (see Blinder, 1980). This problem led the BLS to convert the CPI index to a rental-equivalence basis in its treatment of housing starting in January 1983. The CPI series used for the calculation of inflation in Figure 3 puts the index on a rental-equivalence basis before 1983 in order to provide a more accurate account of inflation in the early 1980s. This series was obtained from the Congressional Budget Office and is described in Huizinga and Mishkin, 1984.

4. For a further discussion of the course of the inflationary process in the United States from 1960 to 1980, see Mishkin 1986, Chapter 25.

5. These estimates were obtained using procedures outlined in Mishkin, 1981, which make use of the rational-expectations assumption. Specifically, the real rates in Figure 5 are fitted values from regressions of the *ex post* real rates on the three-month bill rate, the three-month inflation rate, and a supply-shock variable measured as the relative price of energy in the PPI, all of which are known at the beginning of the period. (See Huizinga and Mishkin, 1986, for an explanation of the choice of explanatory variables.) Because of evidence in Huizinga and Mishkin, 1986, that the stochastic process of real rates shifted in October 1979 and October 1982, three separate regressions are run for the periods January 1953-October 1979, November 1979-October 1982, and November 1982-January 1986.

6. Mishkin, 1986, Chapter 19 has a more extensive discussion of Fed operating procedures during this period and how these procedures might have led to unstable money growth.

7. The adjusted budget-deficit numbers are obtained from Eisner, 1986b. See Eisner, 1986a, for a more extensive discussion of how budget deficit numbers should be interpreted.

8. See Frankel, 1985.

9. Huizinga and Mishkin, 1986.

10. Although the Federal government ran substantial budget deficits in the years 1917-1919 as a result of World War I, there were budget surpluses in every year from 1920 to 1929.

11. Other research analyzing the link between budget deficits and real interest rates does not tend to support a strong connection between them. See, for example, Blanchard and Summers, 1984, and Evans, 1985. Note that financial deregulation, investment tax credits, and oil-price shocks were also not present in the 1920s. Thus, the correspondence between the 1920s and the 1980s of real interest-rate behavior also weakens the case that there were important factors affecting recent real interest-rate behavior.

12. Modigliani, 1971, and Mishkin, 1977, for a discussion of how increases in stock prices affect consumer spending.

REFERENCES

Blanchard, Olivier J., and Lawrence H. Summers. 1984. "Perspectives on High World Real Interest Rates." *Brookings Papers on Economic Activity* 2:273-324.

Blinder, Alan. 1980. "The Consumer Price Index and the Measurement of Recent Inflation." *Brookings Papers on Economic Activity* 2:539-566.

Eisner, Robert. 1986a. *How Real Is the Federal Deficit?* New York: The Free Press.

Eisner, Robert. 1986b. "The Real Federal Deficit: What Is It, How It Matters, and What It Should Be," Northwestern University. Mimeo. March.

Evans, Paul. 1985. "Do Large Deficits Produce High Interest Rates?" *American Economic Review*, 75:68-87.

Frankel, Jeffrey A. 1985. "The Dazzling Dollar," *Brookings Papers on Economic Activity* 1:199-217.

Huizinga, John and Frederic S. Mishkin. 1984. "Inflation and Real Interest Rates on Assets with Different Risk Characteristics." *Journal of Finance* 39:699-712.

Huizinga, John and Frederic S. Mishkin. 1986. "Monetary Policy Regime Shifts and the Unusual Behavior of Real Interest Rates." *Carnegie-Rochester Conference Series on Public Policy.*

Mishkin, Frederic S. 1977. "What Depressed the Consumer? The Household Balance Sheet and the 1973-75 Recession." *Brookings Papers on Economic Activity* 1:123-164.

Mishkin, Frederic S. 1981. "The Real Interest Rate: An Empirical Investigation." *Carnegie-Rochester Conference Series on Public Policy* 15:151-200.

Mishkin, Frederic S. 1986. *The Economics of Money, Banking and Financial Markets.* Boston: Little, Brown.

Modigliani, Franco. 1971. "Monetary Policy and Consumption." In *Consumer Spending and Monetary Policy: The Linkages*, pp. 9-84. Boston: The Federal Reserve Bank of Boston.

Solomon, Robert. 1982. *The International Monetary System: 1945-81.* New York: Harper & Row.

Prospects for Japan's Current-Account Surplus

Kazuo Ueda

Senior Economist, Institute of Fiscal and Monetary Policy, Japan Ministry of Finance

MANY PEOPLE have told me that an American would begin his or her speech with a joke, while the Japanese with an apology! As a Japanese, what is my apology? Well, I am supposed to discuss the papers by Fred Bergsten and Masaru Yoshitomi. But I received Mr. Yoshitomi's paper yesterday, and the Bergsten paper just an hour ago, so it would be rather difficult for me to discuss these.

Instead, I will give my personal views on the kinds of issues discussed by the two authors.

I fully agree with Mr. Yoshitomi that the cause of the U.S. current-account deficit lies in the United States, and any Japanese action would have a very minor impact on the U.S. current-account deficit. But let me, using my comparative advantage as a Japanese economist, focus on the Japanese current-account surplus. I will discuss the near-term prospect of the Japanese current-account surplus — what is likely to happen to it in the next couple of years.

To state my conclusions first: it is very unlikely that we will see a substantial decrease in the current-account surplus this year. It will probably increase by a fairly large amount. What about 1987 or 1988? It might decrease, or it might not decrease; there is a lot of uncertainty there. But I would say, even if it does not decrease, there will be a chance that trade frictions between the United States and Japan will decrease to a considerable extent.

Let me now explain the basis of these conclusions. I will look at the current account from two angles: one, in terms of what will happen in the short run (in 1986), and what will happen in the longer run (1987 and 1988). The other angle is one of the macro-balance, by which I mean the following: I am not just going to look at the current account itself, but I will also look at the savings and investment balance, or the difference between income and expenditures. If you just focused on the current account, it would not be clear if your conclusion would be justified in terms of the balance in the macroeconomy, or in terms of the balance in the goods market. So I will talk about the current account itself, and also the other side of the coin which is the excess of saving over investment or the excess of income over expenditures.

Let me first talk about the current account itself, and what is likely to happen to it in the next couple of years. To see that, what we usually do is to estimate export and import functions, and these can be used to produce forecasts of the current account once assumptions are made about the time paths of the exchange rate, and U.S. and Japanese income growth rates.

I have done thorough calculations for many cases. I examined a case where the exchange rate would stay at 180 per dollar, another case with 160 per dollar; oil price, $30 per barrel, $15 per barrel; U.S. real growth at 1, 2, 3, and 4 percent; Japanese growth, the same.

To summarize the results of the exercise: the Japanese current-account surplus in 1986 is unlikely to decrease substantially. More correctly, it will increase substantially. In fact, for the first four months of 1986, the actual current-account surplus is running at about $20.6 billion, which is about double of last year's figure. So if extrapolated, we will be seeing something like $100 billion current-account surplus in 1986. But I think it will be slightly smaller than that—probably in the range of $65 billion to $85 billion. That is a fairly broad range, but that is what I expect to see for the current account for 1986.

It is very difficult to trace the exact shape of the J-curve, but my simulation results indicate that the current-account surplus will start to decrease either late this year or early next year. If you wait until the end of 1988, the Japanese current-account surplus will decrease, in terms of ratio to its trend GNP, to somewhere between 1 and 2 percent. Thus in a couple of years, we are likely to see a substantial decrease in the Japanese current-account surplus, assuming that the yen will stay at the current level, somewhere between 160 and 180.

But this analysis does not take into account the likely improvement in the service account which is likely to happen in the next couple of years. I have done a back-of-the-envelope calculation about the increase of the service account in the next couple of years. It turns out that the service account will add about 1 percent of GNP to the current-account surplus. So if this is added to the above estimate, the current-account surplus of Japan may not decrease by very much. In any case, the trade account will probably decrease substantially. That is what I get from a direct analysis of the current account.

Next, let me turn to the other side of the goods market: the difference between income and expenditures, or the difference between saving and investment.

This analysis is related to the question of whether we will be able to have a decrease in the current-account surplus merely by a change in the exchange rate, even without an increase in fiscal expenditures in Japan, or a reduction in the budget deficit in the United States. In order to have a decrease in the current-account surplus, we should either have a decrease in savings, or an increase in investment in Japan. In other words, we should have a decrease in income in Japan, or an increase in expenditures.

Now, through what mechanisms will these things take place? We can think about a couple of mechanisms. An obvious candidate is the usual Keynesian story. We are witnessing a very sharp appreciation of the yen, which will lead to a decrease in exports. This will in turn decrease the real income of the Japanese economy leading to a decreased savings. Another mechanism would be the following: we will see very sharp decreases in prices in the Japanese economy as a result of the decrease in oil prices and the appreciation of the yen. This may increase expenditures by households and corporations, which, of course, will lead to the direction of decreasing excess savings. Finally, we could have a policy action within Japan to increase expenditures.

I am going to look at each of these to see whether any decrease in excess savings is likely to happen in the short and long run.

Let me first talk about the terms-of-trade effect on expenditures, the second of the three mechanisms I mentioned. I have estimated saving and investment functions for Japan, to see whether the likely decrease in prices in Japan will increase expenditures. My results suggest that, at least in the short run, expenditures are unlikely to increase. Rather, savings will increase in the short run mainly as a result of the decrease in oil price, which will tend to increase excess savings, or the current-account surplus. So we can't have much hope for the effectiveness of this mechanism.

Next, let me turn to the usual Keynesian mechanism, which would say that a decrease in real income in Japan will decrease savings. My calculations suggest that if the real GNP growth rate in Japan decreases by one percentage point, savings in Japan, relative to trend GNP, will decrease by about 0.5 percent. So if we are to have a decrease in the current-account surplus, say, by about 1 percent of GNP, we should have a decrease in the real GNP growth rate of about two percentage points. However, as I said, the decrease in oil price and other things are likely to increase savings, so even if the real GNP growth rate slows substantially in the Japanese economy, it would be fairly unlikely for savings to decrease substantially. Also, this analysis does not take into account the possibility that investment might decrease as a result of a recession in the economy. If investment decreases, then the excess of savings over investment will increase.

So if I take into account all these factors, at least in the short run, saving over investment is unlikely to decrease, which is consistent with my earlier analysis of the current-account surplus.

What about the effect of policy actions? Well, by June 1986 we have seen decreases in the discount rate three times already in Japan. However, the impact of this on expenditures would be fairly small, maybe not enough to offset a decrease in investment which is likely as a result of a recession. So we can't have much hope here. What about fiscal policy? It is clear that if we increase fiscal expenditures by a substantial amount, it would decrease the Japanese current-account surplus. But obviously, we have to seek a balance between the decrease in the current-account surplus and the increase in the budget deficit; thus, it would be very unlikely for us to be able to increase fiscal expenditures by a large margin. However, let me hasten to add that even if we do not increase fiscal expenditures in nominal terms this year, because we are having a fairly sharp decrease in prices in real terms, fiscal policy is going to be fairly expansionary in real terms in Japan this year.

Let me now turn to a long-term analysis of the savings/investment balance. I think there is a bright picture here. That is, the effect of decreases in prices will, in the longer run, show up in expenditures, so expenditures might increase to some extent, which will decrease excess savings. Also, I would like to point out that what will happen in the next couple of years depends a lot on what is happening now to investment, through supply-side effects. What is happening to investment now? It is going down, especially in the exportable sector. Also, foreign direct investment is increasing by exporting firms. These things will have a negative impact on the competitiveness of the Japanese economy in the next couple of years, which will tend to decrease the current-account surplus.

Also (and here I am borrowing from the analysis by Paul Krugman) even if the Japanese current-account surplus does not decrease, as a result of the improvement in the terms of trade we will not have to increase the quantity of exports by as much as we have been doing in the last decade. So, even if the current-account surplus does not decrease, we will see less export growth by Japanese firms. Also, as I said earlier, even if the current-account surplus does not decrease, we will probably see a fairly sharp decrease in the trade balance. All these considerations suggest that we will see a substantial reduction in tensions between Japan and the United States, or the rest of the world, in the long run.

DISCUSSION: Session I

JOHN OLIVER WILSON:
Bank of America
Can Fred Bergsten comment on the appropriate exchange rates between the dollar and the European currencies for the rest of the 1980s?

FRED BERGSTEN:
I have not done an elaborate analysis of the European outlook for the rest of the decade, but I do not think that we will need nearly as much appreciation of the European currencies over the long run, once we get to some kind of steady-state equilibrium. The reasons I foresee a need for further yen appreciation are largely reasons specific to Japan: the rapid productivity growth and the low inflation rates.

So one might put it this way: what we needed in 1985–86, and continue to need now, is a dollar depreciation against all major currencies. What we may need over the next several years is a yen appreciation against all major currencies, with not-terribly great further movement between the dollar and the Europeans. The yen would then be appreciating against the DM and the others, as well as against the dollar.

RICHARD COOPER:
That is a very good question. Table 2 of Mr. Yoshitomi's paper shows a German surplus, which, when you scale it to economies, is about the same size — only a shade smaller — as the Japanese surplus. When you add Switzerland, the Netherlands, and other smaller European countries, which are also in substantial surplus relative to their GNP, you get what you might call a mark-bloc, which is on the same order of magnitude today as the Japanese surplus. As Mr. Yoshitomi pointed out, at least as compared with the 1980 base, when the U.S. had a surplus, the mark has appreciated much less — in fact, it has depreciated in real terms against the dollar — than the yen. So would it be fair to say that, in your answer to John Wilson, you are putting a lot of weight on the long-term effects as distinct from the current situation?

BERGSTEN:
Yes. Yoshitomi and I apparently agree that it is necessary to get a correction of the continuing large imbalance. Just as a footnote, in his last remarks, Yoshitomi pointed out how the Japanese current-account imbalances will be moving in the right direction by the end of 1987. I agree with that fully. His numbers also underline my point: these imbalances would still remain at levels that are so far from equilibrium that much further correction is needed. So

I think he and I are basically in agreement, at least on the numbers. I do see a need now for more appreciation of the mark against the dollar than yen appreciation against the dollar. Remember I suggested that DM-dollar equilibrium seems about two to one, and the mark, as of June 2 closed at about 2.35. So we are talking about a 15 to 20 percent move in the mark now, whereas the yen has in fact, for a brief moment, been at the 160 level I indicated, and now it is less than 10 percent away from that. So I fully agree, Dick, with your point that, to return to equilibrium in the short run, more movement in the mark than in the yen is necessary. But John Wilson's question was about the end of the decade, and in relationship to my 120 yen to the dollar over the next four years, I would not see the need for nearly as much movement in the mark, and maybe not much at all.

EDWARD LINCOLN:
The Brookings Institution
I have two short questions, one for Mr. Bergsten and one for Mr. Yoshitomi. Fred, it seems that one of the inputs to your calculations of equilbrium exchange rates is an assumption that the elasticity for Japanese exports and imports remains fixed. But as the yen continues to appreciate, don't you think that those elasticities could change fairly rapidly? We are moving into unknown territory.

Mr. Yoshitomi, I understand your explanation of how we might get adjustment without reflationary fiscal policy in Japan, but if there is no expansion of fiscal policy, isn't there a danger that the yen would depreciate and that current exchange rates would not stick?

BERGSTEN:
On your first question, no one can give a definitive answer. One has to be somewhat cautious about making the usual assumptions of the stability of historical economic relationships, whether it's price pass-throughs or income elasticities or price elasticities, when there is a much bigger disequilibrium than we have ever had in the past. I suggested that the dollar became overvalued by at least 40 percent when it hit its peak over a year ago. If that is correct, it doubled or more the previous record currency misalignment of the post-war period, which was about 20 percent at the end of the Bretton Woods period, as revealed by the two subsequent devaluations. We had a smaller misalignment in the mid-1970s. So this has been a much larger disequilibrium, by a large order of magnitude, than before.

Given that, I must admit that one has to be cautious in using historical relationships. Now, given the further appreciation you suggest, whether dynamic effects lead to further changes in elasticities, that is indeed an issue, though I wouldn't be as worried about that.

Nevertheless, you use what you can use. You look at the historical record, you use your best judgment and make adjustments. That is what we've done in all our work. In defense of our numbers, we have used elasticities, price pass-throughs, and all the other key analytic variables that are consonant with those which the whole range of analysts looking at these issues have come up with over the last few years. If there is a structural change, we all have a problem because economic analysis doesn't pick it up very well until after the fact.

MASARU YOSHITOMI:

Regarding the relationship between fiscal deflation in Japan and the exchange rate of the yen, we can refer to three factors in the present context. One is that we assume that without Japanese fiscal expansion, the Japanese current-account surplus will continuously accumulate. Therefore, there is an exchange-rate risk premium associated with Japan's huge net foreign position, and this may explain the further appreciation of the yen. But on this point, as I said, if there is action on the U.S. fiscal side, that will affect the Japanese external surplus very adversely. Therefore, the risk premium associated with the current-account imbalance should be reduced. That is number one.

Second, whether the exchange rate of the yen would appreciate or not because of Japanese fiscal expansion, as was the case in the U.S. over the past several years, depends upon various parameters, particularly money-demand functions, the interest elasticity of money-demand functions, and the elasticity of capital movements in relation to interest differentials. In many models, depending on the estimation of the parameters, we find that for the first few years there might be an appreciation of the yen because of fiscal expansion in Japan, because of the higher interest rate, and so on. But the magnitude of the exchange-rate appreciation is small. So, yes, there would be some positive relationship between the two, but the duration of the relationship is obscure and the magnitude is apparently rather small.

Thirdly, many people say, particularly in discussions in the OECD, that if Japan takes appropriate action for domestic demand expansion, the prospect for Japanese growth would be brighter. Investment opportunities would then become much better from the viewpoint of the foreign investor, and therefore they would increase investment. That would result in higher exchange rates of the yen. But that is a very broad statement, and it is difficult for economists to associate such growth prospects with exchange-rate directions. So I can best reply to your question by referring to these three factors.

TOYOO GYOOTEN:

I have two questions to Fred Bergsten. First, I think it is fair to say that behind any trade imbalance there are structural and non-structural factors. Non-structural factors can be divided into an income-generating part and exchange-rate-generating part. Now, you put particular emphasis on the exchange-rate part. But I wonder, if, say, for the U.S.-Japan trade imbalance in 1985, do you have any idea how one can allocate the imbalance among these different factors?

My second question is, when we talk about the impact of the exchange-rate changes on the trade balance, should we not also consider the speed of such change? As we have witnessed during the last several months, when we have had very rapid exchange-rate changes, then we will have the so-called J-curve effects, and when the speed is very rapid, there is a cumulation of J-curve effects. That is, at first the exchange rate changes, but the nominal imbalance will increase. The markets will react to this nominal increase in the imbalance, so that there will be further exchange-rate changes. That will further accumulate, so that on top of that initial J-curve effect, there will be additional J-curve effects. So I suspect that when we talk about the exchange-rate impact, we should also think about this speed factor of exchange-rate changes.

BERGSTEN:

On your question about trying to disaggregate the U.S.-Japan bilateral imbalance, and estimating how much of it is due to different sources, Bill Cline and I tried to do precisely that in the study we published in late 1985, which now has appeared in Japanese as well. We first asked the question, how much of the increase in the imbalance could be attributed to all the macroeconomic factors, as opposed to trade barriers, unfair trade practices, and the like. We found that we could explain almost all the big increase in the imbalance by macroeconomic factors, not really allowing much, if anything, for changes in trade barriers. We then asked: within the macro-component, how much is due to differential growth rates, and how much is due to exchange-rate changes? We found that the great bulk, at least in our model, was due to exchange-rate change. Certainly in 1983 and early 1984, when the U.S. had its growth spurt picking up from the recession of 1982, income effects substantially increased the U.S. trade deficit. But over the period as a whole, we found something like three-quarters of the deficit to be attributable to price changes through the exchange rate. Now, there are other analysts who reach different conclusions. Some people at the Federal Reserve Bank of New York have suggested that it is about 50–50, that the growth effects and the exchange-rate effects have been about even. They put tremendous weight on the higher elasticity of import demand in the U.S. than in Japan, and suggest that even at equal growth rates in the two countries, the U.S. balance deteriorated because of the higher elasticity of demand. Now there is a big debate as to what the appropriate elasticities are; we used lower numbers in our work, and therefore got a higher effect for the price side as you suggest, but admittedly that is an issue on which technicians can differ. Maybe it's half and half. Maybe it's two-thirds/one-third, but that is the range in which we are talking.

On your second question about the cumulation of J-curve effects: I think you are right, but I don't really see what to do about it. We are paying the price for neglecting the problem for five years. I think the U.S. bears a lot of the blame for that. But when you ignore a problem for five years, and let these massive imbalances build up, the pressure is going to break out somewhere. Where it is breaking out now is in the American Congress and in protectionist actions taken by the White House to try to head off Congressional protectionist legislation, and the trade system is going to hell in a basket. Now while it is unfair and unfortunate when one tries to adjust in one year or two years to the imbalance that was neglected for five, I am suggesting that the price of *not* doing so is even worse, for both our countries as well as for the world as a whole. On the technical point, I agree that there is a cumulation of J-curve effects. That means we have to educate the Congress and the public that it will take some time before the impact of the exchange-rate changes shows up in the published trade data. There are the traditional three lags: from exchange-rate change to price change, price change to volume decisions, volume decisions to published price data of shipments. We know that takes twelve months, eighteen months, maybe more, for the total effects to show up. But if we can at least indicate that the adjustment has gone far enough so that adequate realignment is in train, then I think we have at least a fighting chance to avoid a much worse outbreak of protectionism.

COOPER:

As we break for coffee, I would like to give Fred Bergsten and Masaru Yoshitomi an assignment for our subsequent discussion. As I have heard the presentations and in particular the prescriptions, both are agreed that there should be a substantial cut in the U.S. budget deficit. Mr. Bergsten argues with some urgency that there needs to be in addition to that, some combination of fiscal stimulus in Japan, and further appreciation of the yen and other currencies. Mr. Yoshitomi, however, suggests that a shift into what he calls fiscal neutrality but not expansion, plus no (or very small) further appreciation in the yen, would be necessary to accomplish what appears to be a common objective, namely restoration of sustainable equilibrium.

Both presentations were very interesting, and both presentations relied, behind the scenes so to speak, on extensive simulations. We got glimpses of those simulations. My assignment to the speakers is to tell us whether they share a forecast on common assumptions but disagree about the behavioral relationships of the economies, or whether they really have very different forecasts. Or do they make different but so far unrevealed initial assumptions about, for example, U.S. fiscal policy? I don't know about you but I am a little confused about what 1990 is going to look like on the basis of these two presentations, and why there seems to be so much difference.

[COFFEE BREAK]

YOSHIO SUZUKI:

I would like to ask three questions, one each to Mr. Bergsten and Mr. Yoshitomi, and one to all panelists. The question to Mr. Bergsten is this: you talked about the exchange rate of 120 or 130 vis-à-vis the dollar over the next decade. But judging from the differential of the inflation rates between both countries, do you imply a constant real exchange rate? If so, although Richard Cooper said that there is some discrepancy in the numbers between Yoshitomi and Bergsten about the further appreciation of the yen, I don't think there is much difference because Yoshitomi is talking about policy proposals for a couple of years or so, while Bergsten is talking about the future trend over the next decade.

My question to Mr. Yoshitomi is concerned with interest rates. As one of three conditions for sustaining a real growth rate in Japan of, say, 3.5 percent, you say that interest rates could go down farther to 4 percent for long-term rates, and 2 percent for short-term rates. When talking about the long-term real rate, though, you should keep in mind people's expectations about the underlying rate of inflation. The underlying rate in Japan may be 2–3 percent, in terms of the GNP deflator or Consumer Price Index. So a forecast of a 4 percent long-term interest rate means a very, very low real rate. Also, when it comes to the short-term interest rate, the important deflator is the inflation rate in terms of the GNP deflator when we are discussing business activities. As you know, the GNP deflator has nothing to do with the direct impact of the appreciation of the yen. So during this year or next year, the inflation rate, in terms of the GNP deflator, may be 1–2 percent. A 2 percent short-term nominal rate means a very, very low real rate. So if we try to realize such low interest rates maybe more monetary expansion would exceed a double-digit rate, accompanied by a rekindling of inflation in a year or two. I would like to ask your thoughts on this.

The third question is concerning the targets you have in mind about the future ratios of external surplus or deficit of the host country to its GNP. It seems to me that Bergsten is thinking about the possibility of equilibrium in terms of a zero current-account surplus or deficit, while Ueda and Yoshitomi are talking about the possibility of decline of the Japanese surplus ratio to GNP from the present 3.7 percent to say 1.5–2 percent. Are you aiming at equilibrium at this stage? Or are you thinking that some surplus for Japan and some deficit for the United States will continue?

BERGSTEN:

To answer your last question first, my targets for current account/GNP ratios are as follows: for Japan, I accept Yoshitomi's earlier work which suggests that the equilibrium global current-account position for Japan was about 1–1.5 percent of Japanese GNP, not zero. I do not think, however, that the numbers suggested here by Mr. Yoshitomi or Professor Ueda begin to get us very far toward that level from the current 3.7 percent. I think that is the difference between us; we do agree things are moving in the right direction. I don't think with their numbers we are moving nearly far enough to get anywhere close to 1–1.5 percent which would be an equilibrium. For the United States, I am much less certain. I think there is a very legitimate debate on what should be the U.S. current-account target. Some would even ask whether we should have a current-account target. But accepting that for the moment, traditionally the U.S. has been a capital exporter and a net surplus country on current account. More recently it has been argued that we are the most dynamically growing of the industrial countries, so we should be a net capital importer. I tend to average it out, but with a big dose of pragmatism. If we could get our current-account deficit down to less than 1 percent of our GNP, I would think we would then put to rest a lot of these protectionist pressures, and minimize the drag on our economy. It probably would be sustainable in international financial terms. I am not sure I would stick with that forever, but that should be the first objective.

Now, on your first question as to how much nominal and how much real is in my call for a yen at 120 by the end of the decade, four or five years out, my answer is roughly half and half. You suggested an underlying inflation rate in Japan of 2–3 percent. I think in the U.S. it will probably be 4 percent. So you need 2 percent a year on the nominal exchange rate, to keep the real rate constant. In addition, it looks to me like Japanese productivity growth is going to be running maybe 3 percent a year, perhaps a little more. In the U.S., it is very low now, 1 percent or less; hopefully it will get better than that. But the gap there could be another 2–3 percent. My numbers thus imply an average annual appreciation of the yen of about 5 percent, roughly half nominal and half real.

YOSHITOMI:

I will just touch on the first question of the real exchange rate as well. When Fred Bergsten talked about the 160 yen today, I think that is a sort of equilibrium. At present, we have two kinds of equilibrium exchange rate. Equilibrating what? Equilibrating international price competitiveness, taking into account the structural changes — a sort of modified purchasing power parity (PPP) equilibrium rate. So when he said at the time of the publication of his study with Cline that 190 was the equilibrium, that was the pure PPP rate equilibrating international price competitiveness. If we take into account some structural changes as reflected in productivity growth differentials between the tradable and non-tradable sectors, I might say 175–180 would be the modified PPP exchange rate for 1986. The present exchange rate would be around that modified PPP exchange rate; that would contribute to the correction of the huge imbalances caused by the overvaluation of the dollar over the past several years.

As to the interest rate, I have a different underlying rate of inflation for Japan; at the OECD, we estimate an underlying rate of inflation just at 1 percent for the GNP deflator. For 1986 and 1987, we have a zero rate of inflation in terms of the consumption deflator; the GNP deflator is slightly above that. Therefore, if we take the underlying rate of inflation to be the GNP deflator at 1 percent for the coming several years, nominal interest rates on the order of 2 percent for short term and on the order of 4 percent for long term would be rather appropriate even in terms of real interest rates.

On your question of targets: I don't like the word targets, since we cannot target imbalances because an imbalance is an imbalance, after all. But let's call it the appropriate level of worldwide distribution of international imbalances, and that would be, for Japan, as Fred Bergsten pointed out, 1–1.5 percent of GNP. For the U.S., it would be perhaps slightly negative. Therefore, this appropriate distribution of international imbalances — that is, appropriate for avoiding serious trade protectionism — can be achieved by U.S. fiscal consolidation and exchange-rate changes up to this modified PPP rate. The real question we have now is, in order to unwind the international imbalances we now have, do we really need another misaligned exchange rate? The grossly misaligned exchange rate arose over the period of 1981–85. Because of that aligned exchange-rate relationship, we had large surpluses and deficits, and on top of that investment income, positive and negative, are accumulating every day. So we may need an overshooting in the opposite direction to unwind the present international imbalances. That is a key question we should have in mind.

RYUTARO KOMIYA:

I have a comment on what Fred Bergsten said. I think we agree that exchange-rate adjustments alone cannot cure the balance-of-payments problem. If the United States trade deficit is to be reduced, measures must be taken to increase aggregate savings out of given GNP or reduce aggregate investment and government expenditure in the United States. Consider a very simple model, consisting of two countries, the U.S. and Japan, which are very closely integrated. Suppose that the two economies reached their respective full-employment levels. Even in that situation, there would be a net capital flow from the high-saving, low-investment country to the low-saving, high-investment country. So one cannot predict an equilibrium yen-dollar exchange rate in 1990 or 2000 unless one specifies in detail the size of the budget deficit or surplus and various factors affecting private saving and investment in the two countries.

DIMITRI BALATSOS:
Kidder, Peabody

My question is for Fred Bergsten. You said that if we were to continue with a streak of deficits on the U.S. side on the order of $100 billion, sooner or later we would saturate the world with dollar claims, and therefore we may see a dollar meltdown. Could you be specific? Perhaps you can give us an approximation, how far are we from getting to the point where the rest of the world will feel saturated with dollar claims?

BERGSTEN:

No, I will not and cannot. That is the only honest answer. As you know, there have been those who felt we would have long since reached that point. I was never one of those, but there have been some estimable analysts who have worried that by now we would have had a free fall in the dollar. We did some projections in Stephen Marris's study late in 1985, asking what share of non-U.S. world savings would have to be lent to the United States to finance that baseline number I mentioned, with the U.S. current-account deficit rising to $300 billion. By 1990, close to one-third of all world savings outside the U.S. would have to move into the dollar in order to maintain *ex ante* the capital inflow needed to avoid a lot of broken crockery.

Now we have cut the outlook in half. It would be something on the order of 15–20 percent of world savings. That is much higher than any year to date, which has run 8–10 percent. But that just gives you the parameters.

I don't know of any normative basis on which to make a judgment as to when this is no longer sustainable. If you look at events when currency free-falls have occurred in the past, they have tended to occur late in the process, after the currency has already declined a lot. Then it picks up momentum and moves further. It is often triggered by completely non-economic events — Paul Volcker leaves the Fed, President Reagan leaves the White House. So I really can't give you an answer.

At the same time, I feel confident in saying the U.S. current-account deficit can't go on at these levels forever. Do I have an empirical or theoretical basis on which to say that? In all honesty, no, except to extrapolate how large the share of world savings going into the dollar, and therefore the dollar share of world portfolios would be, and simply to suggest that it would be so much different from any historical experience that it seems hard to believe that it could go on indefinitely.

EDWIN TRUMAN:
Federal Reserve Board

I also have a comment. Dick Cooper raised in his challenge to Fred Bergsten and Masaru Yoshitomi a question about whether their differences lie in forecast models or assumptions. Since Mr. Yoshitomi did mention that his results, he thought, were consistent with the results of the Federal Reserve Board's Multi-Country Model (MCM), I thought it might be useful to comment on that point. I only had available to me some simulations which dealt with the effect of a combined monetary-fiscal stimulus of the same order of magnitude in the major industrial countries, and the effects of that on the current account in various countries. In the MCM, you would get in dollar terms after three years almost twice the effect as in the OECD Interlink model. Interestingly enough, both move in a surplus direction, while the Japanese Economic Planning Agency (EPA) model moves the other way. For Japan the Interlink model generates one-third of the effect as the MCM, in dollar terms, of reducing the Japanese surplus in the current account. Since Japan's GNP is about half that of the U.S., the GNP effect gives a factor of six times. Again, interestingly enough, the EPA model has the other sign.

This seems to be a result of, obviously, a difference in models and in particular the fact that in the Interlink model you get more of a rise in Japanese interest rates than in U.S. interest rates, and therefore, a faster fall-back in Japanese GNP.

I don't mean to suggest where the truth lies in all this: I do mean to question Mr. Yoshitomi's view that Japan's fiscal stimulus will have no positive effect on the U.S. external account. Unfortunately, this — along with Professor Mishkin's citation in his paper of Mr. Emminger — has the effect of suggesting that all the problems of the world can be laid at the U.S. door, because none of the other countries has any effect on anybody else.

KAZUAKI HARADA:
The Sanwa Bank
One question to Mr. Bergsten. As far as I know, the majority of U.S. economists think that the American economy will recover very strongly, and also that oil prices will rebound rapidly towards the end of 1986. If these assumptions are right, will you change your view that the 160 yen would be suitable in the present situation? Don't you agree with the forecast that the yen's rate would get weaker rather than stronger towards the end of 1986?

BERGSTEN:
I think you have asked a crucial question, because in my presentation I could have been much more pessimistic by pointing to the things you mention which could, in fact, push the dollar back up late in 1986. If the U.S. economy does resume 4–5 percent growth, as some think, then we will be back to the growth gap of 1983–1984, at least on my outlook for Japan and Europe. That would put upward pressure on our interest rates, and strengthen the dollar on the exchange markets. That will then make the outlook for the trade and current account numbers even worse. A booming U.S. economy might help fight protectionism, but I think the correlation is more with the exchange rates than the aggregate unemployment rates, though obviously lower unemployment helps. So I worry, in fact, that if the conditions you suggest occur, they will make the trade problem, on balance, much worse than I am suggesting.

Now, two other points. One, I disagree with both those forecasts. I am not one who believes that the U.S. economy will resume very rapid growth in the second half. Nor do I believe that there will be a sharp rebound in the oil price. I am in a minority on that, and my judgment may not be as good as others in that area, but I doubt both. Nevertheless, if both occur, then your question is would I revise my estimate for the equilibrium exchange rate? I would not change my estimate purely from a change in relative economic growth rates; I regard that as a kind of cyclical factor that affects trade balances, to be sure, but really has little direct effect on underlying competitive relationships. So I would not change my equilibrium yen estimate for that. On the oil price, it would depend how far it went.

As I said earlier, the reason that I revised my notion of the equilibrium yen-dollar rate from 190 to 160 was not really the differential productivity growth that Yoshitomi mentioned but a sharp fall in the oil price, which has a differentially positive effect on Japan. All we did was reverse the effect that we had played into that analysis from the sharp rise in oil prices in the second oil shock in the late 1970s. If the oil price went back to $30 a barrel, then I would revise my analysis for the yen-dollar rate closer to 190. If it stays in the $15-$20 range, that is about what we have assumed would be the steady state or average that would emerge after the latest decline, so I would not revise it. In between, maybe a little bit. But my expectation is the oil price will level off somewhere in the $15-$20 range; at that level it would be consistent with the 160 to 1 forecast or normative judgment that I have been suggesting lately.

COOPER:

There may be some general interest in the prospects for the U.S. economy. Perhaps we can ask Professor Mishkin, since his remarks touched on this, for his view on the outlook over the next year. You mentioned the big increase in stock-market valuation, and its effect on consumer wealth. You didn't, I think, mention the depressing effect that the sharp fall in not just oil but energy prices has had on investment. I wonder if you have weighed those against one another.

FREDERIC MISHKIN:

I lean toward the more positive side in terms of U.S. economic activity. In some sense we are having a reversal of the two oil shocks that we have had. But it is not clear that, even if we have a very healthy growing U.S. economy in the second half of 1986 and 1987, we are going to see a rapid appreciation of oil prices. Part of the problem is that predicting oil prices involves a lot of other factors which have been notoriously hard to predict. Secondly, I think the linkage between oil prices and U.S. growth is probably very weak. I have more confidence in thinking that the U.S. economy will tend to be stronger in the second half of this year, rather than thinking that we will see a major appreciation of oil prices in the next year. In fact, even though there are negative aspects in terms of some sectors in the U.S. economy, I think that overall the U.S. economy does benefit quite dramatically from declining oil prices. Clearly, however, the Japanese economy benefits even more because oil's share of its imports is much greater than in the United States.

BEN CRAIN:
Banking Committee of the House of Representatives
A question for Professor Mishkin. I take your argument to be that budget deficits are not the primary cause of high real interest rates. Does that mean then that you also dissent from what I take to be the general view that budget deficits were the primary cause of the trade deficit? If we significantly reduced our budget deficit, but kept real interest rates high through monetary policy, would our trade deficit be reduced or expanded?

MISHKIN:

I think that on this issue saying that the budget deficit was not the major factor in terms of the movement of real interest rates doesn't mean that the budget deficit has no impact on the trade deficit. We are talking about movements of real interest rates: in fact, in Figure 5 of my paper you can see that there was a change of as much of 1000 basis points, from the level in the late 1970s, of real interest rates on short-term bonds; they were on the level of about −2 percent, and currently they are on the order of 4–5 percent. It is still entirely possible that budget deficits had some influence, let's say 100 basis points, which might then mean that that could be an important factor in the trade deficits. I think the key point of the research that I have done on this question is not that budget deficits don't matter at all, but that monetary policy is a much more important factor than most people realize in producing the high real interest rates that we now see.

I should mention also that there is other research which is related to this which looks at the end of hyperinflations, using quite different techniques than are used in the research that I described. This work basically examines when the behavior of real interest rates changes. It turns out to correspond very closely to when the Federal Reserve changes its monetary-policy regime, both in October 1979 and also in June 1920. The end of hyperinflations are also periods when real interest rates decline very dramatically, in fact much more so than we saw in the United States recently. We are currently seeing this in countries such as Argentina where real interest rates are on the order of 20 percent per month, rather than the order of a 5 percent annual rate. This is a very common phenomenon following hyperinflations. So what I am pointing out is just that monetary policy and the monetary policy regime — one which is accommodating and inflationary versus one which is non-accommodating, non-inflationary — can produce major changes in real interest rates. On the other hand that doesn't mean that budget deficits have no impact at all. Secondly, budget deficits do affect the total amount of saving in a country, which can have impacts on the trade deficit. So I think that there still can be arguments that we should reduce the deficit, although we should not think that reducing the deficit is going to eliminate high real interest rates. These may, in fact, be a sign of an economy which is more healthy, because price stability has been achieved.

QUESTION:
My question focuses on the extent to which Japan might stimulate its domestic economy. I have three short questions. The first is the Ministry of Finance has front-loaded a lot of their budget for this fiscal year, as far as public investment goes, in infrastructure development, and have announced a lot of projects such as bridges and airports and highways. I am wondering what is on their minds for the second half, when they will see a shortfall, and on into the next fiscal year, and whether we might expect a mini-boom in government spending, or will they be concerned with their deficit situation and be fairly miserly about further spending?

Is there a passing-the-buck syndrome going on between the Bank of Japan and the Ministry of Finance on who will take responsibility in stimulating the economy? Each side wants the other to take responsibility, either by public investment or by cutting interest rates. Which might play a larger role in that goal?

Finally, what sort of tax reform can we expect next year? I believe the Ministry of Finance has promised tax changes for the next fiscal year. Will that be tokenism or could this be considered to be genuine reform?

COOPER:
I guess that is addressed to Mr. Yoshitomi, although keep in mind that he now lives in Paris, not in Tokyo.

YOSHITOMI:
Yes, there will be a shortfall. But construction companies in Japan know about the shortfall if there is no supplementary budget in the second half. So they may not accelerate their expenditures for investment plans for the first half, but they will try to smooth out their investment plans over the year. So, in terms of actual impact on the economy, there wouldn't be much difference between the two cases.

About tax reform, I think this is really already on the agenda, so there will be quite a bit of modification of the present tax measures.

COOPER:
In their concluding remarks, I wonder if our speakers can address this question. Suppose we follow what is the conventional prescription: the U.S. should contract its federal budget deficit by an amount in the Gramm-Rudman targets on the order of 1 percent a year of GNP, maybe just slightly under that. Other countries should stay more or less on course with their existing policy, with perhaps some modest adjustments such as Mr. Yoshitomi suggests, the Japanese fiscal posture moving to one of neutrality rather than contraction. And, taking into account Professor Mishkin's quotation from Otmar Emminger, that the U.S. is still an elephant, perhaps a smaller one relative to the size of the boat than it was 20 years ago, but nonetheless still substantial. Can the elephant contract substantially, with no offset elsewhere without influencing the overall buoyancy of the boat? In other words, is it fair, or is it appropriate to postulate these adjustments by the countries we are talking about, the two large countries of the world and Europe, without looking at the overall global economic environment? In particular, do we run the risk of a global recession if we follow that line?

BERGSTEN:
I think you have answered your own question, but I will comment on it in the course of saying three or four things, really about Mr. Yoshitomi's presentation where we seem to agree and differ.

I think there was a very large measure of agreement between myself, Mr. Yoshitomi, and Professor Ueda on the *direction* of change that was needed, and the direction in which we are going under current policy. Their projections for 1987 and Ueda's for the longer run are very similar to mine and they indicate things are heading in the right direction. But I think they agree with my conclusion that with present policy, the imbalances both in the U.S. and Japan would be left at very high levels, levels that would be really much too great for the world economy, in purely economic terms, let alone in terms of fighting off trade protection and avoiding the disruptions that I mentioned. Recall that the ten leading Japanese economic forecasters view the Japanese current-account surplus in 1989 as being somewhere between $45 billion and $65 billion. Now, that is a good bit less as a share of GNP than today, but it is nowhere near the 1–1.5 percent that we agree is the equilibrium level. So I really think a consensus emerged from the speakers, to the extent they addressed it, that the adjustments currently underway are grossly inadequate to get back to an equilibrium level.

Second, on policy. I basically agree with what Mr. Yoshitomi said, that the exchange-rate changes by themselves, along with the necessary U.S. fiscal contraction, would account for maybe two-thirds of the necessary adjustments. The issue is, where do we get that other one-third? He and I are agreed that you need another one-third. Yoshitomi suggests two things: one, price pass-through in Japan from the declining oil prices; but Ueda pointed out that in the short run that has actually raised Japanese savings, and made the imbalance worse. Second, Yoshitomi suggested that Japan should expand on the monetary side, and lower interest rates. Leaving aside Suzuki's question about the real level of interest rates, I would worry about that, because it would tend to weaken the yen. If Japan relies on monetary expansion in order to get the needed domestic-demand pickup, then of course the tendency, *ceteris paribus*, is for the yen to weaken again and undo the two-thirds of the adjustment that we agreed would take place from the currency measures plus U.S. budget action.

That leads me to conclude that fiscal neutrality is just not enough in Japan. Yoshitomi's fiscal neutrality just will not go far enough. As I read his numbers, a neutral fiscal policy in Japan would leave a substantial *ex ante* savings-over-investment surplus, and therefore, by definition, would leave that current-account surplus well above an equilibrium level. So I doubt the internal consistency of Yoshitomi's own proposal, and suggest that it will leave us at an excessive level of Japanese surplus. It is going to continue these pressures on the world economy.

In fact, at the conceptual level, I don't really understand the argument for a neutral fiscal stance in Japan, or, in fact, other countries. But Yoshitomi said that if Japan achieves its goal of fiscal consolidation, the right course for the future is to leave fiscal policy neutral. The Japanese economy has had huge shocks from the private sector over the course of the 1980s — a huge expansion in demand through the growth of its trade surplus, and now a sharp decline in GNP growth from the decline in its trade surplus. Those are huge shocks. Why leave fiscal policy neutral in the face of big private-sector shocks on the grounds that it will produce a more stable economic outcome? I would have thought the opposite. You need the knowledge that fiscal policy will adjust to big shocks from the private sector in order to improve the chance of stabilizing the economy. So at both the conceptual and empirical levels, I have very strong doubts about the fiscal neutrality prescription, and therefore would suggest that in the current environment, much more stimulus is needed.

I would also note my agreement with Truman and disagreement with Yoshitomi on the very small effects his model gets on the U.S. external position from macroeconomic changes in Japan or in Germany. I am puzzled by Yoshitomi's numbers. He showed a fairly substantial effect on the external position of Japan itself, from a macro-policy change, but very little ever gets back to the U.S. So the obvious question is, who makes up the difference? That is a zero-sum game. If he assumes that the countries which, in the first round, get the benefit for their trade balances simply do nothing else, maybe it all stops there. But I would have thought that developing countries, for example, would take the additional foreign-exchange earnings, and probably tend to spend them on imports, from which the United States benefits a lot on the export side. So I would have expected a lot more pass-through. My models don't show whether it is six times as great, as Truman suggests, but I would have thought it was considerably more, and therefore I would tend to go in the direction that the Fed's model shows.

Finally, at the start of his comments, Mr. Yoshitomi raised a basic question. If the objective of all this is trying to avoid crazy trade policies in all of our countries, and fight protectionism, what is really the target of this exercise? Is it the U.S. deficit or the Japanese surplus? I think the answer is both, in a direct and indirect sense. There is a close relationship between changes at the margin in the Japanese surplus and the American deficit. It is not one for one; indeed, I have suggested there may be some paradox in the extent of those moves over the next year or two. Clearly, they move in the same direction, and one cannot ask an either/or question. Likewise, given the focus on Japan in American trade politics, the level of the Japanese surplus, I believe, is independently a factor that is going to affect the outcome. Therefore we have to worry about it as an independent variable.

Yoshitomi might have gone on to ask, "Do we worry about the nominal or the real external position?" As I mentioned, our real position is getting at least modestly better this year; the nominal position won't begin to get better until later on. Again, I think it is both. We could not be satisfied with simply a terms-of-trade change, a real gain; the nominal numbers have got to come down fairly substantially.

I don't think the trade numbers, either nominal or real, are the key, although I think the key is more akin to the real external position. The key is really whether the exchange-rate relationship between the dollar and other currencies sharply undermines the competitive position of American industry. When the dollar is overvalued by 20 or certainly 40 percent, you get a wide range of American firms which are normally quite competitive, indeed many who fight trade protection, which suddenly join the steel, textile, and auto people seeking trade protection because they are priced out by the size of the exchange-rate disequilibrium. So the whole balance of U.S. trade politics changes dramatically when the exchange rate gets way out of kilter. I would put the focus there, rather than on the trade numbers per se.

Finally, there is short term versus long term in the J-curve. It is true, as Mr. Gyooten said, that we won't see the trade numbers, in nominal terms at least, begin to turn positive for a year or so even if I got my additional 15 percent decline in the dollar overnight. That, however, I think can be explained. Even politicians will recognize that there are lags in the published numbers. More importantly, when the pricing relationships change, the order books start to change. The exporters start getting better results, the import-competing industries start seeing better results. That information starts coming in to Congress from home and the politics again then start to move back in a more favorable direction. So I think those technical issues can be taken care of if the fundamentals are taken care of. But in addition to U.S. budget action, in addition to direct action on the exchange rate through the G-5 continuing its efforts, it is also going to require a big effort in Japan — more than fiscal neutrality — to pick up the growth of domestic demand and contribute in a macro way to the necessary adjustments.

MASARU YOSHITOMI:
Since Fred Bergsten mentioned the origin of U.S. protectionism, I will start with that argument. He and I agree that exchange rates, particularly misaligned exchange rates, do affect protectionism, particularly in the U.S. If that is the case, since we have been observing substantial change in the overvaluation of the dollar, that should reduce protectionist pressures. I see some inconsistency in his remarks that exchange rates do matter for protectionism, and yet nominal imbalances also do matter. But if we think exchange rates are more important than nominal imbalances, we should really emphasize the importance of the real exchange-rate changes which should correct the sectoral dislocations of competitiveness which have occurred over the past several years. Now, we may see the opposite direction of that dislocation, not in the U.S. but maybe in Japan.

On that point about exchange rates: as I said, in terms of real exchange rates between the U.S. and Japan, the correction is over, but against the DM I don't think that the real exchange-rate correction has been completed. Against particularly the Asian NICs, the correction has got to be done in the very near future. That is an important point which we should keep in mind.

Second, when we talk about equilibrium exchange rates what are we equilibrating? We are equilibrating international competitiveness; we need a modified PPP exchange rate. That's fine, but since we have these huge imbalances, we may need another kind of misaligned exchange rate, that is, an overshooting of the real exchange rate over and above the modified PPP equilibrium rate in order to correct the huge international imbalances. That would depend on the market, and also on the time horizon during which we can reach some equilibrium distribution of international imbalances in the world economy. In 1990, I don't think another huge misaligned exchange rate in the opposite direction will be needed, but that depends upon the market's perception.

About fiscal neutrality: from the Japanese point of view there have been a number of external shocks of the exchange rate, including the overvaluation of the dollar, and "semi-Reaganomics"— not genuine Reaganomics — in 1981 and 1982. Because of these external shocks the external demand for Japanese products increased tremendously. At this time, growth in the Japanese economy was close to its potential. (The growth potential is 4–4.5 percent, and the actual growth rate of GNP just before these shocks would still be 3.5 percent or so — not much gap between the two.) Unless we are really Keynesians, advocating a fine-tuning policy, then given the small gap between growth potential and actual growth, such external shocks had to be accommodated by additional Japanese savings over its own investments in order to avoid overheating of the economy. That coincided with fiscal consolidation in Japan. Without fiscal consolidation over the same period, the Japanese economy would have been overheated.

Today, we would have a different situation in the Japanese economy, and in the world economy. So if we interpret the economic function of Japanese fiscal consolidation over the past several years in this way, then the correction of such external shocks — exchange rates and the U.S. fiscal deficit — might require the opposite direction of Japanese fiscal policy; that is, in order to reach reasonable imbalances or balances in the Japanese economy, the Japanese fiscal deficit, structurally defined, should expand from the present level of 1.5 percent of GNP up to say 4 or 4.5 percent, when we had such figures in 1980–81. Therefore, the real question should be whether we can really unwind international imbalances without expanding structural deficits of the Japanese economy.

But when we raise this kind of question, we should be very careful about what our targets are. If the target is to reduce the U.S. external deficit, which is associated with protectionism, then dollar exchange-rate corrections, including against the DM and Asian NICs, and fiscal consolidation in the U.S. would be enough to reach an equilibrium situation for the world economy in terms of international imbalances. But if the Japanese growth rate couldn't be sustained above 3–3.5 percent for the coming several years, that is a Japanese domestic issue. As I said, in the present OECD projections, Japanese domestic demand is projected to grow by 4–4.25 percent a year in both 1986 and 1987; GNP would grow by 3–3.25 percent a year in each year. Therefore, the negative contribution of net exports to Japanese GNP is about .9 percent of GNP for this year and next year. This is rather substantial. But if we continue along the path I have just described, we would reach a reasonably good situation where we wouldn't have serious protectionism or a possible breakdown of the international trade system. But from the Japanese point of view, that growth rate of GNP, 3–3.5 percent — would that be enough or not? How to take care of that kind of growth rate and the deflationary impact on the Japanese economy is the question for the Japanese authorities.

I personally do not advocate any fiscal expansion today which entails fiscal consolidation tomorrow. This really undermines the stable expectations in the private sector. We should pursue, as much as possible, fiscal neutrality; but if that is not possible, we may need a little fiscal expansion. But we shouldn't advocate fiscal expansion at the outset in order to take care of Japanese GNP problems.

About the U.S. external account: I have been talking about the cross-impact of Japanese fiscal action on the U.S. current account. The reasons for such an asymmetric cross impact are as follows, namely the relative size of the two countries' GNPs, and the exchange rate, and relative import elasticities, which with respect to income is also much higher in the U.S., say, 2.5 to 3 times that of Japan. Recently there is evidence that U.S. import elasticity has risen quite considerably, apart from the exchange-rate price effect. In part, this is an income effect. Also, if we take into consideration the composition of imports of the U.S. and Japan, you will certainly find the U.S. impact on the rest of the world is much bigger, since Japan imports raw materials, especially oil, and the impact on the rest of the world is less. The regional distribution of imports may have a bigger impact for the U.S. than for Japan. So all in all, the cross impact of fiscal action in Japan or the U.S. will be quite different, maybe 1 to 5 to 1 to 10.

Of course, if the non-U.S. major economies as a group — Japan, Germany, U.K., France, Italy, and others — could undertake expansion of fiscal policy simultaneously, that would certainly affect the U.S. external account favorably. But looking at the realistic situation in the world economy, in a policy context, we usually refer just to Japan and Germany. German GNP is much smaller than the Japanese, therefore the impact on the U.S. external account is much less than in Japan's case. Also, German trade is largely intra-regional trade; therefore if we integrate the European economy as a whole, intra-trade is much greater. The share of German imports in GNP, excluding intra-trade in the EEC, would be equivalent to that of Japan. Therefore, taking these factors into consideration, we would certainly find a substantial difference in the cross-impact of fiscal policy between the U.S. on the one hand and Japan and Germany on the other.

So it remains still true, I am afraid, that actions taken by Japan and/or Germany would have much less impact on the U.S. as compared with the impact of U.S. action on them.

There are many more things to say, but one last word about fine tuning. When the Japanese economy is growing at 3–3.5 percent compared with the growth potential of 4–4.5 percent, should we really advocate fine tuning? This brings us back to the issue of the good old days in the 1960s and 1970s, that is, whether fine-tuning policies would generate substantial benefits after all. We would not advocate such policies in the present context, given that the external account of the U.S. can be taken care of by exchange-rate changes and U.S. fiscal consolidation.

Japan and the United States:
Some Observations on Economic Policy

Albert M. Wojnilower
Managing Director, The First Boston Corporation

I AM not at all sure what, if anything, qualifies me to pronounce on U.S.-Japan relations. Perhaps I have been invited because my views allegedly have some popularity in Japan. A paper I wrote for the Federal Reserve was translated into and published in Japanese way back in 1962, but I never visited there until 1984. Possibly the reason why I may enjoy some reputation in Japan is that more than the typical American, although surely less than the Japanese, I think it important to protect the stability and continuity of the social order. Therefore, I am suspicious of policy changes that are advocated on essentially academic or ideological grounds.

No Exchange Stability Without Regulation

I have been particularly skeptical of the claims made in behalf of free and unregulated financial markets. A market is essentially a machine, a very powerful and elegant machine to be sure, but still only a machine that cannot know good from evil. Whether it actually does good or harm depends not on the machine but on the intent and skill of the human beings who connect and operate the machine. This is particularly relevant for financial markets, because such markets deal exclusively in intangible perceptions and anticipations, mobilizing human propensities that evolution has hard-wired into our beings, but which may not be well-suited for use at electronic speed. Participation in financial markets, it seems to me, invokes addictive mechanisms that closely resemble what makes people drive too fast, or drink or take drugs to excess, or gamble in other ways that involve unwarranted risks and costs to themselves and innocent bystanders. Also the sociology of financial markets has much in common with the functioning of "Men in Groups"—the title of a book by the outstanding biologist and anthropologist Lionel Tiger, who points out that males in groups tend to engage in behavior that in the modern environment may be highly inappropriate and, indeed, dangerous to survival.

This, at root, is why I have opposed many aspects of financial deregulation and have done rather well, in my opinion at least, in anticipating its consequences. Echoing James Tobin's remarks here, it was perhaps fifteen years ago that I predicted that the deregulation of international capital flows would lead ultimately to a world in which we restricted trade in order to preserve the freedom of capital flows. Here we are.

Because of the huge and mercurial capital flows, as well as for many other reasons you have heard in these sessions, currency stabilization, so much hoped for in Japan, is a long way off. Such stabilization is desirable, as political leaders elsewhere also are beginning to learn from their constituents, in order to enable people to plan a sensible choice of occupation and residence for themselves and their children. But desirability need not imply feasibility. What I want to call to attention is that achieving even a modicum of currency orderliness will necessitate a large measure of international interest-rate stabilization and coordination. And that, in turn, will be found to entail return to some regulation of financial flows and interest rates. It probably will happen, but not for years.

Meanwhile, the dollar-yen exchange-rate problem seems to me more psychological than economic. As it was neatly put to me in Japan, there really are two dollar-yen rates. One is the observed rate at which current transactions occur. The other is the more favorable rate that governs future planning: it is a hope rather than a reality. I saw little indication that this notional rate has changed enough to motivate the rearrangement of thought habits needed to redress the fundamental imbalance. The implication is that a still bigger shock to the observed market rate is necessary to bring home the urgency of structural change. ("Slow change" or "gradualism" seem to be euphemisms for "no change.") From this point of view the transient dips in the yen, such as from 160 to 175 recently, are unfortunate because they reinforce hopes that the desired rather than the actual exchange rate will prevail. The equilibrating role of the exchange rate is anyhow damped by the failure of Japanese consumer prices to fall as rapidly as they might. It is not so much that this would stimulate demand for imports as that, along with other stimulative measures, it might help to boost aggregate real consumer demand strongly enough so that it competes resources away from the export sector. I doubt that anything less would deflate the Japanese current-account surplus within the short political time frame that is relevant.

Beggar-Thy-Neighbor Policies

Turning to the U.S., we suffered a marked slowdown in industrial growth after the fall of 1984 due mainly to a surge in imports rather than a slackening of domestic demand. Protectionist sentiment intensified but did not immediately become a serious political threat because aggregate employment growth hardly slowed. Soon, however, the import surge was followed by a substantial weakening of exports. This seriously injured the large American multinationals, many of them traditionally free-trade oriented, which now found themselves threatened with deprivation not merely of earnings but of raison d'etre. All along, the U.S. economic upswing has been essentially a small-business experience, in which our industrial giants have hardly shared. For them to accept the loss of foreign markets as well as domestic would be to give up all hope for the future. Thus the large political weight of these companies combined with the growing protectionist groundswell to insist that our international competitiveness must be shored up. Put more harshly, the industrial giants of both the U.S. and Japan, knowingly or not, are pressing their governments as hard as they can to wage beggar-thy-neighbor trade policies against their competitors. In this, sad to say, they draw perhaps unwitting support from American economists who (mistakenly) predict disaster if the trade deficit persists, and from Japanese economists who (mistakenly) predict disaster if Japan's surplus were to shrink rapidly.

The U.S. government, strongly committed to free trade, felt obliged to respond. The Group of Five (G-5) communique of September 22, 1985 (it really should be called the G-1 communique), sent the message that the U.S. was determined to accelerate its economic growth, and to accomplish this primarily through faster growth of industrial exports. We intend to increase our share of the market for industrial goods in the context of more rapid expansion in the world economy. A lower dollar and lower interest rates worldwide are to be the tools. If the other industrial countries are willing to join in more rapid expansion, then their manufactures can continue to grow in absolute terms, though their relative market share will fall if U.S. policies succeed. But if they do not join, we may see no choice but to regress to the contractionary methods of the 1930s, when nations attempted to increase their sales even at the cost of shrinking the global pie.

Everything that has happened since September 22, including the Tokyo summit and subsequent developments, confirms this view of American policy. Notwithstanding mistranslation in Japan of statements by U.S. Treasury Secretary Baker, the American position actually has hardened. Recently Secretary Baker and other officials have promised Congress and the public that next year's trade deficit will be less than $100 billion—probably an impossible objective. For the first time there is a specific target. Fortunately we don't take such official targets too seriously, but failure to make good will lend legitimacy to aggressive exchange-rate and protectionist measures.

Note that the target involves quantity, not price. In Japan, by contrast, attention is focused on the price—the yen-dollar rate—rather than on the quantity of the surplus. I wonder what fraction of the American public—or even the Congress—knows that the current yen-dollar rate is between 100 and 200.

As an economist I believe, for reasons to be stated later, that the G-5 turnabout in U.S. policy was in some respects unfortunate and misdirected. Politically, however, perhaps there was no choice. In any case, now this is our policy. The baby has been born. It may be ugly, but it is our only and, indeed, the world's only baby. It is vital that it thrive.

As Rimmer de Vries and Jim Tobin warned yesterday, more rapid worldwide economic growth is a matter of desperate urgency. Secretary Baker has stated in so many words that the lower dollar alone cannot accomplish our quantitative objective. More rapid growth of world demand is essential. If it is not forthcoming, he implied, we will have to push the exchange-rate policy further, although we know it will be inadequate. Eventually, sharp protectionism will become unavoidable. We happen to have available in the U.S. almost precisely the unemployed labor and industrial capacity we would need to produce for ourselves the three percent or so of GNP that we are importing. We would be happier if we did that. Would others?

Our current policy is a close relative of the beggar-thy-neighbor policies of the 1930s, except that we offer the carrot of expansion. In contrast to the 1930s, the policy is designed to be inflationary rather than deflationary. Indeed, more inflation is what the world badly needs if it is to cope constructively with its enormous debt burden — public and private, internal and external. But the policy is one that easily can degenerate into a restrictive one, if the rest of the G-5 do not participate wholeheartedly — and if, in the likely protectionist reaction, we aimed our cannon at the less-developed countries (LDCs) and newly industrialized countries (NICs) as well as at the industrial powers.

Unhappy Central Banks

Needless to say, central banks by nature are unable to support enthusiastically a policy of worldwide monetary expansion and currency depreciation. For such a policy, who needs or wants an independent central bank? In the U.S., moreover, foreign policy is in the Constitutional domain of the Administration; the Fed can intervene in foreign exchange only under the supervision and instruction of the Treasury. When, as now, economic policy becomes a component of foreign policy, the Fed is disenfranchised. The G-5 agreement caged the central banks. The Bank of Japan, perhaps again because of the ubiquitous translation problems that seem to arise in U.S.-Japan relations, didn't realize this at first and raised interest rates. Even though this helped to appreciate the yen, the U.S. was not pleased. The rates came down, and then some.

Until recently, financial market participants took the subordination of the central banks to be long-lasting. It was assumed that the U.S. government would show persistence and perseverance in its new policy. As a result, although for months there was really no change in our monetary policy and only minimal foreign-exchange market intervention, long-term interest rates and the dollar plummeted. I believe that the previous strength of the dollar, too, can be at least partly explained by the public's belief that the then-prevailing policy regime would persist. Under pre-G-5 policies, there seemed to be no possibility that any currency would ever pose an investment challenge to the dollar or that the economies of the other industrial powers would improve materially relative to the U.S. When the financial public concluded after September 22 that the policy focus had changed to more rapid worldwide expansion, for which the potential was greater outside the U.S. because we were so much closer to full employment, it took down the dollar and launched bull markets in securities everywhere.

Current indications are, however, that the central banks are fighting back. They want to escape. Their apparent view that no one can move to lower rates unless everyone moves (so-called "multilateral surveillance") is tantamount to opposing any movement at all. No wonder the markets have become nervous when the U.S. which instituted the new policy seems to be losing its nerve to lead. As a forecaster I believe the markets' concerns are grossly premature, but I find the concern easy to understand.

Some of Keynes' biographers have concluded that, although a monetarist at heart, he focused his *General Theory* on fiscal stimulation because he despaired that the central bankers of his day would ever be willing to ease decisively. Perhaps they argued, too, as some Japanese (not central bankers) recently told me in defending the Bank of Japan's current posture, "Shouldn't there be a minimum rate below which a discount rate should not go?"

The Competition is From the LDCs and NICs

I have already suggested that U.S. policy is to some extent misdirected. This is because of its excessive emphasis on the exchange rates among the major powers, which tends to reduce the whole matter to a squabble over market shares among a few countries. While the industrial countries are busy contesting one another, they are ignoring the real problem. The competitive "enemy" is not in their group at all. It consists of the LDCs and NICs, countries in which the costs of diligent and increasingly literate labor are lower by quantum differences than in the wealthy countries. As is well known, the dollar has not been declining against the currencies of the poorer countries, so that we should not expect any swift narrowing of our (nonoil) deficit. We are substituting Korean and Taiwanese goods for Japanese at the same dollar price.

While the U.S.-Japan bilateral imbalance is huge, and has grown rapidly, it is nevertheless much less than half the story of what has been happening to U.S. trade these last few years. Indeed the U.S.-Japan problem may be something of a sideshow. The U.S. has simply adapted its internal structure to the new LDC and NIC competition sooner and more flexibly than Japan, which is only beginning to face up to the problem. Much of the tension between the two countries would be defused if Japanese companies were to contract to buy an additional $15 or $20 billion annually of American industrial products. (A much smaller quantity would have sufficed had the decision been taken a year or two ago.) The practical result might well be a corresponding increase in our imports from Japan. At present there are hardly any important American companies that have a vested interest in our having good economic relations with Japan, because they have never managed to get a foothold there. That moderating political force is sadly missing. Why? With the possible exception of automobiles, American entrepreneurship has played a key role in adapting Japanese and other foreign products to the U.S. market. Wholehearted help from Japanese businessmen is needed to sell American products in Japan, just as help from Americans is needed to sell in the U.S.

Manufacturing has been struggling for years in the established industrial countries. Since World War II, indeed, U.S. industrial exports have been strong only when we ourselves were financing them. We gave them away in the Marshall Plan. Then we financed them with huge overseas direct investment. Most recently we gave them away by having our banks finance them with foredoomed loans. The troubles of U.S. industry and agriculture are closely linked to the end of the giveaways.

Although most Japanese probably do not see it that way, Japanese exports also have been strong because they were being given away — given away at too cheap an exchange rate and for a net return consisting mainly of U.S. government securities. I will return to this subject at the end.

The best thing for the industrial countries would be to resume explicit giving. Of course the hysteria over budget deficits stands in the way. In this high-unemployment world people should stop trying to balance budget deficits: it only enlarges them. The U.S. ought to buy from our banks (at substantial discount), and then forgive, the bad international loans they made because our government wanted them to. Then Brazil wouldn't need to run a trade surplus approaching Germany's and we wouldn't have to worry about our banking system. If we provided enough financing, we could boost exports enough to generate a current-account surplus of our own. We are urging enlarged budget deficits on Germany and Japan; the same reasoning would prescribe the same medicine for us.

Bigger Budget Deficits Needed

Much of my forecasting reputation stems from having consistently subordinated the role of budgetary changes as explanatory factors in American exchange and interest rates. In a way, this issue has become moot after September 22; exchange and interest rates have collapsed while the budget deficit grew. If some Japanese still believe that cutting the budget will move interest and exchange rates, do they now want us to pull in our belt in a way that might raise the yen-dollar rate another third? In actuality, the chief consequence of the budget pressures has been the drastic curtailment of our military buildup, a matter that in a country using less than 80 percent of its industrial capacity should not be determined as the inadvertent by-product of a debate over economic doctrine.

The bottom line is that when nominal GNP slows, U.S. interest rates fall. If GNP accelerates, rates rise, regardless of what may be happening to the budget deficit. The critical thing is to be on guard against proposals that treat the world as though employment were full and real resources scarce, when the problem is the opposite. We should distrust advocacies that ask the world's only major engine of growth, the U.S., to shut itself down for the sake of international equilibrium. Then all would fall silent. It would be the equilibrium of the graveyard.

To reiterate, the sensible thing for both U.S. and Japan (and others) would be to resume and enlarge giving. Giving is the most effective form of dumping. Moving production abroad through foreign investment is not nearly as helpful. It has the fatal drawback that it exports jobs. To forestall protectionism, to preserve the value of the dollar-denominated assets owned by Japan and others, and to ease the burden of external debt on borrowers and lenders, it would be wise to give now in order to avoid larger losses later.

We face no serious nearby inflation danger, although the U.S. will have more inflation next year than this. Demand increases in the industrial countries stimulate employment and incomes mainly in the LDCs and NICs. Cheap imports from these countries continue to restrain wages in the rich countries. Raw materials prices likely will remain depressed because of over-supply, displacement by synthetics, and other reasons. For an extended time, the increased inflation will be in profit margins, not in costs. Inflation will become a problem only when labor markets in the LDCs and NICs have tightened sufficiently to weaken their appeal to multinational corporations. The responsiveness of wages to rising employment in such places as Korea or Colombia will determine when inflation becomes serious again. Chances are the world economy will be much happier once it has to deal with that problem than it is today.

Who Loses From the U.S.-Japanese Imbalance?

U.S. policy is not only misdirected but also to our disadvantage. The trade deficits have not done nor do they threaten us harm. Many American industries have suffered, but others have gained; total employment has continued to rise rapidly. While we were adapting our economy to the foreign competition, our standard of living rose and inflation subsided. And we rearmed. All these good things at once.

We have, to be sure, incurred a large volume of externally held claims. But these claims remain almost entirely denominated in dollars. We have just demonstrated how easily we can reduce by devaluation the foreign-exchange equivalent of the debt, in this instance with the cooperation of the very governments whose nationals' holdings we have in effect partly expropriated. Were we to inflate domestically as well, we could also float away the domestic purchasing power of this debt, as we did on a large scale in the 1970s and early 1980s. Who can doubt that we will do these things again in times of stress?

Until we are in reach of full employment, our chief balance-of-payments discipline should be to avoid any action that might put in question our ability to finance ourselves in dollars (which we can print) rather than foreign currencies (which we can't). We are nowhere near to jeopardizing that dollar borrowing power. On this reasoning, however, the U.S. should vigorously oppose the internationalization of the yen, as indeed should Japan. It is impossible for two key currencies to coexist without mortally threatening one another.

Some of our Japanese speakers suggested that each country should put its own house in order. In Japan, people probably are more responsible and better organized than we are with respect to ordering their households so that, even without consultation, each individual family's concept of order will not encroach on its neighbor's. But this cannot be generalized to big-power relations. Major powers cannot rearrange their houses without disturbing their neighbors — especially when all are trying to minimize interference with the freedoms and lifestyle of their own citizenry. Mutual restraint is essential, lest economic frictions poison relationships more important than the economic.

Japan's people save for many reasons, the same reasons that motivate people in all wealthy countries. Perhaps more in Japan than elsewhere, they save for old age. Because of the low birth rate and, in particular contrast with the U.S., the low immigration rate, Japan risks becoming an elderly society with diminished business vitality. The risk is particularly acute if Japan were to slip into a policy of preserving by subsidy its overconcentration of export industries, much as it now supports its farmers in style. If this is how matters drift, the elderly Japanese will, however, own lots and lots of U.S. Treasury securities. When the U.S. again decides, as last September, to meet its obligations in dollars of reduced purchasing power, what recourse will they have? The risk that foreign governments will evade their obligations has always gnawed at international investors but apparently is not yet taken seriously in Japan. The goods that Japan exports have immediate usefulness and value, but the true value of the assets they are purchasing — those electronic impulses on the books of the Federal Reserve — will not be determined until the moment of payment.

I am 56 years old. If I were a Japanese nearing retirement, and enjoyed a life expectancy which in that longevitous country, I am told, would be about 85, I would not look with equanimity on my generation's converting, year after year, $50 billion of current output into financial claims on a foreign nation on which my government seems to exert relatively little influence. I would rather see some of that output sold at home in a way that enabled me to accumulate financial claims on my neighbors. Our social bond and my vote will enable me to collect these claims even in times of stress. Americans are and show every sign of remaining, in contrast with Japan, a short-term oriented, mercurial, polyglot, multiethnic, mobile, and heavily armed people. Claims on such a people need to be accumulated and exercised with care.

Internationalization of the Yen:
Its Implication for U.S.-Japan Relations

Toyoo Gyooten

Director General, International Finance Bureau, Japan Ministry of Finance

SEVEN YEARS AGO I spoke at the Council on Foreign Relations here in New York City on the international role of the yen. It is a great pleasure for me to be given an opportunity today to speak again on this ever-intriguing but somewhat elusive subject. Of course, I am not using the same text.

Indeed, during the last seven years the internationalization of the yen has been discussed both in and out of Japan with increasing earnestness. It seems as if there is a genuine international consensus that the internationalization of the yen is just as desirable as free trade or non-inflationary growth.

When you look into the matter carefully, however, you will find that there is a certain amount of complexity and obscurity. Why is the internationalization of the yen desirable? How can it be realistically achieved? What is precisely implied by internationalization? As far as I know, these seemingly simple questions have not been sufficiently addressed. There are two different angles from which to view the internationalization of the yen. One is more interested in the beneficial impact created during the course of such development. In order to facilitate the internalization of the yen, financial markets in Japan as well as in the Euroyen market need to be deregulated and fostered. Financial institutions both Japanese and non-Japanese, need to be given greater freedom of activity in these markets. Borrowers and investors need to have easier access to yen funds and yen instruments. In other words, this view places greater emphasis on the process of financial deregulation in Japan which becomes inevitably necessary in order to expedite the internationalization of the yen. The process, rather than the goal, is the matter of the highest priority in this view. Most non-Japanese officials and private financiers seem to be advocates of this approach.

The other angle for approaching the issue is to try to assess the impact of the internationalization of the yen (i.e., greater share for the yen in world trade and finance) on the functioning of the international monetary system and the respective role of the U.S. and Japan in the world economy. For the last two decades, we have been discussing the so-called multi-reserve currency system, which would supposedly replace the present dollar-standard system. According to the advocates of such ideas, the yen and the German mark are expected to be used more widely in world trade and finance, so that they would share the burden of the key currency which is now borne by the dollar alone. Better distribution of the burden would enhance stability of the world monetary system.

There are, however, many unanswered questions. Is today's world ready, economically and politically, to accept such a transition? If a change is needed, what would be the desirable pattern of relationships among the U.S., Japan, and Europe? For Japan, particularly, the crucial question would be where to establish Japan's policy orientation vis-à-vis the U.S. and Asia-Pacific region.

Financial deregulation in Japan is certainly an important process toward the goal of the internationalization of the yen. It is a subject which deserves serious attention on an international level. However, I am of the view that we are now at a stage where we should start looking into the subject of the internationalization of the yen by focusing more of our attention on its implications for the world monetary system and the U.S.-Japan relationship.

Let me first take stock of the current phase of the internationalization of the yen. As the backdrop to this development, two basic facts should be pointed out. First, the world economic map keeps changing. While the U.S. economy remains the biggest and the strongest, the process of polarization is progressing. Japan, particularly, has made a remarkable gain. Second, while polarization in the world monetary situation has also been progressing, the U.S. dollar still enjoys overwhelming preeminence and retains the undisputed role as the key international currency.

In 1965, the U.S. held 40 percent of the total GNP of the free world while Japan and Germany shared 7 percent each. In 1984, the shares of the U.S. and Germany declined to 34 percent and 6 percent respectively, while Japan raised her share to 12 percent. With the recent large appreciation of the yen vis-à-vis the dollar, it is likely that, measured in dollar terms, Japanese GNP is equal to one half of U.S. GNP. In the volume of international trade, a similar reallocation has taken place.

When major currencies started to float in 1973, the dollar's share in the official currency reserves of the world was 76 percent as compared to 7 percent for the German mark. The yen's share was truly negligible. In 1984, the dollar's share went down to 65 percent, while the share of the German mark and the yen inched up to 12 percent and 5 percent respectively. The change was certainly not insignificant. It is quite obvious, however, that as a currency, the U.S. dollar still plays by far the most important role in the international monetary system. In 1985, 61 percent of the total issues of international bonds was denominated in U.S. dollars. The Swiss franc, the yen, and the German mark followed with respective shares of 9 percent, 8 percent, and 7 percent.

I said the use of yen in the international marketplace is growing but not quite adequately enough. Let me explain in a bit more detail.

In the last couple of years, a series of important steps was taken to deregulate the domestic financial market and to encourage the development of the Euroyen market. This period coincided with Japan's large current-account surplus and the huge amount of investible funds generated by the private sector. The Japanese interest rate was at an internationally low level. Helped by these factors, the use of yen in the international capital market showed an almost explosive expansion. In 1985, the equivalent of $7 billion of yen issues was made in Japan by non-Japanese corporations, public entities, and international institutions. Japanese banks extended $14 billion equivalent of yen credit to foreign borrowers, and there were $8 billion equivalent of Euroyen bond issues. Thus, starting from an almost negligible position five years ago, the yen has quickly secured the second or the third position, after the U.S. dollar, in the world capital market.

However, in the area of current transactions the yen's role is still lagging far behind the dollar and German mark. In 1985, only 36 percent of Japanese exports and 7 percent of imports were invoiced in yen. Naturally, the yen's use is greater in exports of products, such as machinery, where Japanese exports enjoy strong international competitiveness, and in exports to China and Southeast Asia. The fact that Japan does not belong to a regional economic bloc like the European Economic Community seems to contribute to the smaller role of the yen in trade. Also, primary products, such as energy resources, foodstuffs, and industrial materials, make up for a very high proportion of Japan's imports. Since many of these commodities are traditionally traded in dollars, the yen-invoiced portion of Japanese imports tends to be relatively small. There are, however, encouraging developments which would increase the use of yen in Japanese trade. As an increasing number of Japanese firms are expanding their production bases into overseas markets, the traffic of trade in industrial parts and finished products between parent companies and their overseas subsidiaries is expanding, thereby raising the yen-invoiced portion of Japanese trade.

In summary, in the monetary economy as well as in the real economy, a gradual polarization is taking place with the dollar's decline and the yen's rise. Nevertheless, the dollar's dominance as the key currency is still an undisputable reality. Internationalization of the yen, at present, is not much more than a relatively enhanced role of a secondary currency which complements the primary key currency.

If that is the case, how could and should the internationalization of the yen be promoted? On this point I stress that we have to be realistic in our ambition and balanced in our approach. After all, we can not dictate to the market a preference for a certain currency, and the market assesses a currency as the reflection of the issuing country's total performance. In other words, all that we can do and should do would be to prepare an environment so that the market would find use of that currency attractive. Among many steps which can be instrumental, I believe, under the present circumstances, there are two areas on which I believe we should focus our own attention.

One is to improve the market and provide financial instruments so that non-Japanese participants can invest in yen assets with a high degree of liquidity, safety, and profitability. In this respect, the present situation does not warrant complacency. The degree of non-resident participation in Japanese short-term financial markets is considerably lower than in the similar markets in the U.S. Of course, there is a strong link between the dollar's role as a key currency and the high degree of non-resident participation. Measures have been taken to improve the situation. In 1986, a market has been opened for a new type of short-term government note, steady deregulation of the CD market is scheduled, and, toward the end of the year, the Tokyo offshore market will become operative. These developments, I believe, will facilitate access by non-Japanese to liquid yen assets.

Another area of importance is the structural change in the Japanese economy. Improvement of the yen's market is certainly a necessary condition for the wider use of yen, but it is not sufficient in itself. The yen must win confidence in the market so that it will be built-in, as an integral component, to the normal functioning of other economies. Prudent economic policies, a stable political situation, a reliable international position, and sustainable non-inflationary growth will all contribute to the higher credit standing of the yen in the market. However, these will not suffice. The structure of the Japanese economy needs to be more integrated with other economies through horizontal and vertical division of labor, so that other economies will regard the Japanese economy not just as a trading partner but as a much closer associate in overall economic activities. Overseas direct-investment activities need to be stepped up, together with the transfer of technological and managerial know-how, and with much more active exchange of human resources. Improvement of the climate for investment in host countries is particularly hoped for.

What are the implications of the yen's internationalization to the world monetary system and the U.S.-Japan relationship?

As I stated earlier, the best and the farthest we can envisage, under the present circumstances, is for the yen to steadily increase its role as a secondary international currency to complement the primary currency in the world economy. Even so, the enhanced role of the yen will eventually have no small impact on the international monetary situation.

First of all, what are benefits and costs of being the key international currency? The key-currency country is free of the need to earn foreign exchange in order to finance necessary imports, and is therefore less constrained by the external balance in pursuit of its domestic economic policy. The key-currency country is more immune from exchange risks because trade and capital transactions are largely denominated in its own currency, and it also may enjoy the benefit of being the international financial center.

On the other hand, the key currency country often finds itself in a dilemma in which it has to run a deficit, either on its current account or on its long-term capital account, in order to provide the rest of the world with liquidity. At the same time, it cannot continue to run a current-account deficit because to do so would undermine the credit-worthiness of the key currency. It is also argued that, being the most widely-used currency in the market, the key currency tends to become a target of speculation, and the need to preserve exchange-rate stability sometimes makes it difficult to pursue an autonomous monetary policy at home. Furthermore, it is feared that large holdings of its currency by non-residents would reduce the effectiveness of domestic monetary control.

When the U.S. economy enjoyed the overwhelming share in the world, it could easily absorb the cost of being the key currency and could fully enjoy the accompanying benefits. However, the relative decline of U.S. dominance in the world economy has considerably diminished its ability to absorb such costs. The subtle but fundamental change which took place in U.S economic policy in 1985 seems to indicate the recognition on the part of the U.S. of the new situation.

It is quite reasonable to assume that Japan, with its strong economic position and well-developed financial markets, should be prepared to share the burden of an international currency.

As secondary international currencies like the yen and German mark raise their relative weight in the world monetary system, it is inevitable that we are coming closer to a multi-reserve currency regime. Sometimes it has been argued that because of the shift among reserve currencies, the multi-reserve currency regime is likely to destabilize foreign exchange markets. However, as long as we can maintain a reasonably harmonious situation among major currency countries, the fact that there are enlarged and deep markets for non-dollar currencies should contribute to a better exchange-rate stability. Also, it will enable us to minimize exchange-rate risk by diversifying a portfolio of respective assets. It should be emphasized, however, that in order for a multi-reserve currency regime to function smoothly and to provide stability, the economic performance of the major countries must maintain a reasonable degree of convergence, and for that purpose, policy coordination among them will become critically important. We strongly support the highest level of political will expressed at the Tokyo Summit Meetings in May 1986.

Strong U.S. and Japanese economies built upon a close interdependence are no doubt the cornerstone for world economic stability. It is unprecedented in world economic history that the strongest and the second strongest economies could maintain such a broad, cooperative relationship. In order to preserve the basic structure of beneficial coexistence, however, we cannot afford to be complacent, because the changing relationship will inevitably create friction and increase tension. We shall be constantly asked to review our own economic policies and structures so that we can steer clear of collision while maintaining momentum in the development of each economy.

The enhanced international role of the yen does indeed add another critical element to a sensitive situation. For example, considerable imbalance between the dollar's role in the world monetary system and the U.S. role in the world economy as a whole is imposing upon Japan a unique burden of being the second currency. In spite of its size and strength, the Japanese economy is still very vulnerable to developments in the financial and foreign-exchange markets in the U.S. There is concern that such vulnerability has been increasing recently. The U.S. share in Japanese exports, imports, and overseas investments have increased between 1975 and 1986 from 20 percent to 37 percent, 19 percent to 20 percent, and 28 percent to 45 percent, respectively. Most Japanese portfolio investments are made in dollar instruments. If the interdependence goes beyond an optimum degree, there is a danger that adverse side-effects may well exceed the benefits.

It will be an urgent task for Japan to try to establish a broad direction for her medium- and long-term policy formulation while taking into consideration the development of an increasingly independent Europe, of a desirable relationship with the diversified but dynamic Asia-Pacific region, and the optimum degree of interdependence with the U.S. The internationalization of the yen needs to be viewed from a broad perspective. It is a great challenge.

Recent Developments in the Yen-Dollar Exchange-Rate Relationship

Ryutaro Komiya
Professor, University of Tokyo

MY ASSIGNMENT is to discuss papers by Toyoo Gyooten and Manuel Johnson. But, until last evening I didn't know that Mr. Gyooten would speak on the internationalization of the yen, instead of recent developments in the exchange rate. Moreover, Governor Johnson's paper has not yet been presented. I have chosen, then, to make a few remarks of my own on recent developments in the yen-dollar exchange-rate relationship.

1. My first comment is concerned with the success of the Group of Five (G-5) intervention. The G-5 intervention in September 1985 was remarkably successful in bringing down the dollar exchange rate, which had been very high according to any criterion for nearly four years since 1982. It was similar in several respects to the coordinated intervention in November 1978, although the intervention in these two instances were in opposite directions.

First, the dollar exchange rate before the coordinated intervention had long been much out of line, that is far out of the range that most people thought reasonable.

Second, an international consensus was established among the governments and central banks that the dollar exchange rate had been much out of line and that there was need for coordinated action. Putting it somewhat differently, in both cases the United States authorities agreed to change the laissez faire, non-intervention policy, which they had pursued before the coordinated intervention.

Third, the market participants correctly or not, interpreted the statement announcing the joint intervention and the action of intervention as a signal for forthcoming changes in macroeconomic policies of the countries concerned, especially the United States.

Fourth, the actual amount of market intervention was very small in both cases, compared even simply with the market turnover, not to speak of the total size of financial assets denominated in foreign currencies held by residents of each country.

Thus, it seems to me that the prolonged and substantial overvaluation of the dollar was corrected following the G-5 intervention, not primarily by the central banks' sales of the dollar and purchases of other currencies in the exchange markets. Rather it occurred in response to the announcement of a new direction of macroeconomic and foreign-exchange policies of major countries, especially by the United States, which was taken to be more or less credible by the exchange market participants.

2. My second point is concerned with how to account for the large change in the yen-dollar exchange rate since the G-5 intervention. The yen has appreciated more than 40 percent relative to the U.S. dollar—from about one 240th to one 165th of a dollar—and nearly to the same extent on an effective exchange-rate basis. This is indeed a very substantial appreciation. It is difficult to explain why the yen has gone up so much within such a short period. To begin with, it is not easy to explain why the dollar had been substantially overvalued, and the yen undervalued, for nearly four years before the G-5 intervention. I feel that three factors are among the most important ones in accounting for the large yen appreciation.

First, market participants revised their expectations about the long-run equilibrium rate of the yen-dollar exchange rate as a result of the G-5 and the following joint intervention, as already mentioned. Perhaps they now expect the U.S. government and Congress to be more willing to reduce the budget deficit and to loosen the money supply, leading to lower interest rates and a smaller trade deficit in the United States.

Second, as a matter of fact, since September 1985, the long-term interest rate in the United States has come down considerably, and the difference in the long-term interest rate between Japan and the United States has narrowed by 2 to 2.5 percent between October 1985 and June 1986. According to the formula of the so-called long-term interest parity theory of the exchange rate, assuming that the average time horizon for long-term uncovered investment in bonds is something like ten years, the long-term equilibrium level of the yen-dollar exchange rate is somewhere between 160–180 yen to the dollar, by multiplying these three sets of numbers—namely 2–2.5 percent, ten years, 160–180 yen—one obtains 32–45 yen. In other words, a narrowing of 2 to 2.5 percent in long-term interest rate differentials between the United States and Japan would mean an appreciation of 32 to 45 yen to the dollar; this is about 40 to 60 percent of the recent yen appreciation. Thus, a straightforward application of the long-term interest parity theory explains about 40 to 60 percent of the recent yen appreciation.

Third, the market participants might have become aware of the long-run consequences of the overvalued dollar and the undervalued yen. If the yen-dollar exchange rate remained at the pre-G-5 level, and therefore the U.S. current-account deficit continued to be as high as 3 to 4 percent of its GNP, net U.S. indebtedness to the rest of the world would increase fairly rapidly. It will be bound to weaken the dollar through a process of portfolio selection and a decline in the confidence in the dollar. Conversely, the undervalued yen will lead to rapid accumulation of Japan's net external assets, and sooner or later, will strengthen the yen. Awareness of such possibilities might have led to a revision of people's expectations.

3. My third point is concerned with the international scheme to stabilize exchange rates. As a result of its unexpected and remarkable success, some of those who have long been in favor of the fixed exchange-rate system or some sort of "stable" exchange rates considered the G-5 intervention a beginning of international cooperation leading to a target zone scheme, or some other sort of managed floating system. But, in my view, it is unlikely that such a stable exchange-rate system can be worked out.

First of all, the G-5 intervention was successful because the dollar exchange rate had been much out of line for an extended period, and because major countries were able to agree on a need for joint action. In normal times, it is difficult for countries to agree on appropriate levels for exchange rates of their currencies. As a matter of fact, when the yen appreciated first beyond the 200-yen line, and then the 180-yen line, the international consensus which existed at the time of the G-5 began to erode. At the time of the Tokyo summit, the yen was around 165 to a dollar, and was still tending to appreciate. Japanese industries and the government were almost screaming for help to stop further appreciation of the yen, but none of the other major countries responded to Japan's request for joint intervention in the reverse direction.

One of the beauties of the old Bretton Woods system was that the procedure for the revision of the exchange parity was set down clearly and in detail. The country wishing to change the parity of its own currency, in a situation of "fundamental disequilibrium," proposes the change to the International Monetary Fund, and so forth. After the collapse of the old Bretton Woods, since the Smithsonian Conference, the countries have repeatedly experienced great difficulties in agreeing on the appropriate levels of the exchange rates. In the absence of a formal procedure such as under the old Bretton Woods system, it is nearly impossible for countries to determine the appropriate levels or ranges of exchange rates for individual currencies.

Another major difficulty is that the amount of funds needed for the stabilization intervention would be enormous. So long as each country pursues independent monetary and budgetary policies, it would be difficult to stabilize the exchange rate within a narrow range, or even a 20 to 30 percent range. If countries agree to relinquish monetary autonomy and to use in effect a common, cosmopolitan money, then there will be no problem of exchange rates. But short of such complete monetary integration, stabilization of exchange rates would be incompatible with the free trade of goods and services and unrestricted capital movement.

In short, it seems to me that international cooperation of governments and central banks in the area of exchange-rate policies can be feasible only in an unusual situation in which they find a currency much overvalued or undervalued, and agree on the need to bring back the exchange rate in question to a more reasonable range.

The above would mean that under normal circumstances the exchange rate of a major currency will be basically left free to fluctuate, and will move to wherever the market forces will bring it. This will involve a considerable degree of volatility as observed in the past. Exchange-rate volatility should be viewed as the cost we must pay for maintaining both national monetary sovereignty and the freedom of international movement of goods, services, and capital at the same time.

4. My fourth remark is concerned with views on the yen-dollar exchange rate. There appears to be a division of opinion in Japan as to the current level of the yen-dollar exchange rate between practitioners on the one hand, and economists, especially academic economists, on the other. A popular view on the recent yen appreciation among Japanese practitioners — that is, politicians, policymakers, and businessmen — seems to be that the appreciation since this February is excessive, and that the Japanese economy will be hard hit if the current level of the yen persists. But I think a majority of Japanese economists who specialize in the area of international monetary affairs, and perhaps even of our economist colleagues in the Economic Planning Agency and in the Bank of Japan do not share the popular view. I would think that they more or less welcome the yen appreciation, although many feel that the appreciation has been much too sudden, and will cause great hardship for Japanese export industries because of its suddenness. The appreciation of the yen would correct at least partially the large current-account imbalance of the United States, and lower the pressure for protectionism in the United States. On the Japanese side, too, the current-account surplus in 1985 and 1986 amounts to nearly 4 percent of GNP; this is devoting too large a proportion of GNP to overseas investment, especially in the form of portfolio investment into the United States.

It would be better for Japan to shift resources away from the current-account surplus to domestic expenditures, especially investment in social overhead capital and residential construction. Such a shift has not been facilitated so far, partly because the Bank of Japan was afraid of a further weakening of the yen if the domestic interest rate was lowered, and the interest rate in Japan, especially the real rate of interest, was unusually high, in spite of stagnant domestic economic conditions. The large appreciation of the yen will make it possible for Japan to lower the interest rate, and expand domestic investment.

Although the future course of the exchange rate is always unpredictable, I would be much surprised — and disappointed — if the yen would depreciate much again, and go back beyond the 200 line, provided that there are no unexpected upheavals, such as oil-price shocks, wars in the Middle East, an LDC debt crisis, and so on. In other words, I believe that the recent appreciation up to the 160–180 range is by and large a movement toward a medium-run equilibrium level, rather than away from it or beyond it. Whether the yen-dollar rate will remain in that range, of course, depends on macroeconomic conditions in the United States and Japan, among other things, and especially on the long-term interest rates in the two countries.

The balance-of-payments adjustment process resulting from the large yen appreciation will be a prolonged one, and is likely to be a painful one for Japan. Export industries and import-competing industries will be hard hit, and the depressive pressure on domestic business conditions will be severe. Yet the current-account surplus will not disappear: a surplus amounting to, say, 1.5 to 2.5 percent of GNP is likely to remain even after the J-curve effect will have been fully worked out.

Considering the likely development of Japan's balance of payments and that of the United States in the near future, the present level of the yen could not be said to be an overvalued one. In 1978, the appreciation of the yen beyond the 200 line lasted only for six months, but this time, I would think that a majority of Japanese businessmen expect the persistence of the yen rate in the 160–180 range for a much longer period, even though they talk bitterly about the "excessive" appreciation of the yen.

5. My final remark is concerned with the point that the recent exchange-rate adjustment must be a great relief for many U.S. manufacturing industries, as well as other industries producing tradable goods. For industries competing with Japanese imports it is equivalent to a 40 percent across-the-board surcharge on these competing products from Japan; for industries exporting to Japan it is equivalent to a general export subsidy of 40 percent. So U.S. competitiveness should improve very substantially vis-à-vis Japan, provided that the wage-push and other inflationary pressures are restrained. Competitiveness vis-à-vis other countries should also improve, though somewhat less dramatically.

I do not think the Japanese surplus of $50 billion-$60 billion, or 2–3 percent of Japanese GNP, is a disturbing factor for the world economy. It is a small amount relative to the total saving—and investment—in the world economy as a whole. It is an important source of capital supply for world economic development. What is disturbing is the U.S. trade deficit, not the Japanese trade surplus. Just taking the size of the imbalance alone, the U.S. deficit in 1984, 1985, and 1986 are all between twice and three times as large as the Japanese surpluses in the respective years.

Therefore, in order to save the world's free-trading system from collapsing, I believe it is most important for the United States to take measures for reducing its trade deficit, by whatever the policy options it has available—cutting the budget deficit, lowering interest rates to induce the dollar to depreciate further, or by an export-import link system as I proposed in my paper circulated as background material for this conference.

The Yen-Dollar Relationship: A Recent Historical Perspective

Manuel H. Johnson
Member, Board of Governors of the Federal Reserve System of the
United States

Bonnie E. Loopesko
Economist, Board of Governors of the Federal Reserve System of the
United States

AT THE CENTER of the current debate on international economic-policy coordination lies the question of how to foster and sustain a configuration of exchange rates that contributes to stability in the world economy. Underlying this debate are more fundamental issues: How are exchange rates determined? What forces induce exchange-rate movements that *ex post* are judged to result in misalignments? Common to many recommendations for reform of the exchange-rate system is the notion that exchange rates should move so as to promote better external balance. In this context, the question often raised concerning the yen-dollar relationship is: What level of the yen-dollar exchange rate would be consistent with a more balanced trade relationship between Japan and the United States? Posing the problem in this manner, however, belies the complexity of determining a more appropriate alignment of exchange rates.

Because the issues of exchange-rate alignment and external balance are inextricably linked in public debate, this paper explores their interaction. The analysis highlights the influence of current-account developments on the yen-dollar exchange rate, as well as the reverse. Because the current account and capital account are simultaneously determined, it will also be useful at times to consider the interaction between the capital account and the exchange rate. There is no presumption that bilateral exchange rates should move solely to achieve bilateral trade balance. While promotion of a reduction of Japan's record surplus vis-à-vis the United States is clearly an important, even pivotal, concern with respect to the yen-dollar exchange rate, key structural differences between the Japanese and American economies suggest that balanced trade between them may be improbable and even undesirable for some time.

Section I sketches the broad outlines of the factors driving medium-run swings in the yen-dollar exchange rate over the floating-rate period. The interplay of domestic and foreign macroeconomic policies and developments, major global supply shocks, and the liberalization of Japanese financial markets has produced periods of more-or-less sustained yen appreciation or depreciation. After a brief consideration in Section II of the implications of financial liberalization for the yen-dollar exchange rate, Section III takes a more detailed look at the secular developments underlying movements in the yen-dollar relationship, tracing the evolution over the past two-and-a-half decades of some of the more salient structural features of the American and Japanese economies. Developments in each economy related to productivity, the composition and regional pattern of trade, real wages, the terms of trade, and the savings-investment balance provide insights into the longer-run trends of the Japanese current account and associated pressures for yen appreciation over time. Section IV weighs the relative contributions of changes in the exchange value of the yen and other economic factors in fostering more balanced trade between Japan and its major trading partners, including the United States. A concluding section distills the analysis of the paper and comments on recent and prospective developments in the yen-dollar relationship.

I. *An Historical Overview of the Yen-Dollar Relationship*

In April 1949, the official Japanese exchange rate was established at 360 yen = US$1, and in May 1953 this rate was agreed on with the International Monetary Fund as the par value. It was not until December 20, 1971, after four months of floating following the suspension in August of the dollar's convertibility to gold, that the yen exchange rate was revalued to a central rate of 308 yen = US$1 and wider fluctuation margins were set.

During the preceding 22 years of an unchanged exchange rate of the yen against the dollar, the Japanese economy had undergone a dramatic structural transformation. While in the 1950s Japanese exports were widely viewed as being of such inferior quality that they could not compete successfully with products from the major industrial economies, by the early 1970s Japan had developed burgeoning trade surpluses with many of these same economies. The implied undervaluation of the yen together with the fundamental disequilibrium in the U.S. external accounts were two principal elements of the international imbalance that led to the demise of the Bretton Woods system. After the failure of measures in mid-1971 aimed at diminishing Japan's rapidly increasing trade surplus and despite large net purchases of foreign exchange by the Bank of Japan, the yen appreciated to yen 301 = US$1 (the upper limit of the band around the central rate of 308 yen = US$1) by mid-1972, and remained at about that level until the advent of generalized floating exchange rates in early 1973. In the early months of floating, the yen strengthened further against the dollar, for a total appreciation of 27 percent since 1971.[1] Figure 1, which traces movements in the yen-dollar exchange rate since 1960, shows the yen's steep appreciation over this period.

From 1973 to 1975, the yen depreciated irregularly against the dollar. Throughout 1973, Japan experienced a worsening inflation that was initially

FIGURE 1

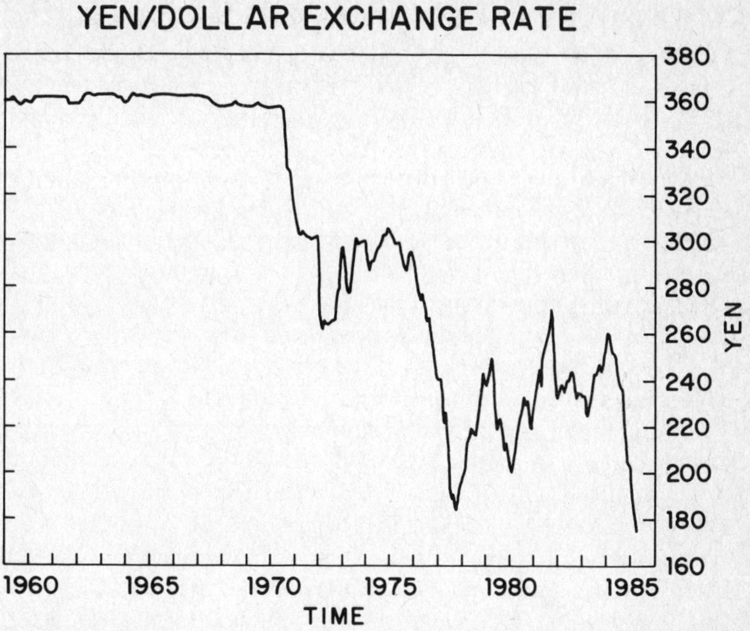

YEN/DOLLAR EXCHANGE RATE

due to an unusual degree of synchronization of the expansions in Japan, the United States, and many other economies. During this period, the strongest OECD-wide boom in 20 years, prices of certain raw material imports surged, including the October 1973 oil-price explosion. The ensuing large wage settlements in Japan set off a wage-price spiral that sent Japanese prices soaring, with wholesale and consumer prices jumping at respective rates of 37 and 26 percent (on a year-over-year basis) at their peaks in February 1974. This was the worst episode of inflation in Japan since the early 1950s. Inflation in the United States, while also accelerating, peaked at 19 percent for wholesale prices and 12 percent for consumer prices (on a year-over-year basis) in November 1974.

The period of adjustment to the first oil shock in Japan lasted several years. The oil-price hike hit Japan just as the economy was showing signs of overheating and the Japanese authorities were already concerned about accelerating inflation. In 1974, the Japanese economy entered an 18-month recession, the most severe recession in Japanese post-war history. In response to accelerating inflation, stagnating growth, and a deteriorating balance of payments, the yen depreciated 16 percent against the dollar between June 1973 and December 1975. After running a record current-account surplus of $6.6 billion in 1972, Japan ran a string of current-account deficits from 1973 through 1975, the first such deficits since 1967.

From 1976 through mid-1978, Japan's current-account surplus rose from $3.7 billion in 1976 to an unprecedented $16.5 billion in 1978, while consumer price inflation dropped to under 4 percent by mid-1973. Tight financial policies in 1973 and 1974 and wage restraint starting with the 1975 spring wage negotiations combined to produce these marked improvements in inflation and the external deficit. From its trough in December 1975 through October 1978, the yen appreciated by 40 percent against the dollar and 34 percent on an effective, or weighted-average, basis. Signs of current-account adjustment began to emerge by mid-1978. Figure 2 highlights the tendency of the exchange rate to respond to current-account developments, for reasons which will be discussed below. Also evident is the tendency for the current account, over time, to respond to exchange rate movements.[2]

The package of cooperative actions announced by the U.S. authorities on November 1, 1978 to stem the dollar's depreciation marked the beginning of a period of dollar appreciation against the yen. From November 1978 through April 1980, the yen depreciated 30 percent against the dollar. Compounding this downward pressure on the yen was the second oil-price hike in early 1979. The resulting surge in import costs, combined with the earlier sharp appreciation, produced a stunning $25 billion drop in Japan's current balance between 1978 and 1979, from a surplus of $16.5 billion to a deficit of $8.8 billion. In an effort to discourage the pattern of speculative hoarding and rapid spread of inflationary expectations that had followed the first oil shock, Japanese authorities quickly responded after the second oil shock with monetary and

FIGURE 2

EFFECTIVE YEN EXCHANGE RATE AND JAPANESE CURRENT ACCOUNT

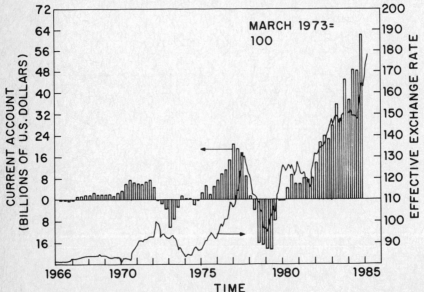

fiscal restraint. These policy actions were instrumental in promoting the moderate nominal wage settlements in the spring 1980 wage round. Although the current account deteriorated further in 1980 to an annual deficit of $10.7 billion, the turnaround in both inflation and the external balance was already evident by late 1980.

The Japanese current account moved back into surplus in 1981. As the current-account surplus increased more than tenfold from $4.8 billion in 1981 to $49.3 billion in 1985, the yen strengthened substantially on a weighted-average basis but passed through two periods of substantial rises and declines against the dollar. From January 1981 through February 1985, the dollar rose steeply against all major currencies, gaining 39 percent on balance against the German mark and 42 on an effective basis. The dollar's net appreciation over those four years against the yen was less, amounting to only 29 percent.

Starting in about 1981, movements in the yen-dollar exchange rate frequently corresponded to changes in the interest differential between yen and dollar securities. In particular, movements in the differential between real returns on yen and dollar-denominated securities, particularly at the long end of the maturity spectrum, started to correlate more closely, though it is important to note far from perfectly, with fluctuations in the real yen-dollar exchange rate. These two series are displayed in Figure 3.[3]

FIGURE 3

REAL YEN/DOLLAR EXCHANGE RATE AND LONG-TERM REAL INTEREST RATE DIFFERENTIAL

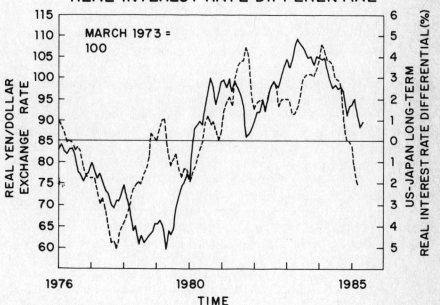

That this correlation between interest differentials and exchange-rate movements became more evident in the early 1980s may not be a coincidence: it coincides closely with the substantial liberalization of Japanese capital markets that picked up momentum starting in 1979. Prior to that time, controls on capital inflows and outflows were instituted or relaxed as a direct means of reversing sharp sustained movements in the exchange value of the yen. Liberalization measures of particular importance were the opening of the *Gensaki* (government bond repurchase) market to non-resident investors in 1979, which offered a powerful channel for international interest arbitrage, and the December 1980 Foreign Exchange and Foreign Trade Control Law which established the general principle that external transactions should be decontrolled subject to prudential guidelines, emergency clauses, and certain residual restrictions that would gradually be relaxed. The 1980 law marked the end of the discretionary use by the Japanese authorities of restraints on capital inflows and outflows to influence the yen exchange rate.

Since February 1985, the yen has strengthened about 35 percent against the dollar as part of a generalized decline of the dollar against the major currencies. In the eight months since the September 22, 1985 Plaza meeting of the Group of Five (G-5), the yen's appreciation has been particularly sharp, rising nearly 30 percent against the dollar and about 20 percent on a weighted-average basis. This most recent period of yen appreciation was initially encouraged by coordinated intervention by Japan and other G-5 countries and by monetary policy actions in Japan, as well as by a widespread perception in the exchange markets that economic factors, such as those discussed in Section III below, warranted a stronger yen.

From this overview of the yen-dollar relationship under floating exchange rates, five main points emerge. First, while day-to-day gyrations in exchange rates may defy explanation in terms of fundamental economic factors, the broad swings in the yen-dollar exchange rate are consistent with our general theories of the relationship between domestic and global economic developments and exchange-rate movements. For example, periods of high Japanese inflation tend to correspond with episodes of yen weakness.

Second, the steep and rapid appreciation of the yen that has occurred in the past 15 months is not entirely outside the range of historical experience. For example, from the third quarter of 1977 through the fourth quarter of 1978, the yen appreciated about 30 percent. However, such sharp exchange-rate movements over relatively short periods do impose considerable burdens of adjustment on Japanese industry.

A third point is that, for Japan, movements in interest differentials began to correlate more closely with exchange-rate swings starting in the 1980s after significant financial liberalization had occurred in Japan. Thereafter, short-run movements in the yen's foreign exchange value are probably best viewed from the standpoint of asset-market models of exchange-rate determination.[4] In these models, short-run exchange-rate fluctuations result from the rapid equilibration of supply and demand in the markets for foreign exchange. Because current exchange rates determined in an efficient financial market already summarize all known relevant information, it is primarily unanticipated developments in a wide spectrum of macroeconomic and financial variables that influence changes in exchange rates in these models.

A fourth feature of the yen-dollar relationship is that there appears to have been a strong positive correlation between Japanese current-account surpluses and yen appreciation. Japan has run current-account surpluses almost continuously since 1965, except during the years immediately following the two oil shocks of the 1970s. Periods of strong yen appreciation have tended to correlate closely with periods of growing current-account surplus, although the appreciation eventually induces a reduction in the surplus as shifts in demand occur in response to the associated relative price changes. In a period of low international mobility of capital, such as that prior to 1979, so-called "flow" models of exchange-rate determination would indicate that trade flows may have a substantial impact on the exchange rate. If strict capital controls prevent a capital-account surplus from emerging to finance a current-account deficit, then the exchange rate will have to depreciate in order to foster a reduction of the current-account imbalance. That link becomes more complicated when financial liberalization permits a high degree of capital mobility across borders.

With capital mobility, current-account developments can still influence the exchange rate through a variety of channels. Unanticipated current-account developments may affect the exchange rate by revealing new information about changes in long-run competitive positions among countries. This channel is discussed further in Section III. In addition, current-account movements may influence the exchange rate through a portfolio balance channel: current-account imbalances result in a redistribution of wealth among countries, and because investors in different countries may have different preferences with respect to the currency denomination of their investments, exchange rates will move to re-equilibrate asset markets. Another channel emphasizes intertemporal considerations and argues that the exchange rate will gradually adjust to prevent current-account imbalances from becoming unsustainably large. This latter hypothesis has appeared particularly relevant in recent years in light of the record U.S. and Japanese trade imbalances.[5] Finally, there are a number of underlying economic developments which influence both exchange rates and current accounts, and which may at times cause them to respond together. Shifts in productivity growth across countries are one example of this type of phenomenon.

The exchange rate, in turn, also influences the current account over time through its impact on the relative price of national outputs. Relative prices of domestic and foreign goods are strongly affected by exchange-rate movements in the short run due to slower adjustment of prices in goods markets relative to asset markets. The impact of the exchange rate on current-account adjustment is discussed in Section IV.

As a fifth and final point, it is worth highlighting the differences between the yen's movements in the past 13 years against the dollar and against other currencies. Figure 4 shows the widely diverging paths of bilateral yen exchange

FIGURE 4

YEN BILATERAL EXCHANGE RATES

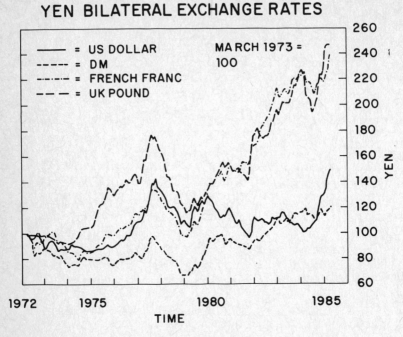

FIGURE 5

WEIGHTED-AVERAGE YEN (EXCL US) AND DOLLAR/YEN EXCHANGE RATES

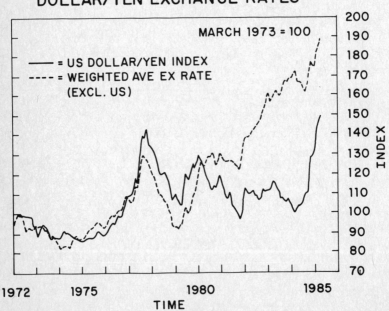

rates against four major currencies. While the yen has made net gains of about 140 percent against the French franc and pound sterling over the floating rate period, it has only appreciated 50 percent against the dollar on balance and just 20 percent against the mark. Of course, differences in inflation and other macroeconomic developments across countries account for much of these diverging movements. From 1973 through the end of the first quarter of 1986, cumulated consumer price inflation has been 72 percent in Germany, 137 percent in Japan, 155 percent in the United States, 249 percent in France, and 327 percent in the United Kingdom.

While developments within the various countries influenced the timing and extent of bilateral movements, it is clear that, overall, the yen has made sizable net gains against virtually all the major currencies over the floating rate period. Figure 5 compares the yen's movements against the dollar and against a basket of nine other major currencies.[6] Because of the yen's relatively uninterrupted rise against the nine currencies as a group in the 1980s while it rose and fell against the dollar, the net appreciation of the yen on an effective basis (excluding the dollar) has been about 90 percent since the start of floating exchange rates in 1973, nearly twice its net gain against the dollar over that period. The remainder of the paper will explore some of the sources of the yen's remarkable strength.

II. *The Impact of the Financial Liberalization Process on the Yen-Dollar Exchange Rate*

Over the past decade, Japan has made substantial progress in opening up its capital markets. As the pace of financial liberalization in Japan has accelerated in recent years, Japan's financial markets have acquired breadth and depth, making yen-denominated securities increasingly attractive to foreign investors. Whereas in the 1970s, capital controls were used extensively to influence the yen, liberalized markets were not restricted anew when exchange market pressures emerged in the 1980s.

In general, it is difficult to determine the contribution of liberalization to the most recent rise of the yen because liberalization has been occurring gradually for years. Many studies have demonstrated that a high degree of interest arbitrage has existed in at least some Japanese financial markets since the late 1970s.[7] Consequently, it was to be expected that further liberalization would probably have little impact on arbitrage opportunities other than to broaden the menu of possible instruments for investment. In part for this reason, there is little evidence to date directly linking financial liberalization and exchange-rate appreciation. For example, the yen weakened against the dollar after the May 1984 Yen-Dollar Agreement announcing further planned liberalization measures in Japan. A strong upward move of the yen did occur starting in February 1985, however. It is, of course, clear that factors other than liberalization also contributed to the most recent rise of the yen.

Other considerations complicate an evaluation of the effect of liberalization on the exchange rate.[8] The impact of liberalization at a particular point in time will depend on whether an excess demand or supply of yen assets relative to foreign-currency denominated assets has developed as a result of the controls in place. For example, it has been argued that the reason for the yen's decline following the 1984 Yen-Dollar Agreement was that Japanese investors at that time had a pent-up demand for foreign-currency denominated assets, and that restrictions were removed on both capital inflows and outflows. While these considerations complicate the analysis of the short-run impact of liberalization measures on the yen's exchange value, it is still clear that, over the longer run, financial liberalization will allow and encourage wider use of the yen in international transactions.

III. *Secular Influences on the Yen-Dollar Relationship*

Much of the descriptive analysis of movements in the yen-dollar exchange rate in Section I focused on relating medium-run movements in the exchange rate to macroeconomic, financial, and balance-of-payments developments. But the yen has exhibited a tendency over the past 15 years to strengthen on balance against the currencies of all its major trading partners. The question inevitably arises as to what longer-term influences might be generating this secular appreciation of the yen.

Differences in relative prices across countries provide a starting point for evaluating longer-run trends in exchange rates. According to the purchasing-power-parity (PPP) theory, if consumers have similar tastes across countries, international arbitrage in goods markets will lead prices of identical goods in different countries, expressed in a common currency, to be equalized over time. From a position of initial equilibrium, if the exchange rate exactly followed a PPP path, the real exchange rate would be constant.

A rough illustration of the deviations from PPP is provided in Figure 6, which displays the path of the yen-dollar exchange rate adjusted for changes in relative wholesale prices in Japan and the United States. While some degree of arbitrariness is inevitably involved in picking a year to represent equilibrium for the yen-dollar exchange rate, it is evident that the yen-dollar exchange rate has not closely followed relative price movements over the floating rate period. However, such evidence should not be construed as necessarily implying an inappropriate path of the yen-dollar exchange rate. Measurement problems caused by differences in composition of price indices across countries complicate PPP calculations. Moreover, a number of factors can warrant sustained deviations from PPP, and this section will examine some of these factors.

Productivity growth. One of the primary factors contributing to improved competitiveness in Japan is that Japanese productivity growth has outpaced that of its major trading partners, including the United States. Figure 7 illustrates Japan's sharp gains in productivity in manufacturing relative to the United States. The chart focuses on productivity in the manufacturing sector since a growing percentage of Japanese exports are manufactured goods — about 85 percent in 1985.

Japan's rate of productivity growth has slowed considerably since the 1960s,

FIGURE 6

WPI-ADJUSTED YEN/DOLLAR EXCHANGE RATE

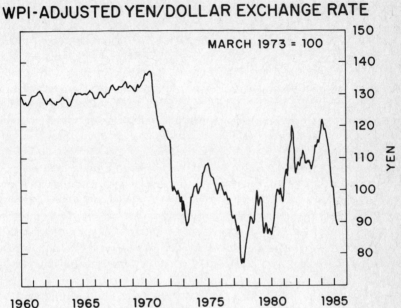

FIGURE 7

OUTPUT PER HOUR IN MANUFACTURING

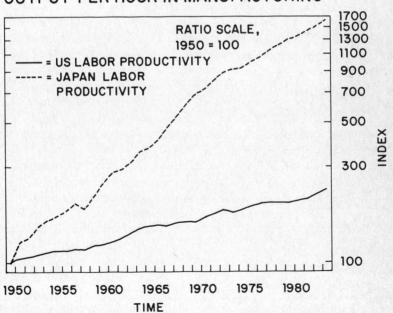

as can be seen in Table 1 below. The remarkably rapid growth in Japanese productivity in the 1950s and 1960s reflected in part the fast pace of technological innovation deriving from a backlog of exploitable foreign technologies. The slowdown in productivity growth in Japan's manufacturing sector over the past 15 years reflects in part the elimination of ready opportunities to adopt foreign technologies and in part structural changes in the composition of investment. As Japan became a more mature industrial economy in the 1970s, a greater share of investment was geared towards the service sector (where productivity was lower), social welfare, anti-pollution and other activities.[9] Still, Japan has maintained faster productivity growth in manufacturing than her major trading partners, while the United States and Germany, for example, have had slower productivity growth in manufacturing than their respective trading partners, as can be seen in Table 2 below.[10] In fact, of the 12 countries considered in the BLS study from which the above table is taken, Japan had the most rapid increases in relative productivity growth in both the fixed- and floating-exchange rate periods. Japan's exceptionally large gains in productivity relative to its major trading partners in the decade prior to the advent of floating exchange rates probably contributed to its growing external surplus and associated pressures for revaluation of the yen in the early 1970s. The sharp appreciation of the yen at the start of the floating rate period was in part an adjustment to these cumulated pressures. The yen has continued to exhibit a tendency towards appreciation over the floating rate period even though the productivity gap has narrowed.

TABLE 1

Productivity Growth in the United States and Japan

	(annual percentage growth in output per hour in manufacturing)	
Period	Japan	United States
1950–59	11.4	2.1
1960–69	14.8	3.0
1970–79	7.7	2.5
1980–84	4.8	3.4

Source: Bureau of Labor Statistics, March 1986.

TABLE 2

Changes in Productivity Growth in Manufacturing
Relative to 11 Trading Partners

	(relative annual percentage changes in output per hour)		
Period	Japan	United States	Germany
1960–73	5.9	–3.9	–0.3
1973–84	3.0	–1.7	–0.5

Source: Dean et al., *Monthly Labor Review*, 1986.

Regional pattern and composition of trade. An important impetus to Japan's rapid productivity gains in manufacturing has been the need to develop a surplus in manufacturing trade to offset a persistent deficit on trade in energy and raw materials. Given an extreme dependence on imported raw materials, Japan typically has run trade deficits vis-à-vis countries classified as developed primary producers (such as Australia, Canada, New Zealand and South Africa) and vis-à-vis oil exporting nations (particularly Saudi Arabia, Indonesia, and Iran). To offset this persistent deficit on primary commodity trade, Japan typically runs a surplus on its manufacturing trade. The dramatic gains in productivity in manufacturing that Japan has achieved relative to its major trading partners, including the United States, have helped Japan achieve a substantial surplus on its trade in manufactured goods.[11]

While Japan exports a growing amount of manufactures to the United States, its imports of food, raw materials, manufactures, and other commodities from the United States have not kept pace, leading Japan to run a trade surplus with the United States every year since 1968. A similar situation currently exists with many of Japan's European trading partners and is a primary source of recent trade frictions. Thus, Japan's longer-run tendency towards trade surplus with the United States and her European trading partners is in part the counterpart of her deficit on raw materials. Still, Japan's gains in competitiveness appear to have surpassed those required just to achieve balance between its deficit on primary commodities and its surplus on manufactures. The result has been persistent current-account surpluses and associated upward pressure on the yen.

Real wage growth. Figure 8 illustrates another factor that, combined with rapid productivity growth, has resulted in improved cost-competitiveness of Japanese exports: real wage growth in the Japanese manufacturing sector has tended to lag behind labor's productivity gains in recent years, except following the first oil shock.[12] This relatively slow growth of real wages is related to the system of industrial relations that prevails in the large Japanese firms. As is well-known, lifetime employment, seniority wage setting, bonuses linked to profits, and company-based unions are key factors contributing to real wage flexibility in Japan. This system appears to strengthen employees' commitment to the company and its long-run vitality, leading to wage settlements that are relatively compatible with company interests. During the annual spring wage negotiations — the so-called *Shunto* initiated in 1955 — company performance is a primary consideration recognized by both labor and management. As was noted earlier, Japanese labor's willingness to accept moderate wage increases in the aftermath of the second oil shock in 1979 despite rising inflation helped prevent the unleashing of a prolonged wage-price spiral. However, while slow real-wage growth helps export competitiveness, it can also inhibit the expansion of domestic demand and hence limit the derived demand for imports.

Terms of trade. Japan's terms of trade have declined substantially since the 1960s, as can be seen in Figure 9. This decline is composed of a relatively slow increase in export unit values and a more rapid rise in import unit values, especially during the periods in the 1970s in which prices of raw materials rose

FIGURE 8

REAL WAGE AND PRODUCTIVITY GROWTH IN THE JAPANESE MANUFACTURING SECTOR

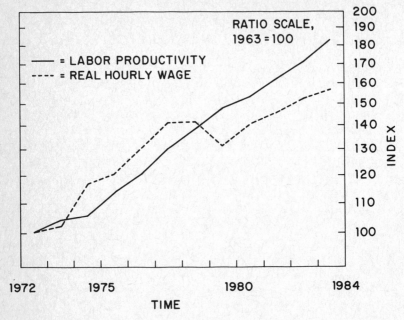

sharply. Of course, some of the movement in the terms of trade reflects exchange-rate changes, but price developments also play a role. A sizable share of Japan's imports consists of raw materials that are purchased in relatively competitive world markets, with oil being an important exception.

In contrast, the pricing strategy of Japanese exporters has tended to enhance Japan's competitiveness. Japanese wholesale prices often increased more rapidly in the 1950s and 1960s than export prices, suggesting that export profitability was squeezed over much of the period while Japanese exporters expanded their world market share. In more recent years, that gap has tended to narrow. Still, Japanese exporters have tended to accept lower profit margins rather than to resort to sharp increases in export prices during periods of rapid yen appreciation. This pricing response has helped improve Japan's competitive position and preserve or increase the global market share of Japan's exporters.

Savings-investment balance. In addition to these factors that have influenced Japan's international competitiveness, secular developments in Japanese savings and investment have contributed to the tendency towards persistent current-account surpluses and associated upward pressure on the yen. From the national-income accounting identity, the total of private savings plus government net savings less domestic private investment represents net national savings, which must equal net foreign investment or, equivalently, the current-account bal-

FIGURE 9

JAPANESE TERMS OF TRADE
EXPORT UNIT VALUE/IMPORT UNIT VALUE

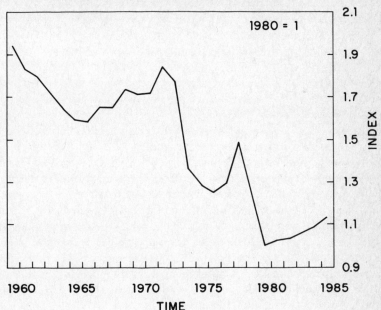

ance. This identity does not, of course, indicate direct causality between any of the elements; for example, shocks to any one of the components must be reflected in the others. But the identity does serve to highlight the fact that a country that saves more than it invests domestically must have, *ex post*, a net capital outflow and a corresponding current-account surplus.

The Japanese savings rate is impressively high by comparison with most other countries, although this has been true only since the mid-1950s.[13] The private savings rate began to rise in the 1950s as the business sector saved after the initial reconstruction process following the war, and as households sought to restore their financial positions in the aftermath of a period of high inflation. The savings rate might have been expected to stabilize after the reconstruction process was complete, but instead continued to rise in the 1960s, albeit at a slower pace. Private investment, in contrast, has not continued to climb along with private savings. During the boom years of the 1950s and 1960s, growth of Japanese private sector investment was extremely rapid, with investment as a share of GNP rising from 8 to 20 percent over the two decades. The government ran a small net surplus over that period, thereby partly financing the corporate-borrowing requirement, while the external sector was in rough balance until the late 1960s. Thus, the strong and rising household savings were absorbed by corresponding increases in the corporate-borrowing requirement.

As Japanese growth slowed in the 1970s, the share of private investment in GNP fell back to around 15 percent and has remained stable at about that level in recent years. The private-savings ratio did not decline in the 1970s, however, and even increased temporarily in the aftermath of the 1973 oil price hike as the heightened uncertainty and rising inflation led households to save more in order to rebuild the real value of their financial assets. Table 3 below presents household savings as a percentage of personal disposable income for 1985 for five countries.

Public-sector spending in Japan generally increased over the 1970s. By 1979, the general government deficit as a share of GNP had reached 4.8 percent, thereby absorbing some of the private-sector savings. Since 1979, however, Japanese fiscal policy has been oriented towards reducing the level of the fiscal deficit, largely by reducing government spending, with the goal of eliminating bond financing of the central government deficit by fiscal year 1990. The Japanese government views fiscal reconstruction as a prerequisite for sustainable noninflationary growth, and for providing scope for the future budgetary demands that will be associated with the aging of the population.

The prospect that this gap between total Japanese savings and domestic investment will be completely eliminated in the near future is small, although some factors may lead to a decline in savings over time. Most studies indicate that demographic factors are key determinants of the high savings ratio in Japan. With the rapid aging of the Japanese population (the share of the population over 65 is projected to rise to 16 percent by the year 2000 and to 22 percent by 2020), those currently in an earlier stage of the life-cycle are saving for retirement. It is likely that, in the future, this factor would imply some reduction in the savings rate; with a larger share of the population over 65, the savings rate should decline. Other reasons cited for the current high savings rate may change less over time. These include precautionary motives (savings for unexpected disasters), housing (the average Japanese home costs nearly eight times average annual income and mortgage interest is not tax deductible), children's education and marriage, and tax-free interest on small savings accounts.

Of these factors, government policy can have most direct influence on housing investment and the preferential tax treatment of savings. Indeed, a report on possibilities for medium-term structural change aimed at reducing the Japanese external imbalance — the so-called Maekawa report released last April —

TABLE 3

1985 Personal Savings Ratios

(percent of personal disposable income)

Japan	22
Germany	13
Canada	12
United Kingdom	12
United States	5

recommended aboliton of the tax exemption on small savings accounts and urged a sweeping reform of Japanese housing policy (through tax deductions for housing, stabilization of land prices, and easing of regulations hampering real estate development). The recommendations of the Maekawa Commission are currently under review by the Japanese authorities.

Is Japan a "Natural" Capital Exporter? Japanese and foreign proposals for measures to reduce Japan's yawning current-account surplus often have acknowledged the importance of both competitiveness factors and the underlying imbalance between savings and domestic investment in Japan. Japan has been urged to stimulate domestic demand, including investment, by taking expansionary fiscal and monetary actions and by adopting measures to discourage household savings. The Japanese authorities have responded recently by promoting a sharp appreciation of the yen to foster improved external balance, and by three ½ percentage point reductions in the discount rate since January to stimulate domestic demand. So far, however, they have refrained from significant fiscal stimulus in light of their deficit-reduction goals. On the United States side, the low U.S. savings rate also contributes to its trade imbalance with Japan, and the Gramm-Rudman-Hollings act is seen as an important step towards reducing United States government dissaving. Still, the recent plunge in oil prices together with the J-curve effects of the yen's appreciation have more than offset the short-run impact of these measures on Japan's current account, and Japan is expected to run an even larger current-account surplus (measured in dollars) this year than last.

The structural features of the Japanese economy highlighted above suggest that Japan will tend to be a net exporter of capital in the years to come. There are few signs that household savings will decline substantially; growth and investment are unlikely to reaccelerate to the fast paces experienced in the 1960s; and some degree of fiscal restraint is likely to be maintained in the near term. The yen's recent substantial gains will probably result in a sizable reduction of the surplus below the current level, although the size of the reduction will hinge in part on developments in the oil market as about one-third of Japan's imports are petroleum and petroleum products. Nevertheless, the remaining surplus deriving from the structural features of the Japanese economy could be quite large.

The concept of a structural surplus in a country's external accounts is rather vague; it is intended to highlight the importance for the path of the current account of differences across countries in endowments, preferences, and other fundamental characteristics of an economy. As a consequence, there is no precise way to calculate the size of the structural surplus, nor does the assertion that a surplus is structural imply that it is not influenced by policies. As suggested above, structural adjustment policies are being discussed. Moreover, the influence of macroeconomic policies on exchange rates, interest rates, and other variables will strongly influence the actual path of the current account and can offset some of the underlying structural forces.

Should we be concerned that Japan is a net capital exporter? Are measures to reduce savings in Japan really desirable from the standpoint of world welfare? Forcing a reduction in Japanese savings would tend to reduce Japanese net foreign investment and hence to raise the level of interest rates abroad. Instead the focus should be on encouraging the most efficient and equitable global redistribution of Japanese savings. If relative real returns in the United States continue to decline and the fiscal deficit narrows, it is likely that Japanese foreign investment will gradually diversify away from U.S. investments. It might be hoped that rates of return on investment in developing countries would be attractive enough to draw a substantial portion of these Japanese funds.

An interesting recent analysis from the World Institute for Development Economics Research (WIDER) suggests that since Japan will be unable to absorb fully its domestic savings, it will need to continue to rely on current-account surpluses in order to continue channeling excess savings abroad.[14] WIDER proposes that to counteract the global contractionary impact of any reduction in the United States' fiscal and trade deficits, Japan should "redirect" the surplus towards financing productive capital formation in the developing countries. Japan's savings represents a large potential source of investment in developing countries. If the reforms advocated by Treasury Secretary Baker in Seoul in October 1985 are implemented on a substantial scale, Japanese funds could be drawn to the Third World as more coherent macroeconomic policies help attain such goals as sustained lower inflation and enhanced use of market pricing which in turn promote more attractive investment opportunities.

IV. *The Role of the Yen Exchange Rate in Japanese Current-Account Adjustment*

For the part of the Japanese current-account surplus that is not structural in nature, the issue arises of how best to encourage rapid adjustment. The Plaza meeting in September 1985 recognized the importance of both yen appreciation and stimulation of Japanese growth in promoting more balanced trade between countries. So far, a substantial yen appreciation has been the principal outcome of this process. To obtain an idea of the relative importance of income and relative price influences on Japan's trade balance, we have gathered evidence from the Federal Reserve Board staff's Multi-Country Model (MCM).[15]

According to the parameters of the MCM, the price elasticities for Japanese trade indicate that Japanese exports are highly responsive to relative price changes, while Japanese imports are much less responsive to relative price movements. In fact, of the five country models included in the MCM (the United States, Japan, Germany, the United Kingdom, and Canada), Japan faces the highest price elasticity of demand for its exports and has the lowest price elasticity of import demand. This would suggest that the recent sharp yen appreciation, if allowed to be fully reflected in prices, will result over time in a sizable reduction in the volume of Japanese exports but a less substantial increase in imports.

The relatively weak estimated response of Japanese imports to exchange rate-

induced changes in relative prices is probably related to the commodity composition of those imports: 60 percent of total imports are fuel and raw materials
that are relatively difficult to substitute away from in the production process
when their relative prices rise. Consistent with this view, estimates from the
Japanese Economic Planning Agency's macroeconometric model indicate that
the relative price elasticities of fuel and raw materials imports are about one-
sixth the size of the relative price elasticity of manufactured imports for Japan.[16]
In contrast, about 85 percent of Japan's exports are manufactured goods, including 70 percent machinery and industrial equipment, for which relatively
close substitutes exist in the world market. As a result, importers of Japanese
goods can more easily switch to cheaper alternative sources of manufactured
goods.

What impact will the 35 percent appreciation of the yen against the dollar
in the past 15 months have on Japan's bilateral trade surplus with the United
States? A very rough calculation based on the MCM equations suggests that
the yen's recent 35 percent rise against the dollar could over time result in as
much as a $20 billion reduction in Japan's current $50 billion trade surplus with
the United States. (J-curve effects lasting up to one year, according to MCM
simulations, would prevent this improvement from becoming apparent immediately.) This simple calculation assumes that the yen appreciation occurred as
a *deus ex machina*, so that other effects of any policy changes that may have
encouraged the appreciation are not considered. Also the calculation implicitly
assumes that real income growth is maintained in Japan. To the extent that real
income growth slows, the reduction in the surplus will be less. Of course, any
estimates based on historical experience provide at best a rough guide to the
current situation; we may well be in uncharted territory. Still, this calculation
illustrates that the yen's recent rise could make an important contribution towards reducing Japan's current-account surplus.

Efforts to stimulate domestic income growth in Japan and thereby to induce
an increased demand for imports could also help foster external adjustment.
However, while the effect of Japanese domestic demand expansion on overall
imports may be sizable, results from the MCM suggest the effect may not be
as great on Japan's imports from the United States: the estimated income elasticity
of demand for imports from the United States is quite low, while the income
elasticity of demand for total Japanese imports is greater. In particular, the responsiveness of Japan's imports from developing countries to increases in Japanese real income is substantial, roughly twice that of imports from the United
States.

On the export side, Japan's exports to the United States are highly responsive to changes in U.S. income. However, one would hardly want to recommend a recession in the United States to improve our bilateral trade balance
with Japan. Still, these results may help explain why Japan's trade surplus with
the United States soared in recent years as the United States economy expanded
rapidly.

V. Concluding Remarks

The interaction between the exchange value of the yen and the Japanese current account has served as a unifying thread throughout this paper. The yen's exchange value appears to have played a potent role in fostering current-account adjustment in Japan, but exchange-rate movements have not sufficed to maintain external balance. Another central theme of this paper has been that developments affecting Japan's current account have had an important influence on the longer-run course of the yen-dollar exchange rate. The sizable gains in competitiveness and the tendency for total savings to exceed domestic investment have contributed to a tendency towards persistent Japanese current-account surpluses and an associated tendency for the value of the yen to rise, except in the wake of major disruptions such as the oil-price shocks of the 1970s.

It is interesting to note that an examination of policy analyses in 1972, just prior to the commencement of floating exchange rates, points to a striking parallel between the adjustments recommended for the Japanese economy at that time and those offered today, almost 15 years later. For example, the 1972 OECD *Economic Survey* stated:

> A determined policy of import stimulation would seem an indispensable complement to the revaluation. . . . It would take the wind out of protectionist sails in foreign markets and contribute to welfare. . . . It could also assist growth in many of Japan's developing partner countries. . . . While it is clear that relative cyclical positions played a large role in explaining the record current surplus last year, the striking tendencies registered in the Japanese trade balance with Western industrialized countries from about 1964 onwards pointed clearly to a growing fundamental disequilibrium. A sizeable and timely revaluation was, in these conditions, a prerequisite for Japan's continuing integration in world trading relations. The revaluation was also desirable from a domestic standpoint. . . . The effects of the revaluation may, however, take some time to come through. . . . It is in the interest of both the international economic scene and the domestic economy that quick progress should be made in reducing domestic slack and increasing the weight of social consumption. Given such progress, the revaluation is likely to prove a major act of post-war Japanese economic policy, rather than an unavoidable short-term move. (pp. 44–45)

The tendencies in Japan towards growing trade surpluses and insufficient domestic absorption were thus already apparent in the early 1970s. The subsequent decade was punctuated by periods of prolonged adjustment to the two oil-price shocks. Now those same tendencies have resurfaced. Despite the initial hopes of some proponents of floating exchange rates, the move to flexible rates has not resulted on average in a reduction in external imbalances between Japan and her major trading partners, although sizable adjustments have tended to occur with rather long lags.

All of this points to the need to rely on factors other than just exchange rates to bring about better balance in the world economy. Measures to stimulate domestic growth in Japan could make an important contribution to improved external balance. The more income expansion the Japanese authorities encourage, the less yen appreciation is required to foster more balanced trade.

In light of the strains already imposed on Japan's industries by the yen's appreciation to date, expansion represents an important potential impetus to further external adjustment.

There currently appears to be a scope for both monetary and fiscal actions. Given the recent strength of the yen, further reductions in the Japanese discount rate could probably have a salutary influence on the domestic economy without adverse exchange-market effects. Also, fiscal stimulus could be provided without severely compromising Japan's longer-run commitment to reducing the central government's budget deficit, since the fiscal measures could help set in train a self-sustaining recovery in domestic investment and spending. Whatever the medicine, it is clear that actions to stimulate the domestic economy would provide some boost to imports and help lift Japan's economy from its current doldrums.

NOTES

For helpful comments, we are grateful to members of the Division of International Finance, in particular to Edwin Truman and Karen Johnson, and to Dale Henderson. We would also like to thank Joerg Dittmer for excellent research assistance.

1. Throughout this paper, we adopt the convention of calculating percentage changes in exchange rates based on rates expressed as the domestic currency price of foreign currency, e.g., yen/dollar.

2. In chart 2, the quarterly current account is seasonally adjusted at an annual rate, and the effective exchange rate index is the Federal Reserve Board staff's ten-country trade-weighted average exchange rate.

3. The real exchange rate and real interest rate paths are obtained by adjusting the nominal values for movements in the consumer price index. In this way, we abstract from the influence of differential inflation in the United States and Japan on the two series.

4. For an exposition of models of this kind, see Frankel and Mussa, 1985.

5. See, for example, Paul Krugman, 1985.

6. In chart 5, the index of the yen's value against a basket of 9 currencies is calculated based on the Federal Reserve Board staff's trade-weighted index, dropping out the United States trade share and renormalizing on the 9 remaining shares.

7. Recent studies include Richard Freeman, 1984, Jeffrey Frankel, 1984, and Sumimaru Odano, 1986.

8. Freeman, 1984 provides a useful discussion of the impact of liberalization on the yen exchange rate.

9. Richard Marston, 1986, studies trends in productivity in different sectors of the Japanese economy over the floating-rate period.

10. The BLS calculates relative productivity as the ratio of the productivity index of the reference country to the trade-weighted average index for 11 trading partners. Rates of change are computed from the least-squares trend of the logarithms of this ratio.

11. Paul Krugman, 1986, provides additional details on the manufacturing surplus and primary commodities deficit in Japan, and compares the Japanese trade situation to that of Germany and the United States.

12. The real wage in chart 8 is hourly compensation in manufacturing, national currency basis (BLS, March 1986), divided by the wholesale price for manufacturing industry products. The productivity data is the same as in the table on page 13 (BLS, March 1986).

13. This section draws on the interesting study of Japanese savings by Randall Jones, 1986.

14. For a more detailed description of this proposal, see the WIDER Report, 1986.

15. Sean Craig of the Federal Reserve Board's Division of International Finance kindly provided the estimates and calculations from the Japan sector of the MCM model.
16. See "EPA World Economic Model," 1984.

References

Dean, Edwin, Harry Boissevain, and James Thomas. 1986. "Productivity and Labor Cost Trends in Manufacturing, 12 Countries." *Monthly Labor Review*. March.

Economic Planning Agency (Japan). 1984. "EPA World Economic Model, February 1984 Version." EPA World Econometric Model Discussion Paper Number 16.

Frankel, Jeffrey A. 1984. "The Yen-Dollar Agreement: Liberalizing Japanese Capital Markets." Policy Analyses in International Economics, Number 9. Washington, D.C.: Institute for International Economics.

Frenkel, Jacob A. and Michael L. Mussa. 1985. "Asset Markets, Exchange Rates and the Balance of Payments." In Ronald W. Jones and Peter B. Kenen, eds., *Handbook of International Economics* Vol. 2, pp. 679–747. Amsterdam: North Holland.

Freeman, Richard. 1984. "Aspects of Recent Japanese Financial Market Liberalization." Mimeo. Washington, D.C.: Board of Governors of the Federal Reserve System.

Jones, Randall S. 1985. "Japan's High Savings Rate: An Overview." Japan Economic Institute Report Number 46A. Washington, D.C.

Krugman, Paul. 1985. "Is the Strong Dollar Sustainable?" National Bureau of Economic Research Working Paper No. 1644.

Krugman, Paul. 1986. "Is the Japan Problem Over?" Mimeo. New York University Conference on Trade Frictions. New York.

Marston, Richard C. 1986. "Real Exchange Rates and Productivity Growth in the United States and Japan." Mimeo. American Enterprise Institute Conference on Real-Financial Linkages.

Odano, Sumimaru. 1986. "Integration and Efficiency of Japanese Financial Markets." Mimeo. Tokyo: International University of Japan.

Report of a Study Group of the World Institute for Development Economics Research (WIDER). 1986. "The Potential of the Japanese Surplus for World Economic Development." Tokyo.

International Imbalances and the Search for Exchange-Rate Stability

Rimmer de Vries
Senior Vice President, Morgan Guaranty Trust Company

EVERYBODY is clamoring for stability. But how can we obtain stability when we have such huge imbalances?

We are living in a world in which imbalances actually are getting larger. In the late 1960s and early 1970s, during the first balance-of-payments crisis of the United States, we were very concerned about current account imbalances of $3 billion, $5 billion, and $10 billion. Next came a crisis of major proportions: the OPEC surplus moved up to $65 billion—the end of the world monetary system, according to many. Then there was the second OPEC surplus, almost twice as large, which led to the debt crisis. Now we have an even larger imbalance, with the U.S. current-account deficit at around $150 billion. We desperately need a mechanism to monitor, contain, reduce, and finance these imbalances.

From an adjustment and financial point of view, the first OPEC surplus in general was handled very well, but the second was not handled nearly as well. The uneven adjustment and financing in the second was a major contribution to the international debt crisis. The American economic expansion eased the less-developed countries' (LDC) debt crisis, but also added to the U.S. balance of payments deficit.

Thus, we now have two crises with us. The first is the LDC debt problem. The balance-of-payments deficits of these countries are no longer so immediate an issue, because they have been very much reduced; but there is the continuing problem of the great overhang of the debt. The second crisis is the United States imbalance. The first and second initiatives of Treasury Secretary Baker are directed to those two major issues, which are still very much with us. In the year since the initiatives were announced, we have made some progress, but not enough.

I am very much in favor of both initiatives, because I think the world is at a crossroads. We can either go the route of unilateral actions and nationalistic policies, or take the road to cooperative, international, global action.

To foreigners it may seem strange that the United States is taking a global view—no more benign neglect, but an activist global view. If we don't succeed, though, we will have to take unilateral action that means defaults, protectionism, and inevitable global economic decline. Obviously, the preferred way is the international cooperative approach.

I was very glad to receive the other participants' papers. My technical staff ran some of the policy suggestions from Mr. Yoshitomi's paper in our model and produced Table I. It details various scenarios that would accomplish a narrowing of our current-account deficit to $50 billion, a target that I think would be politically acceptable. A $50 billion imbalance in the current account of the United States would be eventually about equal in magnitude to our payments on interest, and would stabilize our debt-to-GNP ratio at around 8 percent.

The three major variables we can use to attain this objective are U.S. growth, foreign growth, and exchange rates. Using the assumptions from Mr. Yoshitomi's paper—which would leave foreign policies and exchange rates unaltered by and large—the only way to reach a $50 billion current-account deficit is through a severe recession in this country with a 3 percent to 5 percent cumulative decline of output. We all use different models, but a recession is obviously inevitable under these assumptions on policies inside and outside the United States. We cannot eliminate the budget deficit without tight fiscal policy. We cannot have lower interest rates in this case because they would weaken the dollar, contrary to our assumptions. In fact we would have to tighten monetary policy to support the dollar. This combination of tight fiscal and tight monetary policies would create a recession.

These conclusions should not be so surprising. After all, this combination is frequently the IMF prescription for developing countries. However, it is to-

TABLE 1

Economic growth and exchanges rates*: the adjustment trade-off tables illustrate combinations of foreign economic growth and dollar depreciation consistent with a U.S. current account deficit of $50 billion in 1988 and U.S. real GNP growth for 1986–88 of

	3% per annum Dollar trade-weighted index (1980–82 = 100)		1.5% per annum Dollar trade-weighted index (1980–82 = 100)	
	Unchanged (= actual June 3, 1986) 107	15% depreciation 90	Unchanged (= actual May 12, 1986) 104	15% depreciation 90
Japan				
Real GNP growth	6.3	3.7	5.5	3.0
Real domestic demand growth	7.0	4.7	6.3	3.8
Yen/$	171	135	171	135
Germany				
Real GNP growth	5.8	3.5	4.7	2.6
DM/$	2.27	1.65	2.27	1.65

* Growth rates are annual averages for 1986–88 and exchange rates are 1988 averages.

tally unacceptable politically in this country. Thus it is not a course of action we can take.

We have to look at other variables, particularly the trade-off between exchange rates and foreign growth, as portrayed in this table. I used another version of this table in a small group. And they said, "You darned two-handed economists! You always have two options." "Of course," I responded, "we have five fingers on each hand, so I can give you ten variations, as well." There are many possible combinations of foreign growth, American growth, and exchange rates. This table shows that to attain the $50 billion target for the current-account deficit, while maintaining today's exchange rates (about 170 yen and 2.25 marks per dollar) and 3 percent growth in the United States, Japan will have to produce 7 percent domestic growth and Germany at least 6 percent. Then exchange rates could be stable. On the other hand, if they are not willing to move that far, and produce at the most only 4½ percent domestic growth, then the exchange rate of 135 yen per dollar will inevitably result.

There is another alternative: a kind of growth recession in the United States. The table shows that with a 1½ percent rate of growth in the United States — a growth recession — and today's exchange rates, Japan and Germany still need more stimulus than is provided for by existing policies.

Obviously, one can argue about some of those models or technical assumptions. Still, if I look at this table and these numbers, I find that we are at a crossroads. We heard from the speeches being made at the monetary conference in Boston that most of the officials say "no" to more expansionary policies. The Germans say "nein." The Japanese say "yes," but they do not seem to have a word for "no" in the Japanese language, so their "yes" means "no."

That leaves us in a stalemate: we cannot have exchange-rate stability without changes in domestic policies. So the road ahead is going to be fairly rough. I do not know whether I would use the word confrontation, but we are getting into a much tougher situation. Profit margins have been squeezed by dollar devaluation and yen and mark appreciation, but we have not solved the problem of the imbalance yet. And I think there has to be some give over the summer months.

Let me make two final comments. However much the issues of target zones, purchasing power, and so on have been discussed, it is very difficult to pinpoint an effective target range without knowing the policy environment. Each particular set of U.S. and foreign growth policies produces a different exchange-rate target zone that is appropriate. I find these things so interrelated that it is very hard to say what the rate should be. Using a very narrow purchasing power parity approach, a measure we produce every day, it would take a 2.10 mark and 190 yen to go back to the average of 1980–1982. Obviously, that would not go very far in narrowing our trade deficit or current-account deficit. Because 50 percent of U.S. trade is with countries whose trade is relatively insensitive to our exchange rate, or whose currencies move with the dollar — such as the Canadian dollar, the Mexican peso, and the currencies of all of Latin America — the whole improvement in the current-account deficit and the trade deficit really has to occur within a very narrow group of countries: Japan and Western Europe. We may even have to exclude Britain from this area. That is part of the issue: we must have very major changes in exchange rates within the industrial countries.

Finally, I would find it very appealing to institutionalize the G-5 or the G-7 framework. As our imbalances are rising, we desperately need an institutional framework other than just the OECD, which is probably much more representative of individual countries. It is difficult for the OECD to take a global point of view. We need international economic management by key industrial countries. I stress this approach, rather than a U.S. recession, because deflationary forces still dominate inflationary forces in today's world. There is too much unemployment in Europe and in the United States. There is virtually no growth in Latin America or in much of Southeast Asia. Many European countries and Japan are, if anything, tightening their policies. Maybe we are even tightening in the United States, since the budget deficit is being reduced and monetary policy may be tightening mildly. At the same time, the United States must narrow its trade deficit, which would take another $100 billion of stimulus out of the world economy. There is low inflation, in some European countries and Japan even negative inflation at the wholesale level — thank God for the oil price decline!

That is why I think it is urgent to look from a truly global point of view and have a consistent economic policy framework in which we stress more growth in those countries that can afford it. There is plenty of room for the expansion which is so desperately needed.

Discussion: Session II

JAMES TOBIN:

I would like to make two remarks. In regard to the internationalization of the yen, I was wondering whether it does not make a lot of difference in discussing internationalization of a currency that we are on a floating-rate system rather than a fixed-rate system? The advantages or disadvantages of being a key currency are a lot different now than they were under the Bretton Woods system.

Second, I have observed from living through the last 40–50 years as an economist that in the days when capital transactions and currency transactions were not so much internationalized, but trade was more internationalized, things were a lot better. I don't see the great advantage of internationalizing trade in paper and nationalizing commodities.

QUESTION:

I'd like to follow up that comment and ask the following question to Mr. Gyooten. Isn't one of the perceived difficulties in obtaining a long-term equilibrium exchange rate a result of a dichotomy that is getting wider between two different types of markets? On the one hand, we have deregulation promoting large capital flows; on the other hand, in the tradable goods area, we see increasing market sharing and product cartelization. So in that environment how is policy to function to strike an equilibrium exchange rate?

TOYOO GYOOTEN:

You have a very good point. Certainly the deregulation of the capital and financial markets in all major economies has encouraged a very active flow of capital. I think at least in certain instances this has aggravated the volatility of exchange rates in the market. However, if we are talking in a long-term perspective, I am not that sure whether expanded capital movements would always contribute to less stable exchange markets. While, as I briefly touched upon in my presentation, I think if you have a larger market certainly there will be more speculation, quite often speculations cancel each other. You may have, relatively speaking, a more stable market in the long run. So I am not of the view that in order to achieve exchange-rate stability we should try to at least manage transactions among major markets.

On the trade side, I also agree with you that today the role of trade in determining the exchange rate has been very much reduced compared with ten years ago. In those days, it was quite possible for us to have a reasonably accurate idea about the direction of the movement of the exchange rate, if you looked at movements in the current account. But now, as you know, in the Tokyo market alone, every day $5 billion or so of exchange transactions are taking place, and there are probably twice as many swap transactions. So if you multiply these numbers by 250 days and then add other financial-market transactions, the total annual amount of transactions is by far greater than the current-account transactions. So I'm quite in agreement with you that trade is now playing a much-reduced role in exchange determination. But that may imply that we can count more on the basic trends in economic fundamentals, rather than those phenomenal aspects of the economy, such as the current account in the balance-of-payments.

So, in conclusion, I may say that the current-account transactions are not playing a great role, and that capital transactions have certainly grown enormously now, so what will be the final determinant of the exchange rate? I think we have to come back to the very fundamentals of the economy itself. In that sense, I think there is a much greater need for better coordination of policies, and better conversions of economic performance, at least among the major-currency countries.

FRED BERGSTEN:

A comment on Professor Komiya's statement, and a question to Mr. Gyooten.

Right at the end of Professor Komiya's remarks, he mentioned the idea of a linkage between export and import transactions as a second- or third-best way to achieve adjustment of the current account. I mention that because I think it is a very dangerous idea because it would be readily accepted in the U.S. Congress. American Congressmen would be only too happy to link export and import transactions, but not in the way he suggests, which has a healthy purpose from an economic perspective. They would like to achieve bilateral trade balances on a country-by-country basis. If that idea proceeded very far, I am afraid we would all be in big trouble!

A question for Mr. Gyooten: at the very end of your remarks, you made an extremely provocative reference to the optimum level of interdependence between the United States and Japan. You suggested that maybe that interdependence had moved too far too fast. You said that after having talked about the desirability of further liberalization of the capital markets, internationlization of the yen, etc. What do you have in mind in terms of possible means to limit the extent of interdependence, assuming for the moment that one wanted to do that?

GYOOTEN:

You raise a very good point. Probably that is the most critical part of my presentation. As I said, I have no quick answer, because I think that is a very difficult question. But I believe we cannot dictate the international transactions either in trade or in capital markets. We have to prepare the environment so that goods and capital flow more evenly among different countries.

I mentioned direct investment, and that is one area I am very much concerned about now. I think that Japan needs to invest more in the developing world, but for many reasons they have not been developing as we have wished.

Also, in terms of exports, in the past some Japanese industries have concentrated on certain markets alone. They were motivated by profit incentives, so there is nothing wrong perhaps with their attitude in the short term. But I think to do business in this world now all private enterprises should have a long-term view as well as short-term profit motives. If you rely on those long-term views, I think they may have different ideas about diversification of their markets. So this is the kind of approach I think we should concentrate on in the future.

RYUTARO KOMIYA:
I proposed the export-link system on a multinational basis, as you said. I doubt very much whether the U.S. Congress would want it on a bilateral basis. What is the advantage of having it on a bilateral basis?

BERGSTEN:
To get rid of the trade deficit with Japan! Unfortunately that is their motive.

HUGH PATRICK:
A question for Mr. Gyooten. In Japanese financial internationalization, there seems to have been a bias in that the barriers to the outflows of Japanese capital abroad have been reduced, whereas there has been less done to attract short-term capital inflows. In particular, there has not been the development of a good market in riskless short-term securities, namely Treasury bills. Perhaps you cannot, or you may not choose to, comment on that, so I simply want to make the point that the effect of policy is biased toward capital outflow rather than being neutral.

My question is one simply of confusion about the purpose of the government's policy on the internationalization of the yen. There are two ways to interpret what is going on. One is that the Ministry of Finance regards internationalization as a desirable objective and is taking active leadership to encourage it. The other is that internationalization is driven by market forces, it is inevitable, and there is nothing the Ministry of Finance can do to stop it; all it can do is to try to react in as constructive and sensible a way as possible. I would like to get some feel as to which is the appropriate interpretation of Ministry of Finance policy?

GYOOTEN:
You were graceful enough not to put your first statement as a question, but a comment! I think you are right. In the past, I think, deregulation resulted in a greater outflow of capital rather than an inflow of capital into the Japanese market, for many reasons. There were some structural problems, and there were some cyclical issues at that moment, but it is true that deregulation resulted, in fact, in greater outflow than inflow. We are now trying to improve this im-

balance by taking measures to improve our short-term domestic financial markets. I hope that correction of the situation will be achieved in the due course of time.

Now, to your second question. As you said, there was no national consensus, so to speak, on the internationalization of the yen. There are many views on whether we should internationalize our currency or not. There are many fears that internationalizing the currency will simply result in volatility of the exchange rates, and undermine domestic monetary policies. But there was this inevitable international trend which nobody could resist, and if one cannot resist a trend, I think the question is how to make the best use of it, accommodating our economy to the trend, so that it can best contribute to and compete in the world economy.

So I think the present position is now pretty well established that we are now basically in favor of the internationalization of the yen. But as I pointed out in my presentation we should not be too ambitious, and we have to take a balanced approach to that, otherwise this will create more confusion both internationally and domestically.

MASARU YOSHITOMI:

Mr. Gyooten, you mentioned the implications of the internationalization of the yen for the monetary system and macro policies. You also said that because Japan is the second-largest economy, and has the second-strongest currency, Japanese authorities should share the burden of having one of the key currencies. If we apply this idea to the present situation, what kind of policy coordination would you suggest? We can say that in the States we need fiscal consolidation; in Japan, we need more domestic demand expansion. But suppose I asked the following nasty question to you. Because of this rather important implication of the internationalization of the yen for both countries' macro policies, many people talk about the adverse impact of Japanese fiscal consolidation on the Japanese external surplus. They say that putting your house in order in terms of fiscal consolidation is fine from your point of view, but for the rest of the world the impact of such fiscal consolidation in Japan is too serious. Therefore, why don't you moderate fiscal consolidation, or even give it up, when the U.S. commits itself to fiscal consolidation? How do you view this sort of policy coordination required for the present context?

GYOOTEN:

I think everybody should try to put their house in order. I think in the Japanese case we are in the process of doing that. But I cannot agree with the view that we are now taking conservative fiscal policies. We are running large deficits every year. We are diverting 20 percent of our expenditures to interest payments. So you cannot say that our fiscal policy is an easy one. Even if we continue this conservative or prudent fiscal policy while the U.S. is also trying to follow a similar policy, I don't think there will be any conflicts of interest between our two countries. Certainly, in the past, there were some excessive weaknesses in our fiscal situations, and both of us are now trying to improve that, and what's wrong with that? If our economy can grow at 4 percent or so, I think we shouldn't be too pessimistic about that.

[COFFEE BREAK]

TOBIN:

Some of the speakers today, notably Fred Bergsten and Rimmer de Vries, said that we need a further depreciation of the dollar and a considerable further appreciation of the yen. Also, several speakers, including Japanese speakers, said there was not much advantage in the expansion of the domestic economy of Japan in relation to rectifying the U.S. current-account imbalance.

I noticed Governor Johnson said that the Japanese could lower their interest rate, and encouraged them to do so; but if the United States would not do that, and what I read about the Federal Reserve is that they don't seem to be prepared to do that now, then wouldn't that be pulling more funds into the United States, and appreciating the dollar again, making our current-account position worse? Perhaps we should be telling the Japanese, either prepare to go along in another multilateral reduction in interest rates, which, as Mr. de Vries said, would be good for the whole global economy which is weak and deflationary rather than inflationary, or else stick to fiscal expansion of their economies.

The bigger question I suppose for the U.S., and I don't know if Governor Johnson can be induced to comment, is this: given the weakness of the American economy, given the fact that during the J-curve phase the current-account balance actually is a negative influence on aggregate demand, what reason is there to defend the dollar by monetary policy and to refrain from letting interest rates go down further?

YOSHIO SUZUKI:

I would like to raise one issue along the same lines as what Professor Tobin has just said. It is concerning Governor Johnson's final remark about the scope for easing Japanese monetary policy further. He said another reduction in the discount rate might be possible.

The monetary growth rate at the moment, over the previous year, in terms of M2 plus CDs, which is the intermediate target of the Bank of Japan, is 8.4 percent. It is accommodative enough to stimulate domestic private demand. Further cutting the discount rate will no doubt increase that monetary growth further. Won't it be too high?

I would like to draw your attention to the fact that the recent large appreciation of the yen has been accompanied by improvements in trade terms, so eventually it must have an expansionary effect upon the Japanese economy. But in the transition period, such as this year, the deflationary effect upon tradable-goods sectors will be larger than the expansionary effects upon the non-tradable-goods sectors. People, then, are anxious about the possibility of a recession this year.

But prices and wages in the Japanese economy are very flexible, so the adjustment process is always short. Interest rates have already responded to the high monetary growth rate: 5 percent in long-term rates, 4 percent in short-term rates are low enough to sustain the present economic growth path.

Also, I would like to say that monetary policy under the floating exchange-rate regime should be assigned to maintaining internal equilibrium, such as price stability and sustained growth, and not to external objectives, such as the exchange rate. If we seek to target our exchange-rate level by using monetary policy, the final result would be inflation in Japan and deflation in the United States. So I don't think that there is any scope for monetary policy to stimulate our private domestic expenditures any further.

QUESTION:
My question to Mr. Gyooten is why not a Japanese interest equalization tax? The United States had that in the 1960s.

GYOOTEN:
I didn't say that I was complaining about the capital outflow from Japan now, so I am not too sure whether I should propose an interest-rate equilization tax to control it. Secondly, there are various factors behind this capital outflow. Certainly, the interest-rate differential is one, but exchange-rate risk is another. Quite recently, as you may know, the bulk of the capital outflow from Japan has not been necessarily attracted by the interest-rate differential between the dollar and the yen. It is obvious that even with a rapidly reducing interest-rate differential there has been very little change in our capital outflow. So I think it means that the interest-rate differential now is not really playing the major role in the capital transfer between our two countries.

QUESTION:
I wanted to ask Rimmer de Vries whether he is suggesting a resurrection of the international Keynsian economic policy toward major industrial nations?

TOBIN:
Let's hope so! [Laughter]

QUESTION:
Do you both agree?

DE VRIES:
Well, I wouldn't necessarily call it Keynesian. It simply makes good common sense. I have been working on a paper on the international capital markets, and we have a beautiful quote of Keynes from *The Economic Consequences of the Peace* in which he describes the situation before World War I. That is a Keynesian world where there was free movement of trade and capital. I think there is very much need for that.

QUESTION:
Well, in adolescence, he had one point of view, and when he grew up he had another point of view. Nothing wrong with that.

TOBIN:
Maybe we can analyze the issues rather than using names which seem to have different connotations for different people.

DE VRIES:
Professor Komiya said that a $60 billion dollar surplus on the current account, "only" 3 percent of GNP, is very sustainable. The same argument can be made for a $150 billion current-account deficit. But it is not politically sustainable. The economist might say that this is very small in terms of GNP, but that is not the way Congress looks at it. There are political limitations to running these huge imbalances, along with economic and financial implications. In a world of free capital movements, major political offsets, and a tendency to run larger and larger imbalances, we need an effective mechanism to monitor these issues from a global point of view.

KOMIYA:
If that is the problem, the problem is how to educate politicians. It is a task for economists in the United States. If the problem is a political problem, not an economic policy problem, then can you discuss it in rational economic terms in the United States? One must ask how one can educate politicians and the public.

DE VRIES:
It is not only a political problem, it is also a financial problem.

QUESTION:
One question to both Professor Komiya and Mr. de Vries. How do you evaluate the power of the Group of Five (G-5) intervention into the foreign exchange markets? In other words, do you regard the intervention by G-5 as only a trigger towards the yen's appreciation? Or does G-5 intervention still have power, along with some political maneuvers, to control the level of the main currencies, such as the yen, dollar, and the Deutsch mark?

KOMIYA:
The G-5 intervention was successful in a very unusual situation. The dollar had been very high for an extended period, and almost all knowledgeable people agreed that it had been too high. Governments were able to agree on bringing the dollar down to a more reasonable range.

But nowadays, there are great differences of opinion among major governments, so there is no possibility of such agreement now, and hence no possibility of a successful joint intervention.

MANUEL JOHNSON:

I would just like to make a few comments on this discussion. First, I agree with what Professor Tobin said; this is really not a time to assign labels to different views. What is required right now is quite a bit of common sense just looking at the global economic situation.

When I look at it I see a number of things that are fairly obvious. One is I see a lot of slack worldwide. As Rimmer de Vries says, unemployment rates are still high both in Europe and the United States. Our unemployment rate has performed fairly well, especially in terms of the employment rate in general. So I would think that we have come a lot further than the Europeans have, although there are structural differences.

The Japanese situation is also different; even though the unemployment rate is traditionally low there because of flexible wages and prices, industrial production has been anemic in Japan. I think that some of this has to do with the re-strengthening of the yen, the dramatic strength of the yen recently. I think that, in fact, this has further reduced potential inflation. The appreciation of the dollar had a tremendous impact on the U.S. domestic inflation rate, and of course the yen appreciation would be expected to have a similar impact on Japanese inflation rates. The oil-price decline is also part of that whole scenario, and has been a much greater benefit to the Japanese, and I should say to Europeans (aside from the British) as well. They are all 100 percent importers of crude oil, whereas the United States has a large, significant amount of domestic crude-oil production, and therefore the picture on the oil-price decline is a little more mixed here. So the relative gains to potential economic growth are biased more toward Europe and Japan than they are to the United States.

That doesn't mean the United States can't continue to expand. I think that any country that still has only 79 percent industrial capacity utilization still has room for expansion. We don't have to just start talking now about full employment potential growth, because I don't think we are at that level on a global basis.

But, clearly, the relative shift in potential growth and in capacity falls to the major trade-surplus nations. I don't think there is any doubt about that. The United States over the last four years has been the major global force in economic expansion. Four years down the road, however, the United States now has a $150 billion trade deficit, and our major trading partners have a surplus. Considering that fact, there is a logical direction for policy change. I think it implies that the surplus nations have more of a responsibility in engendering domestic growth than the deficit countries. That is fairly clear.

It is even clearer when you look at the potential growth situations in the trade-surplus versus the trade-deficit countries. As I mentioned, the oil-price decline has had more relative benefits for the surplus nations than for the deficit country. At the same time, there is more slack capacity in those countries.

In response to Professor Tobin's question about whether we would correspond with this rate reduction, first of all I think a lot would depend on the performance of our own domestic economy. Aside from that, I think it is very clear that we shouldn't be expected to provide the same degree of stimulus that the surplus industrial countries should provide. So I think that the central bank in the United States will certainly concentrate on trying to stabilize prices domestically. But I think that is also consistent with continued reasonable real economic expansion. However, given the fact that it has a $150 billion trade deficit, and has had the traditionally strong currency up until just recently, I don't think the United States should be expected to perform in real terms at the same pace that other countries with large trade surpluses and a lot of slack capacity should.

Clearly, there is a relative direction for domestic policy movement. I won't put labels on it; I just simply say it is obvious.

PATRICK:

There seems to be a clear divergence of perspective here between Americans on one side and Japanese on the other. As I have heard today's discussion, all the Americans have said, "Clearly, it's obvious, for the reasons that were given, that Japan and Germany should grow faster." As I have heard the Germans and the Japanese and the others say, "We're not yet sure that we are prepared to take the steps to grow faster." So I think there is a real difference of perspective on this point, while there is general agreement that the U.S. should reduce its budget deficit.

If growth does not happen, I think we have to consider again the implications of Rimmer de Vries's table, which suggests that we can anticipate a substantial, continued depreciation of the dollar and appreciation of the yen and the other currencies. That seems to me the only thing that is going to give, because everything else is really stuck in domestic politics, or caution, or inertia. Yet we have this market force in which the fundamentals suggest continued dollar depreciation.

So I have come away from this discussion feeling very much that we are in the same situation as we were back in September 1985; the dollar is less overvalued, but it is still overvalued. But now we don't have a consensus, so we aren't going to have intervention. Economists for several years said, "It is inevitable that the dollar is going to go down." Then for a long time it didn't go down; finally it fell, proving fundamentals were at work. I derive from this the same conclusion: finally, the dollar will depreciate, but I worry about what Fred Bergsten said — it may go down in a very hard landing sense. I would like to ask Rimmer de Vries where he disagrees with me on this.

DE VRIES:

When the G-5 meeting took place at the Plaza in September 1985, most people interpreted it simply as an exchange-rate agreement, but it is now seen differently. Today we see the trade-offs more clearly; we see that what we need is much more complicated than just a quick deal on exchange rates. The focus should really be on economic growth from the global point of view. You can see the progression in thinking in the speeches of our Secretary of the Treasury as well.

I think that the issues now are sharper and better focused and perhaps we are getting the mechanism in place. Some progress has been made. I don't want to go into the LDC debt issue in detail, but obviously the other critical issue right now is Mexico, where it is essential to get domestic reforms started. A lot of work has been done on that as well.

So some education is behind us. We have sharpened the issues, the agenda is better, and now we have got some action. Everybody is waiting for the U.S. budget-deficit reduction and tax reform.

But it ought to be very clear to all that either we take an international cooperative approach, or we go in the other direction. I grew up in Europe in the 1930s, and I do not like that world of nationalistic, protectionistic, beggar-thy-neighbour policies. We do not want that.

But we cannot have stability with the enormous amount of imbalance we now have. In this very dangerous period, we must educate people and politicians here, and in Japan, Germany, Mexico, and elsewhere.

Japan's Financial Market: Present Conditions and Outlook

Toru Kusukawa
Deputy President, The Fuji Bank, Ltd.

IN THIS ERA of instant global communication and internationalization of the worldwide financial marketplace, it is sometimes difficult to believe that any nation can continue to adhere to its own distinctive traditions and institutions.

Most of us in Japan know that we, too, must change in response to the current climate of deregulation and innovation in the global financial marketplace. We will have to adapt our policies, markets, and institutions in order to keep pace with and support our nation's own economic growth — and in order to assure Japan's place in the global economy. Change *is* underway, with much more to come, as I shall discuss.

First, however, it must be understood that there are very fundamental socio-cultural differences between Japan and America that color even our respective views on the issues involved in deregulation. In the United States, the rule of market discipline has long been firmly established. The primary role of government here is to ensure fair trade, as typified by the Fair Trade Act. Government intervention is limited to areas where market mechanisms do not operate efficiently. In the area of banking as well, the role of government is merely to safeguard the fair and efficient working of market mechanisms based on free competition and self-reliance.

By contrast, we Japanese have not traditionally shared such complete faith in free competition and self-reliance as a basic rule for social conduct. Reliance on government regulation has long been ingrained in our attitudes, and when something goes wrong, we resort to the convenient expedient of blaming the government.

Therefore, any effort to truly internationalize our financial markets must be preceded and accompanied by a conscious effort to change some very fundamental perceptions and perspectives. That effort has begun.

I believe it would be instructive to review some of the changes that have already been made, some that we will be making, and even a few that I think will have to come as Japan responds to progress and change in the international financial marketplace.

The tempo of financial deregulation in Japan has quickened since the appointment of the Yen/Dollar Committee in 1984. Although there is no denying that these deregulation measures have been instituted partly in deference to the wishes of Western countries, they are essentially a natural result of the expansion of our domestic economy. More specifically, they can be attributed to three factors which indicate that deregulation will continue in Japan:

First is the growing maturity of the Japanese economy. As their incomes have increased, both individuals and corporations have accumulated substantial financial assets over the years. These increased financial assets have made the Japanese people increasingly conscious of the kind of return they get on their investments, and emphasis has lately been shifted from liquidity of assets to yields. In order to satisfy such needs, financial institutions have had to devise products carrying unregulated interest rates, and higher-yielding instruments.

On the other hand, business demand for funds has tended to be much less vigorous since our economy has become considerably more mature than it was in the 1960s and 1970s. In such circumstances there is little danger that interest rates will soar, even if lending rates were allowed to float with the market.

The second factor adding to the pressure for early deregulation of the financial market is the massive offering of government bonds that has been going on continually since the second half of the 1970s. The huge amounts of government bonds outstanding on the market have led to the development of a secondary market. Their yields, established through the market mechanism, have come more or less to dictate the coupon rates of new government bond issues. The linkage established in this way between the government bond coupon rates and market rates has also been instrumental in spurring deregulation of interest rates on other financial instruments.

The third factor is an increase in international financial transactions, which has accompanied the internationalization of the Japanese economy. As a result, our domestic market has become much more closely tied to overseas markets, to such an extent, in fact, that financial deregulation in major markets overseas has an immediate impact on the Japanese financial market. Any delay in financial liberalization on our part would probably cause a substantial shift of financial transactions to overseas markets, thus "hollowing out" our domestic market.

Such has been the background spurring the deregulation of the domestic financial markets. Up to now, however, the major thrust of this deregulation drive has been directed at easing the restrictions on interest rates. It is fair to say that short-term rates and coupon rates on debt securities have now been almost completely deregulated.

Among all the interest-rate categories, our regulatory agency has treated the deposit rates with utmost discretion. No significant step toward deposit-rate deregulation has been taken since 1979, when certificates of deposit were introduced to corporate treasurers as new financial instruments carrying unregulated interest rates. In 1985, however, the government authorized the issue of money market certificates carrying interest rates which vary according to prevailing market rates. Regulation of interest rates on time deposits in extra-large denominations was eased in October of the same year. As plans stand now, interest rates on large-denomination time deposits will have been completely deregulated by the spring of 1987. This will be followed by the deregulation of interest rates on small-denomination time deposits. For the present, there is no plan to deregulate interest rates on passbook accounts, but this will come up on the agenda sooner or later.

Another issue crying out for early reform is the statutory separation of different business areas. In this respect, Japan still has a long way to go.

The present financial-market system basically adheres to the principle of separation of different business activities. Long-term credit banks, for example, were established which specialize in long-term loans. To help them raise long-term funds, they were given special authority to issue bank debentures with maturities ranging from three to five years. Similarly, only a limited number of financial institutions known as "trust banks" are authorized to manage trust assets; and the securities business is separated from banking—a rule modeled on America's Glass-Steagall Act and strictly enforced in Japan.

It is fair to say that specialization such as this and the separation of different areas of business has played an important historical role in Japan. It helped specialized financial institutions gain expertise in their respective fields and was instrumental in supplying long-term funds needed by business corporations during the period of postwar economic reconstruction.

However, in recent years, as the Japanese economy has matured, the system has outlived its usefulness. The effects of deregulated interest rates on the Japanese economy will not be fully realized without the removal of the regulations separating business areas.

Sources of funds for commercial banks in Japan are confined at present to relatively short-term deposits. However, if we are to meet adequately the changing and diverse needs of our customers, and at the same time hedge against risks associated with interest rate fluctuations and availability, we must secure means of raising long-term funds ourselves. Authorizing commercial banks to issue bank debentures could be one solution toward that end.

In the area of trust services, the Japanese government has recently authorized foreign banks to establish wholly owned or majority-owned subsidiaries to engage in the trust business. This has made the separation of the trust business from commercial banking virtually meaningless. Consequently, we believe that a relaxation of the rules separating long-term banking from short-term banking, and the trust business from commercial banking, holds the key to maturing the financial-market system of Japan in a way commensurate with its economic strength.

Next, I would like to touch on the separation of banking from the securities business. Before the war, banks were authorized to engage in a wide range of securities transactions including the underwriting of corporate bond issues. Since the enactment of the Securities and Exchange Law in 1948, however, its Article 65, which was modeled after the Glass-Steagall Act in the United States, has severely restricted involvement by banks in the securities business. After the war, the United States implemented a variety of institutional reforms in Japan, which have contributed to the modernization of our country. We Japanese are grateful for this, but from our perspectives as bankers, the introduction of Article 65 based on the Glass-Steagall Act was rather unfortunate.

Since the separation of banking from the securities business was instituted following a U.S. model, it should not become a cause of financial-market friction between the United States and Japan. With the European countries, however, which have adopted the universal-banking system, the separation of banking from the securities business has become a bone of contention. To accommodate their wishes, the Japanese government authorized European banks to engage, for all practical purposes, in the securities business, provided the vehicle was not a majority-owned subsidiary.

Whether or not we should continue to separate banking from the securities business has become a subject of serious debate in Japan as well as in the United States. The real issue, however, is not which system better suits the particular conditions of each country, but which is superior as a financial system, taking into consideration the possible detrimental impact that concurrent operation of banking and underwriting might have on sound banking principles. Realistically, this type of debate can eventually lead to the coexistence of markets which separate banking from the securities business with ones in which the two are not separated. However, this poses practical difficulties for all concerned.

When restrictions on external financial transactions were the norm rather than the exception, maintenance of a financial-market system unique to a given country was justifiable. Today, however, liberalization of external financial transactions has become a universal trend, a trend which is expected to strengthen in the coming years. Given the fact that geographical boundaries have been practically eliminated as far as financial transactions are concerned, it has become increasingly irrelevant in my opinion for a few countries to stick to the system of separating banking from the securities business.

Therefore, the industrial nations should join forces toward eventual relaxation of this separation while taking care to implement necessary measures to minimize adverse side effects arising from possible conflicts of interest, if any.

Meanwhile, the participation of foreign banks operating in the trust and securities businesses in Japan has created a situation which exposes Japanese financial institutions to unfair competition with their foreign counterparts in the domestic money and capital markets. Some of the American banks have started providing trust-asset management services on top of their banking services. If they wish, European banks which provide universal-banking services can also engage in trust and securities businesses along with banking. More recently, foreign banks were also authorized to float Euroyen bonds. All of these are privileges which have been given to foreign banks but denied to Japanese commercial banks.

In addition to the separation of business areas, there are two other problems confronting Japanese banking institutions. In Japan, as in other countries, non-bank institutions have become increasingly active in the consumer-finance and credit-card business. What really concerns me is the fact that these non-bank institutions have lately been actively encroaching upon the traditional preserves of regular banks, namely, the settlement of financial transactions and deposit taking. More specifically, securities firms are offering money market funds and cashing services by means of extensive cash-dispenser networks. Credit-card companies offer consumer loans through similar networks. Given the proliferation of such financial services provided by non-bank institutions, a serious examination of their impact on the integrity of the traditional banking system and on the effectiveness of the nation's monetary policy has become extremely important.

The second problem involves regulation of the primary capital ratio or risk-asset ratio. In Japan, monetary authorities have been primarily concerned with controlling interest rates and the business activities of individual banks, and have not paid too much attention to their primary capital ratios. However, as the deregulation of interest rates and business activities takes hold, the regulatory agencies will be paying greater attention to the primary capital ratio and other financial ratios of the banks under its supervision.

The trend toward internationalization has clearly reached Japan. We cannot ignore it. An increasing number of foreign banks are showing active interest in the Japanese financial market. The participation of some of them in the trust business in Japan is a typical manifestation of this interest. When a Japanese bank was driven to the verge of bankruptcy, one of the foreign banks reportedly proposed to buy it out. This episode also serves to dramatize the keen interest which foreign banks are taking in the growth potential of the Japanese financial market.

Another area of great interest to foreign banks is the ability of the Tokyo market to serve as a source of yen funds and as a yen-dominated investment market. With the growth of the Japanese economy into the second largest in the free world, the role of the yen as a financing and investment currency has increased dramatically. For our part, we realize it is in the best interest of our country to develop the Tokyo market into a leading international financial center. An offshore market is scheduled to be instituted in Tokyo this fall on the model of New York's international banking facility. This, I hope, will give the Tokyo market an increasing international importance.

As I said earlier, however, we know that for the Japanese financial market to become international in the true sense of the word, further liberalization of the domestic market system is inevitable. In addition to the deregulation of the interest-rate structure and the separation of business areas I mentioned earlier, further development of the money and capital markets, including Treasury bills, will be necessary. An exemption of non-residents' interest income from withholding tax should also be seriously considered.

We are making progress. We will continue to reexamine our institutions and systems in the context of the new, international marketplace and to make the necessary changes.

The Internationalization of Investment Banking

Frederick Whittemore
Managing Director, Morgan Stanley & Co.

WHEN I WAS INVITED to give this speech, I wasn't quite sure what the internationalization of the market really meant, but after Mr. Kusukawa's remarks, I now can honestly say that our Japanese friends from the banking industry sound just like our friends from Bankers Trust, Morgan Guaranty Trust, and all the other bankers who would like to put us investment bankers out of business.

I would like to discuss what I believe is happening in the securities markets: the recent innovations in these markets; their relationships to each other; and the strategy that Morgan Stanley and our competitors in Japan and around the world are developing to maximize our business franchise. We believe that there is a very competitive atmosphere developing, which we all must share and shape in different ways.

The globalization of the securities markets is a grand and exciting prospect. It is exciting because it brings enormous opportunity, and it is grand because fundamental shifts in the world market in the 1980s seem to be taking place more rapidly than in prior generations.

Why are these fundamental shifts happening? To give you some perspective on this, we have to look back before the period of relative economic growth of the 1980s, to the 1970s — the inflation decade. This prolonged period of inflation then forced some fundamental changes on us in this decade.

What we have done in the marketplace here and abroad is institutionalize the volatility. Prices of securities no longer move in eighths and quarters, but by much larger swings up and down. We can no longer expect to establish the kind of stability in marketplaces that we had come to expect in the past. I think many of us in the business, and many who write for the newspapers, still yearn to recover the price stability which we have had in prior years. A fundamental part of understanding the securities world at this point is to see that a return to stability is just not possible.

The institutionalization of investment is the fundamental trend that has driven the reaction to volatility, the reaction to inflation. This reaction has involved the creation of new products to defend against inflation's effects, and protect and preserve investment performance.

The rise of pension funds in the United States and elsewhere has been the principle vehicle of this institutionalization. When our fathers or grandfathers bought insurance in the Depression of the 1930s, they thought that they were protecting their families. Insurance companies — and I say this in a mean way on purpose — have huge asset bases, which they invest very profitably. Their asset investment activity is more successful than their insurance function, in terms of preservation against inflation, and as a means to provide for the economic need for which they were created. Now, I don't mean the insurance companies are not innovative and changing; of course they are. However, the pension fund has taken over the investment decision-making process in many of our markets, and particularly in the United States. There is no question that the mutual funds, trust activities, and all the other myriad activities which represent institutionalization have done the same thing. Most of the activity on the New York Stock Exchange today is institutional business, trading in huge blocks of shares. (See Figure 2.) We are no longer in the era of the taxicab-driver investor. Investment decisions are made by others, and they are made more professionally.

What changes has this institutionalization required of us?

First, institutions require lower costs. Over ten years ago, we in the U.S. securities industry went to negotiated rates. The British are struggling to get to negotiated rates; the Canadians are struggling to get to negotiated rates. The institutions are driving everyone of us towards lower costs for large transactions. The notion that the small transaction of John Q. Public should cost the same as the large transaction of the trust company has been reassessed and rejected.

Second, the institutions have pressed for much more comprehensive and sophisticated professional advice. They want better information, and they want it quicker.

Third, they have also driven for faster settlement, because they have learned that they cannot afford to leave their money in the banks over the weekend at high rates, just as we have learned. This results in substantial technological costs, and results in large clearance facilities, and an emphasis on systems control. If you recall, 15 years ago, in the 1970 period, a great many Wall Street firms were having trouble with a back-office problem of not being able to add and subtract. We have now learned to add and subtract, and the biggest part of our budget is a systems mechanic. In this regard, I consider the stock-exchange mechanism in this country something of an operating antique. We in the business spend substantial amounts of money to get orders there, and substantial amounts of money to get orders back. The system is being encroached upon slowly as the biggest practitioners in it have a better systems mechanic than the New York Stock Exchange itself does. That is an incendiary statement; it is meant to be. But this drives us to provide the lower costs that our customers require; it is where we spend our money.

You can't spend money without making it first, and that requires a whole series of mechanisms to protect the investor. In the inflationary decade of the 1970s, your grandfather's portrait or your silverware were more important investments than your securities. We have come through periods of dramatically high interest rates; yet now that we seem to have put the genie of inflation back in the bottle, our real interest rates have become higher than they were with high inflation. High real interest rates have also driven change.

The internationalization of the market is not new. Obviously, there has always been, in Switzerland, Britain, Amsterdam, and so forth, a real interest in the internationalization of investment. This country was substantially built by investment from abroad. In the 25 or 30 years after the Second World War, Americans spent substantial amounts of capital building or buying abroad from here. Now, however, we recognize that we are no longer as strong as we must be, and other capital markets, principally Japan, principally Europe, have risen to become full partners in that process.

So the internationalization of investment is a fundamental change to which we all are reacting. I shall discuss what this change means in different marketplaces. But the competition of technological new products is very dramatic. I remember people saying in the 1960s that the Eurobond market would be a few hundred million dollars at most; it has now grown to be many billions. It is now grown to be an active competitor — an unregulated marketplace in a world where other major marketplaces are regulated. But I think the interesting thing is that in 1985, by our calculations, some 75 percent of the bond trades and issues were backed or supported by some sort of an interest-rate swap. There are many ramifications from that. No longer do corporate treasurers allow themselves the full risk of having an international business and not being able to protect it on their balance sheets. Between the investment banks like ourselves and the commercial banks, this is an area of competition but of cooperation; we seem to be able to help that treasurer protect his balance sheet and his income account. He now can trade and have the full benefits of that business still stay with him. He doesn't necessarily lose it when people meet in the Plaza Hotel; nor does he gain artificially when they don't meet in the Plaza Hotel.

Let me summarize the forces driving the globalization of investment:

- Institutionalization of funds, which I have discussed.
- Deregulation of markets.
- The trend toward privatization — when governments sell state-owned enterprises on the public markets, such as Mrs. Thatcher has done in Britain with the sale of British Telecom and other businesses. This, of course, expands the supply of equity.
- Effects of technology.
- Increasing global competition.

Let me elaborate on some of these factors further.

Figure 1 provides some perspective on how substantial the Eurobond market really is. At the bottom is a chart showing when, for Triple A credit instruments, the Eurobond market has an advantage over the U.S. market. We show this to treasurers to be honest with them and to defend the fact that the United States has a market you should use. If the market is going to go to Europe, in that sense, and the U.S. market in its credit arbitrage is not always more advantageous than the Eurobond market, with that kind of track record, obvi-

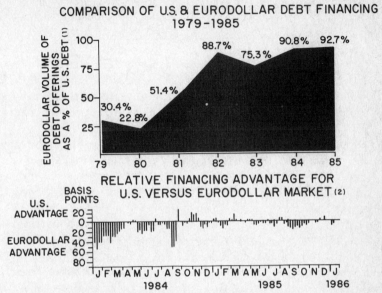

FIGURE 1

GLOBALIZATION OF THE CAPITAL MARKETS

COMPARISON OF U.S. & EURODOLLAR DEBT FINANCING
1979-1985

(1) INCLUDES TOTAL DOLLAR DENOMINATED STRAIGHT CORPORATE FROM ALL ISSUERS DEBT IN EURO AND U.S. MARKETS RESPECTIVELY.
(2) FOR 10-YEAR AAA CREDIT.

ously those firms who are going to chase U.S. credit are going to go to Europe to do that business. So if it means competing with universal banks in Europe, or if it means competing with Japanese securities firms, or British securities firms, we have all been chasing our clients wherever they are going.

The next figure shows the impact of institutionalization on the equity markets.

Figure 2 shows the percentage of trades of 1000 shares or over relative to the New York Stock Exchange volume, and the block trades of 10,000 shares or more as a percentage of New York Stock Exchange volume. In 1985, the respective ratios were almost 90 percent and more than 50 percent.

Much of the activity in U.S. corporate stocks involves American institutional and individual investment. Relatively little, in terms of the volatility of funds, is foreign investment, at least as recorded in the U.S. Federal Reserve flow of funds data. We cannot tell who owns the money that Citibank or Morgan Guaranty Bank trades. But foreign investment as a percentage of that is still relatively modest.

In Figure 3 one can see that U.S. institutions have started to recognize they must chase performance on a worldwide basis. They no longer can just cherry-pick the Big Board, or even the U.S. market for all of their performance criteria. They must compare an automobile company in Europe versus an automobile

FIGURE 2

INSTITUTIONALIZATION OF THE U.S. EQUITY MARKET

TRADES 1,000 SHARES AND OVER AS A % OF TOTAL NYSE VOLUME

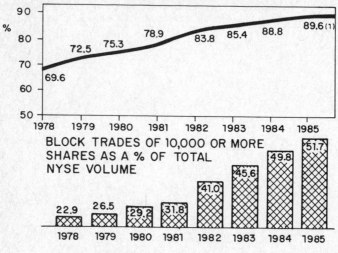

BLOCK TRADES OF 10,000 OR MORE SHARES AS A % OF TOTAL NYSE VOLUME

(1) THROUGH NOVEMBER 1985

FIGURE 3

NET U.S. PURCHASES OF FOREIGN EQUITY

1975–SECOND QUARTER 1985

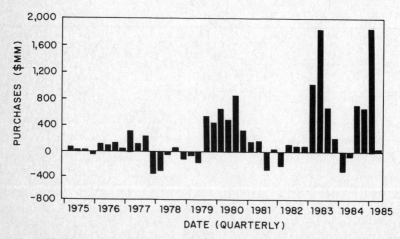

SOURCE: U.S. TREASURY, MORGAN STANLEY

FIGURE 4

ADRs OUTSTANDING [1]

1980 – 1985

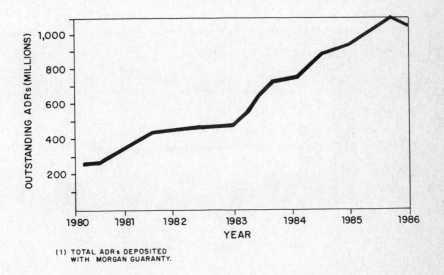

(1) TOTAL ADRs DEPOSITED
WITH MORGAN GUARANTY.

company in Japan versus an automobile company in Detroit. The marketplace must do what the trade-related place has done; opportunities must be seen for investors across borders.

Figure 4 shows the growth of the American Depositary Receipt (ADR) market in the early 1980s. It was not so long ago that companies outside the United States used to say, "We can't come to New York. We don't like the SEC. We can't stand having to disclose all the things we disclose; we actually have to write a registration statement, we'd have to put the Chairman's salary in. A terrible thing to do." But the ADR market — in lieu of the actual shares — is the important bridge which has brought institutional investment here into foreign equities. If you were a substantial company trying to grow in Europe, and you were competing against the I.B.M.s of the world, or the General Motors or whatever, you don't have the equity market to use, except on a local basis, unless you can come here, where the equity market is broad. Take Scandanavia: a Farmacia will come to this market and will be competing with companies who must raise their money for growth on mezzanine finance. They must find tricky ways to do things to take equity risk. So the United States market is trying to develop a mechanism to do this; we are trying to interest investors, and we have parades of companies coming in. We are finding ways to take advantage of the value, the liquidity, the breadth of interest that can be developed in equity markets here.

FIGURE 5

MARKET CAPITALIZATION
OF SELECTED STOCK MARKETS

(AS OF 12/31/85)

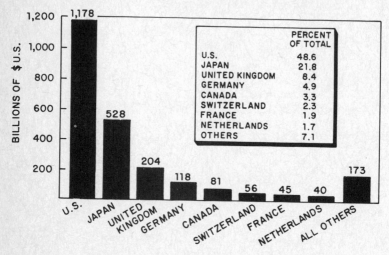

	PERCENT OF TOTAL
U.S.	48.6
JAPAN	21.8
UNITED KINGDOM	8.4
GERMANY	4.9
CANADA	3.3
SWITZERLAND	2.3
FRANCE	1.9
NETHERLANDS	1.7
OTHERS	7.1

NOTE: U.S. DATA REPRESENT MARKET CAPITALIZATION OF STANDARD & POORS 500 STOCKS.

FIGURE 6

APPRECIATION OF WORLDWIDE EQUITY MARKETS

DURING CALENDAR 1985

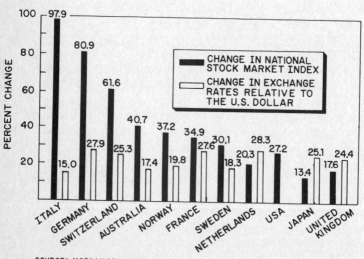

SOURCE: MORGAN STANLEY CAPITAL INTERNATIONAL PERSPECTIVE

FIGURE 7

ANNUAL TURNOVER AS A % OF
TOTAL MARKET CAPITALIZATION (1)

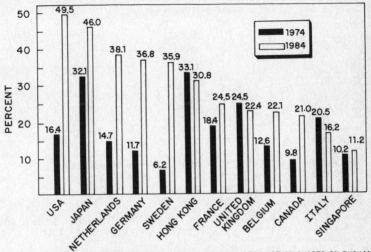

(1) DATA REFERS TO COMMON STOCKS ONLY. DATA INCLUDES FOREIGN SHARES ON EXCHANGES WITH THE EXCEPTION OF THOSE LISTED IN GERMANY AND THE NETHERLANDS.
SOURCE: MORGAN STANLEY CAPITAL INTERNATIONAL PERSPECTIVE, MARCH 1985

Figure 5 shows market capitalization at the end of last year, to give you some perspective on where investment really is going. Much of it is United States, but notice how much of it is in Japan. Notice that we are in a far different relation than perhaps we were five and ten years ago.

Figure 6 shows what happened in these markets during 1985. Italy is the one that grew the most—I maintain that Italy has good credit in two out of every ten years. But the fact is that the United States and Japan did not have the same appreciation of equity markets in 1985. If you are a performance-driven investor, investing other people's money, you cannot afford to ignore other markets. The John Templetons and the George Soroses of the world are at the forefront of reaching out to find other markets abroad and take that kind of risk. The technology that we are all providing and trying to develop is supporting that exercise.

Figure 7 shows the turnover in trades; it is a measure of liquidity if you will. If you are a company in France trying to raise equity and competing against a U.S. company that can go to a market where its investors can easily sell, and you have a very tightly controlled bourse in France, your competitors have a major advantage.

Table 1 shows how much overseas investment is happening with U.S. pension-fund growth. This shows both by Fortune 500 companies and by the amount of pension assets—who is reaching out and who is staying in the U.S. cocoon.

TABLE 1

International Investment Trends of
U.S. Corporate Pension Plans

	Percent of corporate pension plans investing internationally							Will start investing	Total participation
	1979	1980	1981	1982	1983	1984	1985		
Fortune 500 rank[1]	%	%	%	%	%	%	%	%	%
001–100	23	34	47	49	49	53	64	8	72
101–200	19	29	29	34	29	37	40	10	50
201–300	10	9	20	23	23	34	42	3	45
301–400	1	16	16	25	27	22	21	15	36
401–500	4	5	8	7	9	7	9	7	16
Pension plan assets	%	%	%	%	%	%	%	%	%
Over $1 billion	26	40	59	60	63	65	77	5	82
$501–1,000 million	24	27	42	60	33	41	43	12	55
$251– 500 million	18	24	32	32	32	39	35	13	48
$201– 250 million	5	18	20	22	24	29	37	12	49
$151– 200 million	15	22	17	27	19	30	24	9	33
$101– 150 million	12	7	19	21	24	15	17	10	27
Total companies	8	13	17	18	19	20	26	8	34

Source: Greenwich Research Associates.
(1) The 500 largest U.S. industrial companies ranked by yearly sales as compiled by Fortune magazine.

Notice that the substantial companies in this country are reaching outside of the United States market abroad to invest; the larger companies are doing the most of this.

Table 2 shows pension fund assets in different countries. This is that pension-fund mass that I spoke of earlier, and shows how much of it is in the United States, and how much of Britain's total assets are in foreign countries. Britain

TABLE 2

1985 Total Pension Fund Assets in Selected Countries

	(U.S. $ billions)		
	Total assets	Holdings of foreign securities[1]	Percentage of total
United States	$860.00	$16.0	1.9%
Britain	95.0	21.0	22.1
Netherlands	77.0	6.2	8.1
Japan	60.0	5.0	8.9
Switzerland	55.0	4.4	8.0
West Germany	24.0	0.7	2.9
France	6.5	0.1	1.5
Rest of Europe	12.0	1.0	8.3

[1] Includes both debt and equity securities.
Source: Estimates of InterSec Research Corporation.

is a capital society, not necessarily an earning society today, but a capital society as an investment mechanism. Notice how Japan is just really beginning to move.

Let me say what the strategy is for investment banking firms such as Morgan Stanley.

We are chasing the internationalization of this investment. Let me be more or less bottom-line oriented about this. Morgan Stanley, Goldman Sachs, First Boston, Salomon Brothers and the rest of the major securities firms in this country are all seeking to build a very substantial three-legged stool. We are seeking to build a user market position and market share here.

We are in far different businesses and many more businesses than we were five years ago. For example, we cannot have an international-investment activity without trading currencies; it used to be that we did that at Morgan Guaranty and Citibank in New York, and now we do it in our own firms. Another example: you cannot have a significant business if you don't securitize kinds of assets that used to be done in the banking system. Mortgages have been a major growth area for all of us. We must reach into the interest-earning business, without calling it a "b-a-n-k." If you look at the income statement of Merrill Lynch, taking the interest earned and the interest paid, and look at the spread difference in relation to the amount of earnings, you will find that 35 to 40 percent of their earnings are made just as an interest spread.

Surveying our competition in the world, the British merchant banks are behind us on the global business. For many years they thought that being an accepting house, with little capital, was enough. They are really just now organizing themselves to go abroad, to deal with the fact of negotiated rates, and to buy brokers and jobbers. Deutsch Bank has moved its trading operation to London, but it is such a fundamental part of the German economy that we think it will always be an instrument of Germany rather than an instrument of the market. The Swiss banks can buy us and sell us any day when they want to, but they are basically preservators. Their rationale in the world is to find assets and preserve them, not necessarily to be an intermediary.

So our major competitors in the next few years, obviously, will be from Japan, albeit with their own form of the Glass-Steagall Act. There is no question that the amount of capital coming from Japan will be followed and chased by Japanese securities firms and banks, as U.S. firms have followed American capital. Even the barriers of culture are rapidly resolving themselves. So for the next ten or twenty years we expect to be competing mostly with Japanese securities firms.

Our other major competitors are U.S. banks. We believe that the banking system with its rich traditions deserves and needs the Glass-Steagall Act. The banking system has the subsidy of the United States Government behind it and that it has preferred and organized monopolies in certain areas of the marketplace. It has a deposit protection system, paid for by the United States Government which we do not share. We believe that we operate in an area of risk and risk-taking which they properly should be restricted from entering. We believe that the reasons that the Glass-Steagall Act was put into place in the 1930s have current validity as well. We would like the Glass-Steagall Act to be preserved but we expect that Congress will chip away at it. We would hope to preserve it at least in equity securities.

But in any event, we are taking advantage of a three- to five-year window, before the banks become full-fledged competitors, to become as large and as powerful as quickly as we can.

Since this is a very capital-intensive business we just went public, as have other firms on Wall Street. We are all raising funds in order to get large enough quickly enough in order to take advantage of the capital opportunities that are there. I could say that some other way, but that is the truth.

One quick word about the economy, because I know this is an economic event, and you have lots of highly paid economists here. In the last five weeks, interest rates in this country have gone up about 75 basis points, give or take. Every time Mr. Volcker coughs at a reporter it changes the interest rate, as we all know. But there was a great deal of concern as to whether the Japanese investor was going to chase our government bond market down in level. That concern is still there. There is a concern that the weak dollar has changed that. There is a concern that the stimulus of the change in the dollar rate is going to drive growth in the third and fourth quarters of this year. Frankly, I believe, on a bilateral trade-weighted basis that the dollar hasn't changed enough. I believe that we are not going to have a stimulated economy in the latter part of 1986, driven by the change in the market. I believe the problem is that we are going to have relatively low growth. Germany and Japan seem to be having low growth too. Growth, but low growth, at the moment. What does this mean? We've also had an oil-price drop. We have institutions, at least in this country, who are concerned for the viability of their loan system. The banks must revalue their loans; they must be realistic. Investment banks will help them restructure (we hope!). But the fact is that I believe the combination of these factors calls for a further reduction this summer in interest rates.

The Dark Side of Financial Innovation

Franklin R. Edwards
Professor and Director, Center for the Study of Futures Markets,
Columbia University

I. *Introduction*

Financial innovation can increase competition, promote efficiency, and improve the allocation of risk in the economy. In doing so it can change the nature of risk in the financial system, change who bears this risk[1] and either increase or decrease risk to the overall system. A recent study of innovation by the Bank for International Settlements (BIS) concludes:

> A main conclusion of many observers with respect to new financial instruments is that market participants, at least those with access to all markets, are able to adjust their profiles of most categories of risk more precisely with the new instruments than previously. Overall, this enables credit to be extended by lenders to borrowers, while the various categories of risk historically associated with credit extension can be separated and spread more widely and, in particular, can be transferred to those who can absorb it by an offsetting exposure or to those who specialize in management of risk for a fee.[2]

There is another side to financial innovation that often goes unrecognized: innovation exacerbates a serious regulatory problem that we already have, and one that may lead ultimately to a financial collapse. Indeed, if the present regulatory structure continues unchanged, the long-run effect of financial innovation is to increase the likelihood of a financial collapse.

The Bank for International Settlements' study is concerned about this as well, and even pays lip service to the possibility. It fails, however, either to identify the seriousness of the problem or to recognize the reasons why such a collapse may occur. The study simply states:

> The above argument is often extended to reach the conclusion that banking innovation is an unambiguous social good. That is, the effects in the aggregate are the simple sum of effects for individual economic agents, without any significant negative side effects (externalities). The possibility of negative side effects should be examined in detail, in terms of the various types of systematic risk described above. Sufficient data are not available to approach these questions with empirical economic models, but it is possible to examine the use of instruments by market participants and attempt to hypothesize about how markets for them might react in times of stress and how such reactions might spread through the financial system.[3]

There is no conclusion on this issue in the report.

II. *Innovation and Risk*

Innovations have changed the nature of bank risk in several ways. First, some types of assets that banks have customarily held will in the future display more market risk. This is because banks have traditionally employed historical-cost-accounting, so that changes in the market value of their assets were not reflected in their statements, even though these values were changing. This made some sense because it was often difficult or impossible to determine an accurate market value for these assets, other than when the asset was either acquired or sold, or at its maturity. Recent innovations, however, have made it possible to assign market values to assets like securitized loans and contracts. Thus, in the future banks will have to recognize and actively manage these risks, and suffer the consequences of adverse market moves.

Second, assets or contracts that do not involve an extension of credit, such as currency swaps, contain substantial credit risks that banks will have to manage carefully. Credit risk, long familiar to banks as lenders, is the risk that the counterparty (borrower or any party committed to a future exchange under given terms, as in a currency swap) will fail to perform — in other words, he will default. Institutions engaging in swaps, options, long-dated forward exchange, providing letters of credit, or purchasing revolving underwriting commitments face huge aggregate volumes of credit risk at all times. These risks have been recognized and partially managed by trading foreign exchange or using repurchase agreements, but these techniques cannot be used to offset contracts whose longer-term maturities create credit exposures orders of magnitude greater than that which is customary.

Finally, innovation has been one way that banks and other financial institutions have circumvented regulations designed to keep them from taking "too much" risk. Thus, regulations that have been relied upon historically to limit the risk exposure of our financial system have been rendered ineffective.

Traditional regulation or prudential oversight has not addressed these new developments. It has not been flexible and adaptive enough to close the regulatory loopholes opened by innovation. More important, the existing regulatory structure actually encourages institutional risk-taking by subsidizing it. As a consequence, it provides an incentive for institutions to innovate around existing regulations in order to increase their risk exposures to levels far beyond that which would be prudent (or profitable) in a world without regulation (where the ultimate regulators are competitive market forces).

III. *Innovation, Financial Stability, and Regulation*

The rapid and widespread innovation of new products, techniques, and strategies that has overtaken financial markets in the last few years might well be viewed as a force of 'creative destruction.' While innovations have given us new ways to manage a more volatile and unforgiving economic environment, they may nevertheless be sowing the seeds of a future financial collapse. While this view may seem unnecessarily alarmist, to those of us who have studied the complex interrelationship between government regulation and financial institutions it does not seem so.

Unlike most industries and markets, the health of financial institutions and markets depends critically upon maintaining the proper balance between government and industry. In the United States, the availability of last-resort lending from the Federal Reserve, together with widespread deposit insurance, results in a federal guarantee of the soundness of our financial institutions and, indirectly, of the stability of the financial system.

Recent innovations and political exigencies have overwhelmed this structure of federal guarantees. Deposit insurance coverage has become far more extensive than is suggested by a formal reading of the law (and certainly more extensive than that envisioned in 1933 by the founders of deposit insurance). *De jure* guarantees are only the tip of the iceberg; *de facto* guarantees extend to a wide variety of formally uninsured financial liabilities. Partly for political reasons, and partly because of the deficient information systems and the defective insolvency concepts employed by U.S. regulators, the aggregate value of deposit-insurance guarantees has become much larger than is either generally recognized or supportable under the present system.[4] The magnitude of this federal guarantee continues to grow, and is administratively out of control. The insurance reserves of U.S. insurers are inadequate to meet the *de facto* financial insolvency that even today exists in our financial system, and the staffs of these insurance agencies are overwhelmed by the magnitude of the task with which they are faced and by the inadequacy of their tools. They are facing a *de facto* financial disaster and they are helpless either to resolve it or to slow its relentless pace.

Financial innovation is making the problem worse. It expands the opportunities for risk taking, increases institutional risk exposure, and makes the extent of the federal guarantee greater than ever. This is happening because of the complex relationship we have between government regulation and private financial institutions. Financial institutions do not operate in a completely free-market environment. They are supported by a system of federal regulations and guarantees which have the effect of undermining or weakening the heralded 'invisible hand.' Depositors and other creditors tend to rely on federal guarantees to protect them, and, as a consequence, fail to impose on financial institutions the requisite market discipline. Institutions can take on additional risks without paying the full "market price" for such risks. As such, they receive a federal subsidy equal to the differential between the true price of such risk and what they actually pay. The aggregate value of these subsidies to all institutions equals the present federal guarantee given to our financial system.

This guarantee is growing daily. As institutions take on new risks they receive additional federal subsidies. Thus, by increasing their risk-exposures they are able to increase profitability. Innovation, by opening up new lines of activity and new products, feeds the incentive towards risk-taking. Further, the effectiveness of the traditional regulatory checks on this tendency has been eroded by competitive pressures and political exigencies. Regulators have been forced to find expeditious short-run solutions, rather than confronting the problem directly. The result is that the long-run problem is made worse because short-run policies have encouraged the very kind of institutional activity that leads to more insolvency.

Unless we can curb the incentives for risk-taking that are created by the presence of *de facto* federal guarantees, or reprice and redesign the existing system of *de facto* deposit insurance to bring incentives into line with a sustainable system of federal guarantees, we are headed for a financial disaster. A system must be established that either restores market discipline and shifts the main burden of institutional insolvency to the stockholders and creditors of financial institutions and away from federal regulatory agencies and taxpayers, or resurrects a system of regulatory constraints consistent with our present federal guarantees.

Government officials, industry spokesmen, political representatives, and academics in the United States are debating a number of proposals for restoring market discipline. If history is any guide, however, such reform will only become possible after the occurrence of a financial crisis. Regulatory reforms undertaken in a crisis atmosphere, however, almost always result in the adoption of short-sighted measures, more suited to the immediate crisis than to the long-run failings of the system. To avoid a financial disaster and the undesirable financial reforms that will almost certainly follow such a disaster, we must move quickly to adopt reforms which will restore market discipline and provide a stable financial environment.

IV. *Policy Prescriptions*

There are a number of reforms being discussed which offer promising avenues to financial stability. At the heart of all of these is the goal of making deposit insurance a viable system. Historically, deposit insurance has worked well, but only because there existed constraints which prevented financial institutions from operating freely. These constraints have been eroded by recent innovations.

Federal deposit insurance presently imposes an explicit *ex ante* (flat) premium on deposit liabilities, regardless of an institution's exposure to risk. To control the incentives toward risk-taking that this system encourages, deposit-insurance administrators have to monitor institutional risk taking and penalize institutions when they go beyond boundaries deemed financially prudent. In the past, regulators were assisted in this task by an elaborate system of constraining regulations which prevented institutions from engaging in "risky" activities and from exposing their institutions to excessive risk. The permissible activities were well understood by regulators, as were their implications for institutional soundness. Even so, the system was vulnerable to "insolvency creep" as institutions discovered ways of taking advantage of the system.

In the adaptive and innovative financial environment of today this "creep" has become a "gallop." As institutions enter new businesses at an unprecedented pace, and find new ways to increase their already high leverage (through off-balance sheet activities such as "swaps"), the mispricing of deposit insurance becomes even greater. Today's flat insurance premiums have little relationship to current institutional risks. Further, the *de facto* extension of deposit insurance to formally uncovered liabilities (such as large banks and large depositors), together with this increase in mispricing, has resulted in a meteoric rise in the value of the federal insurance subsidies and guarantees. The ability of government to sustain these subsidies is questionable.

Reform must reduce the mispricing of deposit insurance and place the federal insurance agencies on a sound footing. A promising proposal to accomplish this is to adopt a system of risk-based insurance premiums, together with reducing *de facto* insurance coverage to levels more compatible with the long-run soundness of the insurance agencies.

The desirability and feasibility of adopting variable risk-related insurance premiums has been hotly debated. I will not repeat the arguments for and against it here. The consensus is that such a system can succeed in reducing institutional incentives to increase risk. However, there are two key problems in devising a system of risk-based premiums, and these are made more difficult by the present innovative environment we now have.

First, the institutional flexibility which the present free-wheeling competitive atmosphere offers makes it imperative that regulators adapt their policies and premiums quickly to keep up with market developments. If risk-related premiums are to succeed, insurance agencies will themselves have to be more flexible and responsive than in the past. A proposal that has been advanced to achieve this result is to inject competition into the federal deposit insurance system, among the insurance agencies themselves.[5] These proposals deserve serious consideration.

Second, a system of *ex post* procedures for settling up gains and losses among an insured institution, its stockholders, creditors, and the insurance agency needs to be worked out in order to further reduce the moral-hazard problem. This is potentially the most troublesome issue because of the prevailing legal institution of limited liability. To completely eliminate the endgame gambles that failing institutions are prone to take, the liability of stockholders would have to be extended beyond what it is now. Just how far is disputable. Treating bank (or financial institution) stockholders differently from other stockholders may create new problems which are difficult to anticipate.

Along with risk-related variable insurance premiums, there should be a reduction in the *de facto* coverage of deposit insurance. The basic coverage should not be raised beyond the present *de jure* limit ($100,000), and should possibly even be reduced. The argument in favor of setting some upper limit on deposit insurance is related to the usual one for deductibles in insurance. The more risk an institution pays for by having to pay market prices for its "deposits," the more its choice of risky activities will conform to market principles. Consequently, the potential insurance subsidy will be reduced, and the risk to the insuring entity will be less.

While limiting insurance coverage has the potential for increasing the probability of bank runs, and of increasing the costs of such runs, the long-run gains from introducing more market discipline into the financial system outweighs this potential cost. The prevention of bank runs, and the maintenance of short-run stability of the financial system, should in any case be left to the central bank in its capacity as lender-of-last-resort. If financial institutions are essentially solvent, as they would be under a more enlightened regulatory system, short-term liquidity problems can be handled by the central bank.[6]

An important point to recognize is that the present system of deposit insurance and federal guarantees is actually making the financial system less, and not more, stable. Thus, an important purpose of reforms is to eliminate this propensity to make matters worse. It is essential that this be done before it becomes too late to restructure the system.

There are two related reforms that deserve some mention: accounting and disclosure. The present accounting system allows an institution to carry assets at book value as long as scheduled cash flows remain reasonably current. This historical-cost accounting relieves pressure on managers to disclose the true state of their institutions, and permits them too much flexibility in determining how and what to report. In addition, it enables deposit insurance agencies to postpone taking action to minimize their own risk exposures. Historical-cost accounting, therefore, weakens both the market-discipline effect that would accompany the disclosure of more accurate information and the political discipline that might lessen the willingness of deposit insuring agencies to take still more risk.

Market-value accounting is a desirable goal to work towards. It is implicit in the concept of risk-related deposit-insurance premiums; it is administratively feasible; and, it is essential if we are to achieve the managerial discipline that flows from the use of market discipline.

Currently, the adoption of market-value accounting would result in the disclosure of large unrealized losses. This is basically a problem of transition from one accounting system to another. The current environment of low interest rates, however, provides us with an unusual opportunity for making this transition. Together with a permissive regulatory approach, a low-interest-rate environment presents us with the best opportunity we have had in a long time to make the change.

A final and related issue is disclosure: should greater mandated disclosure of information be required? Is it necessary for market discipline? This is a moot issue for large financial institutions, since they already have publicly traded stock and are therefore subject to Securities and Exchange Commission disclosure requirements. In addition, in competitive securities markets, such as we have now, there is a strong incentive to disclose and communicate useful information to investors. Further, given the existence of a desire to disclose favorable information, it is doubtful that a firm could benefit by not also disclosing unfavorable information. Financial institutions that choose not to disclose will probably be small institutions. Such institutions are not subject to much market discipline in any case because they have few or no uninsured deposit liabilities. They face only the discipline of regulators. Thus, while on its face requiring greater disclosure seems attractive, it would in reality serve little purpose. It may also impose unnecessary disclosure costs on the system.[7] Finally, whether or not private institutions are forced to disclose more to the public, the adoption of market-value accounting will force deposit-insurance entities themselves to have to disclose the true state of affairs to Congress and to the public, a clearly desirable goal.

In summary, the steady stream of financial innovation will continue to change our financial system and structure. There is no turning back. Coupled with appropriate and wise regulatory and central-bank policies, the emerging financial system will be better than we have ever known. Without changes in our regulatory system, however, all the gains from innovation may be lost in the collapse of some major segments of the financial system. Time is running out. The risk of financial instability is growing. We must adapt our current system of government guarantees to present market realities. Bankers and government officials, both in the United States and elsewhere, should recognize the risks and get behind sensible reform proposals. With the fate of the U.S. financial system goes the world's financial system.

NOTES

The author has benefited from discussions with Ian Giddy of New York University's School of Business Administration.

1. For a description of such risks, see Appendix 1.

2. Bank of International Settlements. *Recent Innovations in International Banking*. April, 1986. p. 197.

3. *Ibid.*, p. 198.

4. Edward J. Kane, "Valuing and Eliminating Subsidies Associated with Conjectural Government Guarantees of FNMA Liabilities." Unpublished paper. May 1986.

5. For example, by allowing the FDIC to compete with the FSLIC, or both to compete with some form of private deposit insurance, we may be able to obtain more institutional efficiency and flexibilty.

6. See F. Edwards and J. Scott, "Regulating the Solvency of Depository Institutions: A Perspective for Deregulation." In F. Edwards, ed., *Issues in Financial Regulation*. New York: McGraw-Hill, 1979, pp. 65–105.

7. See G. Benston, "Financial Disclosure and Bank Failure." *Economic Review, Federal Reserve Bank of Atlanta*. March 1984.

APPENDIX I

Comparative risk table

Instrument	Credit risk	Market risk	Settlement risk	Market liquidity risk
Currency options	Writer for premium amount until paid, buyer for cost of replacement until exercised.	Limited for buyer, unlimited for writer.	Premium amount on payment date, principal amount for both parties if exercised. (One party pays currency A, one pays currency B.)	Exchange and OTC options new, liquidity of markets untested under stress. Liquidity of exchanges superior to OTC markets, also partially dependent on liquidity of market for underlying.
Interest rate options	Same as above.	Same as above.	Same as above except one party delivers cash, the other securities, if exercised. (Could be net amount if cash settled.)	Same as above.
Currency swaps	Default cancels future obligations. Risk limited to replacement cost. May be principal risk if agreed in original contract.	Equal to rate change on principal and interest amount.	Contractual amount on successive payment dates.	All OTC contracts: limited liquidity.
Interest rate swaps	Default cancels future obligations, risk limited to replacement cost. No principal risk.	Complex: equivalent to bond of equal maturity on fixed side. Risk to fixed payer in swap if rates have fallen, to fixed receiver if rates rise. Small on basis swap. No market risk on principal amount.	Interest payment amount only on successive payment dates.	All OTC contracts: limited liquidity.

Appendix I (cont'd)

Instrument	Credit risk	Market risk	Settlement risk	Market liquidity risk
NIFs/RUFs	Principal amount for holders of paper, same as other guarantees for writers of standbys.	Writers of standbys face risk they will be called on to lend at below-market spreads if market conditions change.	Principal amount on payment date for borrower.	Liquidity of paper largely untested.
Forward rate agreements	Mostly cash settled, credit risk limited to amount of market risk.	Equal to market risk on deposit.	Limited to amount of market risk if cash settled.	Small market, limited liquidity.
Euro-bonds	Same as onshore bond.	Same as onshore fixed rate bond.	Largely same as onshore market.	Markets well developed, but secondary market less developed than major onshore markets.
FRNs	Same as bond.	Same as on short-term paper.	Largely same as onshore market.	Relatively new market, liquidity untested, thin secondary market.
Securitised credits	Derivative from credit risk of underlying asset, sometimes with explicit insurance back-up.	Same as conventional instrument of similar maturity.	Generally equal to similar conventional instruments, although some have payment date concentrations.	Markets well developed for long-standing instruments, less clear for new instruments. Thin secondary markets.
Asset sales (with recourse)	Equal to credit risk of selling institution.	Fixed by terms of sale.	Limited.	Limited liquidity.
Asset sales (without recourse)	Buyer takes credit risk of underlying debtor.	Set by terms of underlying credit.	Limited.	Limited liquidity.

Comparative Studies of Financial Innovation, Deregulation, and Reform in Japan and the United States

Yoshio Suzuki

Director, Institute for Monetary and Economic Studies, Bank of Japan

I.
A GENERAL FRAMEWORK FOR STUDIES ON FINANCIAL INNOVATION, DEREGULATION, AND REFORM

GENERALLY SPEAKING, at anytime and in any country, financial innovation arises as a device for the private financial sector to solve or to circumvent conflicts between the newly developing economic and technical conditions, and the old statutory framework and regulations which played an important role in the past but have become obsolete. Financial innovation is further promoted when the financial authorities recognize the obsolescence of the existing statutory framework and deregulate them. The whole process of this interaction between the private financial sector and the regulator forms a history of financial reform. The financial innovation, deregulation, and reform facing us today is merely an example of this story.[1]

The common background against which financial innovation has proceeded in every industrialized country since the 1970s is that they have the common economic and technical conditions which have emerged simultaneously during the past decade, and that the old financial framework more or less failed to cope with these newly developing conditions.

Also, the speed and spread of financial innovation differs from country to country because the extent of the newly developing economic conditions and the types of old statutory framework and regulations are different in each country, so that seriousness of conflicts between them varies from country to country.[2]

In my view, there are four common economic and technical conditions that developed in the past decade: first, the high and volatile interest rates due to worldwide inflation since the first oil crisis in 1973; second, the application of technological progress in computer and telecommunications to financial transactions; third, more active international shifts of funds among industrialized countries since the global floating of exchange rates in 1973; and finally, the increase in public-sector deficits resulting in a large-scale issue of government bonds which has stimulated development of open markets in the financial system. These conditions have created potential demand for and supply of new financial instruments and services.

Along with these four newly emerging economic and technical conditions, there existed financial regulations that were incompatible with the new financial environment. First of all, there was regulation of interest rates on financial instruments provided by financial intermediaries; second, there was strict statutory distinction among financial businesses, such as banking, securities, and trust businesses; and third, there existed exchange control and other regulations which have separated international and domestic financial markets.[3]

It may not be necessary to elaborate on the conflicts that occurred during the past decade between these four newly developing conditions and the three major characteristics of the old financial framework that led to financial innovation. To make sure, however, let me present only a few examples. Conflicts between high and volatile interest rates and interest-rate regulations have been the background for a lot of innovative financial instruments with market-oriented interest rates. Also, with technological progress in computers and telecommunications, many kinds of cash management services and retail banking services have been developing in order to circumvent the strict distinction among the scope of the various financial businesses. Further, to solve the conflict between the active movement of international funds and the statutory segmentation of international and domestic financial markets, Euromarkets and offshore markets have played an important role.[4]

II

COMMON FEATURES OF FINANCIAL INNOVATION IN JAPAN
AND THE UNITED STATES

It seems quite natural, from the point of view just expressed regarding the motivations for financial innovation, that Japan's experience has more in common with that of the U.S. than with that of European countries. This is because Japan shares a more common statutory framework with the United States and because the newly emerging conditions are similar in both countries. For example, Japan has regulations concerning interest rates on deposits which the United States also had until quite recently through Regulation Q, while European countries, such as Germany and Britain had deregulated interest rates on deposits longer than a decade ago. The Securities Transaction Law in Japan and the Glass-Steagall Act in the United States both define strict statutory distinctions between the banking and securities businesses, whereas in Germany, Switzerland, and Holland, for example, there prevails a universal-banking system in which one financial institution can combine both the banking and securities businesses. As to the newly developing conditions, technical progress in computers and telecommunications is very rapid and has been more quickly applied to the financial business in Japan and the United States than in Europe.[5]

As a result, conflicts between high and volatile interest-rate regulation, and those between technical progress in computer and telecommunication and the strict statutory distinctions between the banking and securities businesses are much more serious in Japan and the U.S. than in Europe. Therefore, innovation in financial instruments and services is more similar in Japan and the United States than in other industrialized countries, including European countries.

For instance, financial innovation in the securities business first took the form of *Gensaki* and the medium-term Government Bond Fund in Japan, which are just counterparts of the Repurchase Agreements (RPs) and the Money Market Mutual Funds (MMMF) in the United States. The counterattack from the banking business to overcome the resultant disintermediation was, in both countries, creations of Certificates of Deposit (CDs) and Money Market Certificates (MMCs). Cash Management Accounts (CMAs) connecting demand deposits in banking and investment trust funds in securities firms have also appeared in both countries.[6]

The common process of financial innovation in Japan and the United States has also resulted in similar approaches to deregulation of interest rates and the scope of financial businesses.

III
DIFFERENT ASPECTS OF FINANCIAL DEREGULATION AND REFORM IN JAPAN AND THE UNITED STATES

However, the speed and spread of financial deregulation has been different in the two countries. For example, the United States has finished deregulating interest rates except those on demand deposits, whereas Japan is still in the course of it. Japan has eliminated the statutory distinction between banking and securities businesses as far as government securities are concerned, while the United States has not yet made significant steps towards deregulating either these statutory distinctions or the prohibition of interstate banking.

Differences in Objectives and Regulatory Structures

The different aspects of financial reform seem to me to arise because, despite the similarities between Japan and the U.S. discussed above, there also exist unique features of financial regulation as well as economic conditions in each of the countries. These features have caused the different speed and spread of financial innovation, deregulation, and reform.

First of all, in spite of the superficial resemblance of regulation and statutory framework, the philosophy, targets and structure of regulation are not necessarily the same. Regulation in the U.S. has been primarily designed to restrain competition in order to limit risk, especially for banks, though it might be disputable whether it has actually functioned effectively. The competitive constraints were focused on intermediation finance, whereas direct markets in which competition was not restrained were closely monitored and a system of financial disclosure was enforced. The structure and objectives of regulation in the U.S. were strongly influenced by the collapse of the banking system during the Great Depression. At a later stage, regulation also came to be regarded as an important part of a social policy to support the housing sector through savings and loan associations (S&Ls) backed up by the development of the mortgage market.[7]

The structure of regulation in the United States has also a unique aspect. There exists a multiplicity of U.S. financial regulators, partly as a result of dualism. Even at the federal or state level, however, there exists a multiplicity of regulators. The most important regulators at the federal level are the Federal Reserve System, Federal Deposit Insurance Corporation, Federal Home Loan Bank Board, Federal Savings and Loan Insurance Corporation (part of the Federal Home Loan Bank Board), National Credit Union Administration, and the Securities and Exchange Commission.[8]

In Japan, regulation looks as if it had similarly constrained financial markets, but the nature of regulation differs in at least three ways. First, regulation was not designed to encourage mortgage or any type of consumer credit, but was more concerned with accommodating industrialization, and investment- and export-led high economic growth. Second, regulation was far more extensive, especially regulations over interest-rate movements and restrictions designed to isolate domestic finance from the international financial system. Not only interest rates on intermediation finance, but those on instruments in direct markets such as bonds and debentures in the primary market were also regulated. The severe isolation from the international system was necessary to keep such extensive regulations. Third, in Japan, there is a much simpler, more unified regulatory structure. The Ministry of Finance (MOF) and the Bank of Japan, are the major regulators followed by the Ministry of Posts and Telecommunications (MPT) which regulates only postal savings accounts. This distinction between Japan and the U.S. has an important bearing on the reform process in each country.[9]

Different Structures of Financial Systems

The contrasting nature of regulation in each country has naturally resulted in the different structures of financial systems.

First, securities markets in Japan are considerably underdeveloped compared to those in the U.S. The U.S. possesses broad and deep securities markets in both spot and futures contracts. The securities markets cover the complete term structure from very short to very long maturities. The government and business sectors are the main participants. The government securities market plays an important role as a base for the entire securities market, as a liquidity base for intermediation finance, and as the focal point for monetary policy conducted via open-market operations. On the contrary, Japan's long-term securities market has not developed until recently because (1) interest rates in the primary market of bonds and debentures were regulated; and (2) government budgets were balanced or deficits were small until the early 1970s. Therefore, there was no need to develop a securities market for government debt. As a result, corporations were not able to use the securities markets as a main source of funds. Short-term securities markets for Treasury bills (TBs) and commercial paper (CPs) do not exist or remain small, and that for bankers' acceptances (BAs) just started last year. The main short-term markets consist of the interbank market for call loans and commercial bills (similar to the federal funds market in the U.S.) organized before World War II, the *Gensaki* trade that emerged in the late 1960s, and the large bank CD market authorized in 1979. The one exception is that the secondary market in government bonds has grown dramatically since 1975 despite the limited development of primary markets in Japan.[10]

Second, the counterbalance to the underdeveloped direct markets in Japan is the more important role played by Japanese banks in intermediation finance as compared to the U.S. banking system. Thus, the high ratio of indirect to direct finance is one of the most significant differences between the Japanese and the U.S. financial systems. In 1973, 93.2 percent of the flow of funds was transferred through financial institutions compared to about 75 percent for the U.S. A major outcome of liberalization since the early 1970s has been a continual decline in the importance of intermediation. In 1984, the intermediation share declined to 87.6 percent, which is, however, still higher than that for the United States.[11]

One reason for this contrast is that Japanese intermediation markets are not influenced by the dualistic system of chartering, organization, and regulating as in the U.S. Since the National Bank Act of 1864, the concept of dualism has been an important characteristic of intermediation finance in the U.S. and accounts for the presence of constraints against interstate banking, the variation among states in their regulation over intrastate banking, and the large number of major depository institutions. Private depository institutions alone in the U.S. as of December 1983 included approximately 15,400 banks, 3,513 S&Ls, 534 mutual savings banks, and 19,203 credit unions. In addition, there are a large number of nondepository financial institutions (finance companies, private pension funds, insurance companies, securities companies, etc.) as well as nonfinancial firms offering financial services, such as Sears Roebuck & Co. In contrast, in Japan the number of financial institutions is considerably smaller. As of 1985, there were 87 banks (13 city banks, 64 regional banks, 3 long-term credit banks, and 7 trust banks), 1,024 institutions for small businesses, 6,122 institutions for agriculture, forestry, and fisheries, and several hundred other institutions (insurance companies, securities companies, etc.).[12]

Differences in Economic Environments

Another reason for the rapid and even abrupt deregulation in the United States and the gradual deregulation in Japan with respect to interest rates can be seen in the newly developing conditions in the two countries. Although Japan and the United States have shared, as noted above, the common economic and technical conditions which have emerged during the past decade as the main stimuli of financial innovation, the most influential one among the aforementioned four conditions is not the same in both countries. In the United States, high and volatile inflation rates played an overwhelming role in forcing deregulation of interest rates, while in Japan increases in public-sector deficits with the resulting developments in the bond market has given rise to the pressure for deregulation of interest rates.[13]

It is said in the United States that the Federal Reserve failed to achieve noninflationary monetary growth throughout the 1970s. As a result, inflation and expectations of future inflation generated high interest rates in securities markets and rendered Regulation Q binding. Thrifts such as S&Ls were the most sensitive to high interest rates because they obtained funds from short-term deposits and allocated funds to long-term, fixed-rate mortgages. Prior to 1966, thrifts were not subject to Regulation Q ceilings; however, as interest rates increased significantly in 1965 and 1966, Regulation Q was extended to thrifts. This merely exposed thrifts to greater liquidity or disintermediation pressure; consequently, combined with their limited asset diversification powers, problems in the thrift industry threatened the stability of the entire financial system. Regulation on deposit rates, which had been functioning as a social policy measure to support the housing sector, turned out to be an obstacle to housing finance. Thus, by the late 1970s, the conflict between existing financial regulation and the failures of monetary policy generated intense pressure for rather abrupt deregulation of interest rates.[14]

In the case of Japan, the inflation rate has been low and stable since 1977 after the bitter experience of 1973-74, and the interest rate has not been as high and volatile as in the U.S. The primary catalyst for financial reform was generated not by inflation, but by the sudden end of the high-growth period in 1973, and the impact that slower growth had on the flow of funds. The end of the rapid growth reduced the role of the corporate sector as the primary deficit unit. Instead, the appearance of a significant increase in government deficits made the government the primary deficit unit.[15]

In order to issue a large quantity of government bonds smoothly, the authorities were obliged to decide the interest rate on syndicate issues of long-term government bonds in line with the market rate and to deregulate sales of government bonds by the syndicate members to the secondary market. In addition, the government started to issue medium-term government bonds through tender. These deregulations naturally resulted in the development of the primary and secondary markets for government bonds, which in turn caused financial disintermediation since interest rates on intermediation instruments were still regulated. The pressure for deregulating deposit rates thus emerged in Japan.[16]

In both Japan and the U.S., financial disintermediation created a pressure for deposit-rate deregulation, but the nature of the pressures as catalysts for financial reform was different. Inflation in the United States made it inevitable for the authorities to deregulate hastily, whereas in Japan exensive regulation of interest rates together with no inflation makes the liberalization process more gradual and cautious. Also, since 1975 the Japanese authorities have been willing to keep regulated rates more in line with market rates than U.S. authorities.

IV

Prospects for Future Financial Reform in Japan

Although the process of financial reform in Japan has not been very rapid, it will further proceed steadily, since the conflicts between the new economic and technical conditions and the old regulatory framework, discussed in the first section of this paper, will continue to stimulate financial innovation which will in turn make further financial deregulation and reform inevitable.

Interest Rate Deregulation

First of all, with respect to deposit-rate deregulation, Japanese banks already provide some instruments with deregulated rates today. They are CDs of one to twelve months with a minimum unit of 100 million yen, MMCs of one to twelve months with a minimum unit of 50 million yen, time deposits of three months to two years, with a minimum unit of 500 million yen, and deposits denominated in foreign currencies. Since the minimum units of MMCs and liberalized time deposits are to be reduced and the longest maturity of MMCs is to be prolonged to two years by spring 1987, deposit rates which will remain not to be deregulated are (1) those on time deposits whose minimum unit is smaller than the minimum unit of MMCs and (2) those on demand deposits, or short-term deposits whose maturities are shorter than three months.

In regard to (1) small unit deposits, small unit MMCs with a minimum unit of, say, several hundred-thousand yen will be introduced within two or three years if MPT agrees to MOF's proposal that banks and postal savings offices should have the same rule to determine the market-oriented rate on the small MMCs and their minimum denomination. However, complete deregulation of small deposit rates cannot be foreseen because deposit rates of the postal savings office would not necessarily be determined on the market principle, since postal savings offices are public institutions whose objective is not profit maximization but the supply of public goods. In the case of complete liberalization, deposit rates offered by postal savings offices on the basis of policy decisions by MPT would become the leading rate of small unit deposits in the financial system, because they are large enough to have an oligopolistic share in the market. This would distort fund allocation and would also hinder the effectiveness of monetary policy.

Concerning (2) interest rates on demand or short-term deposits, deregulation is not yet discussed openly, but *de facto* cash management services for businesses and *sogokoza* (demand deposits with overdraft facilities using time deposits as collateral) for individuals are functioning like demand deposits with higher interest rates provided by time deposits or investment trust funds. As was the case in the United States where cash management services or accounts were eventually replaced by the money-market deposit accounts (MMDAs) or

Super NOW accounts, it is not unlikely in Japan that demand deposits with market-oriented rates will finally be introduced in the future.

Besides deposit rates, there is another area of possible interest-rate deregulation in Japan, since regulation is extended to the field of direct finance. Treasury Bills are issued at a fixed low rate so that almost all of them are bought by BOJ, which sells some to the private sector at market rates at a loss in order to create a TB market. However, this market still remains small. Deregulation of TB rates in a form of, say, a tender issue is strongly desired, because the resultant creation of a large TB market will become the core of open money markets and the focal point for monetary-policy transmission.[17]

A commercial paper market is also another area of innovation that may evolve, but issuing CPs is not yet permitted. This is primarily due to the so-called "collateral principle," which has been a unique aspect used to limit risk in Japanese financial markets and was established after a series of credit panics towards the end of the 1920s. Bank loans to customers, call loans in the interbank market, and bills and bonds issued by business firms are in principle all secured by the collateral.

This can be contrasted to the case of the United States where financial transactions have been secured by a system of financial disclosure and rating, being established following the bitter experience in 1929. In the case of Japan, predominance of indirect finance by banks compensates for a lack of disclosure and rating system, because financial information on borrowers is exclusively disclosed to lenders through a long-term customer relationship between "main" banks and client business firms. In the open market, the collateral principle limits risk instead of a disclosure and rating system.

However, interest-rate deregulation followed by development of a direct market for private securities and the internationalization of financial transactions are now pressing the Japanese financial system for alteration of this collateral principle. Exceptions to that principle have already been introduced with the emergence of Euroyen bonds and domestic bonds issued without collateral by big businesses since 1984, and call-loan transactions without collateral since 1985. The quantity of financial transactions without collateral will continue to increase.

Thus, a meaningful financial disclosure system is a necessary condition for stability of the future financial system in Japan. It will cause the development of broad and deep corporate securities markets. Obviously, the financial system has functioned without a U.S.-style financial disclosure system; however, this may no longer be possible if the result of liberalization and internationalization is to increase the role of direct finance for nongovernmental borrowers. In addition, regulators need a more continuous flow of information on at least the major financial institutions to assess risk exposure, especially if the banking system becomes more directly involved in the securities markets. Also, market mechanisms for evaluating risk are likely to appear. Japanese finance cannot continue to rely exclusively on the collateral principle, customer relationships, main-bank systems, or government administration to assess risk. If a more market-oriented system is the ultimate goal of liberalization, then an improved financial disclosure system together with the emergence of reliable rating companies should become part of that goal.[18]

Deregulation of the Scope of Financial Businesses

Deregulation of the scope of financial businesses in Japan will not have to overcome as many serious barriers as in the United States.

This is partly because Japan has no multiplicity of financial regulators. Japanese financial intermediaries are smaller in number and more homogeneous under a unified regulatory structure. For example, although names are different, city banks, regional banks, mutual loans and savings banks (*Sogo* banks), credit unions (*Shinkin* banks), and credit cooperatives are functionally engaged in the same kind of deposit banking, and have almost the same business scope. Long-term credit banks and trust banks, which have their own special fields in long-term finance, are also engaged in the same short-term finance as deposit banks.[19]

Therefore, statutory distinctions between short- and long-term finance and between banking and trust businesses are not so solid. Indeed, the former distinction is *de facto* disappearing on the asset side, since all banks are dealing in both short- and long-term lending now.

However, the statutory distinction between short- and long-term finance on the liability side still remains, so that it has become a cause of a mismatch between assets and liabilities accompanied by interest risk and liquidity risk. From the point of view of a sound banking system, deregulating the statutory distinction on the liability side as well is desirable in order to get rid of this mismatch. In addition, if this deregulation is delayed, the statutory distinction on the liability side, which is already circumvented by deposit banks accepting long-term deposits denominated in foreign currencies, will eventually be circumvented further in the course of deregulating international financial business, such as issuing long-term CDs, and borrowing long-term funds by deposit banks in the Euroyen market.

Regarding the statutory distinction between banking and trust businesses in Japan, it is not so strict as in the U.S., because Japan has not erected such a "Chinese wall" concerning the exchange of information and personnel within a bank. Besides, since new entry into the trust business by foreign banks was permitted in 1985, the trust business market today is not a strictly segmented market, but becomes a contestable market. Therefore, conflict of interest will be more or less prevented by the surveillance and the selection of market participants.

Another reason why deregulation in Japan will not be so hard as it has been in the U.S. is that the relationship between Japanese banks and securities companies is already closer than in the U.S. Although neither Japan nor the U.S. have a universal-banking system such as Europe has, banks in Japan are allowed to operate closely with securities companies in forming syndicates to purchase government debt. Banks are also permitted, with securities companies, to become dealers in the government-bond market, and banks can hold corporate bonds and corporate equities in their investment portfolios. These activities exceed those permitted U.S. banks.[20]

In the future, it is quite likely that the distinctions between short- and long-term finance and between banking and trust businesses will get blurred further, and all kinds of banks will become more homogeneous. Accompanying a more homogeneous banking circle will be a decline in the number of institutions through the process of affiliation and merger, and wholesale banking, retail banking or both will be selected as a main area of business by each institution.

With respect to postal savings offices, whether they should be denationalized and divided into smaller groups will be examined. The final decision on this cannot be foreseen at this time.

Large banks will further expand their business in the government securities market, and securitization of loans will make prohibition of private securities business much more obscure.

One of the most important problems facing Japanese financial authorities in the course of deregulating these areas is how to keep stability of the payment system in which not only deposit banks but also securities companies and other non-bank institutions are to be involved, and in which electronic fund transference is to prevail. The lucky conditions for Japan compared to the United States are: a unified regulatory structure; a small number of financial institutions which are rather homogeneous and less weak; and stable macroeconomic performance limiting credit and other risks. Since too large a safety net would cause moral-hazard risk to rise, effective supervision by the financial authorities as well as a stable macroeconomic performance will have to be the most essential measure and condition for stability of the future payment system.[21]

Internationalization of the Japanese Financial System

The process of aforementioned deregulation concerning interest rates and the scope of financial businesses will be accompanied by internationalization of the Japanese financial system, because entrance into the Japanese financial markets will become much easier for foreign financial institutions, and because the Japanese financial system will be much more integrated with overseas financial markets. The start of the offshore market in Tokyo this fall will enhance this trend.

Judging from the possibility that Japan will become the largest net lender country in the world through the accumulation of the current-account surplus, Tokyo will be one of the three major world financial centers, following London and New York. In addition to the common roles of international financial centers, such as financing the balance of payments of other countries and providing financial facilities to the global activities of domestic, foreign, and multinational enterprises, Tokyo may further perform the function of financing rapid growth of the Pacific Basin countries as well as providing markets for yen-denominated borrowings and lendings. This will increase the role of the yen as an international currency.

The Tokyo market as an international financial center will become a mixture of both the London market, which is mainly engaged in lending foreign currencies to non-residents, and the New York market, which is specialized in providing dollar-denominated financial facilities to non-residents.

The speed of internationalization of the Japanese financial system will depend crucially upon development of the securities market, which was discussed above.

NOTES

1. Suzuki, 1983a, 1984a, 1984b; Suzuki and Yomo, 1986; Silber, 1983.
2. Suzuki and Yomo, 1986; Akhtar, 1984; Bingham, 1985.
3. Suzuki, 1984a, 1986; Korea Federation of Banks, 1984.
4. Akhtar, 1984; Suzuki, 1984a.
5. Suzuki and Yomo, 1986; Akhtar, 1984; Cargill, 1985.
6. Cargill, 1985, 1986; Cargill and Garcia, 1982, 1985; Suzuki, 1984a, 1986; Wenninger, 1984.
7. Cargill and Garcia, 1982, 1985.
8. Golembe and Holland, 1983; Cargill, 1986; Kane, 1977, 1981.
9. Suzuki, 1980, 1984b; Bank of Japan, 1973; Cargill, 1985; Hamada and Horiuchi, 1984; Horiuchi, 1984.
10. Working Group of the Joint Japan-U.S. Ad Hoc Group on Yen/Dollar Exchange Rate Issues, 1984; Sakakibara and Kondoh, 1984; Cargill, 1984; Suzuki, 1983a, 1983b.
11. Suzuki, 1983b, 1984a, 1984b.
12. Bank of Japan, 1973; Cargill, 1985; Royama, 1983-4; Suzuki, 1980, 1984b, 1986.
13. Suzuki, 1984a, 1984b; Korea Federation of Banks, 1984; Cargill, 1985.
14. Cargill and Garcia, 1982, 1985.
15. Suzuki, 1983b.
16. Suzuki, 1984a, 1984b.
17. Suzuki, 1984a; 1986.
18. Cargill, 1985.
19. Bank of Japan, 1973; Federation of Bankers Association of Japan, 1985.
20. Cargill, 1985.
21. Benston, 1986; Corrigan, 1982.

REFERENCES

Akhtar, M.A. 1984. "Financial Innovation and Monetary Policy: A Framework for Analysis." *Financial Innovation and Monetary Policy*, Bank for International Settlements, March.
Bank of Japan. 1973. *Money and Banking in Japan*. Macmillan Press.
Benston, G. (ed.) 1986. *Ensuring the Safety and Soundness of the Nation's Banking System*. MIT Press.
Bingham, T.R.G. 1985. *Banking and Monetary Policy*. OECD.
Cargill, T.F. 1985. "A U.S. Perspective on Japanese Financial Liberalization." *Monetary and Economic Studies* 3(1), May. Bank of Japan.
Cargill, T.F. 1986. *Money, the Financial System, and Monetary Policy*. Prentice-Hall.
Cargill, T.F. and G.G. Garcia. 1982. *Financial Deregulation and Monetary Control*. Hoover Institution Press.
Cargill, T.F. and G.G. Garcia. 1985. *Financial Reform in the 1980s*. Hoover Institution Press.
Corrigan, G. 1982. "Are Banks Special?" *Annual Report*. Federal Reserve Bank of Minneapolis.
Federation of Bankers Associations of Japan. 1985. *The Banking System in Japan*.

Golombe, C.H. and D.S. Holland. 1983. *Federal Regulation of Banking 1983-84*. Golombe Associates, Inc.

Hamada, K., and A. Horiuchi. 1984. "The Political Economy of Japanese Financial Markets." Paper presented at Japan Political Economy Research Conference, August.

Horiuchi, A. 1984. "Economic Growth and Financial Allocation in Postwar Japan." University of Tokyo Working Paper, August.

Kane, E.J. 1977. "Good Intentions and Unintended Evil: The Case Against Selective Credit Allocation." *Journal of Money, Credit and Banking*, 9(1), February.

Kane, E.J. 1981. "Accelerating Inflation, Technological Innovation, and the Decreasing Effectiveness of Banking Regulation." *Journal of Finance* 34(2), May.

Korea Federation of Banks. 1984. *Financial Innovation and Financial Reform*. First International Symposium on Financial Development, December.

Report of the Working Group of the Joint Japan-U.S. Ad Hoc Group on Yen/Dollar Exchange Rate Issues. 1984.

Royama, S. 1983-84. "The Japanese Financial System: Past, Present, and Future." *Japanese Economic Studies 12*.

Sakakibara, E. and A. Kondoh. 1984. *Study on the Internationalization of Tokyo's Money Markets*. Japan Center for International Finance, Tokyo, June.

Silber, W.L. 1983. "The Process of Financial Innovation." *American Economic Review* 73(2), May.

Suzuki, Y. 1980. *Money and Banking in Contemporary Japan*. Yale University Press.

Suzuki, Y. 1983a. "Interest Rate Decontrol, Financial Innovation, and the Effectiveness of Monetary Policy." *Monetary and Economic Studies*, 1(1), June. Bank of Japan.

Suzuki, Y. 1983b. "Changes in Financial Asset Selection and the Development of Financial Markets in Japan." *Monetary and Economic Studies* 1(2), October. Bank of Japan.

Suzuki, Y. 1984a. "Financial Innovation and Monetary Policy in Japan." *Monetary and Economic Studies* 2(1), June. Bank of Japan.

Suzuki, Y. 1984b. "Monetary Policy in Japan: Transmission Mechanism and Effectiveness." *Monetary and Economic Studies* 2(2), December. Bank of Japan.

Suzuki, Y. 1986. *Money, Finance, and Macroeconomic Performance in Japan*. Yale University Press.

Suzuki, Y. and H. Yomo. (eds.) 1986. *Financial Innovation and Monetary Policy: Asia and the West*. The Proceedings of The Second International Conference, The University of Tokyo Press.

Wenninger, J. 1984. "Financial Innovation in the United States," *Financial Innovation and Money Policy*, BIS, March.

Discussion: Session III

JAMES O'NEILL
Marine Midland Bank
How does Mr. Whittemore see the outlook for foreign-exchange stability, given all these trends in financial markets and the economy?

FREDERICK WHITTEMORE:
In the short term, I hold out very little hope. I believe that currency volatility is part and parcel of what I have been talking about. People who try to bring currencies together talk about finding a time when everybody's inflation rate, growth rate, and economic policies are in sync. I don't see that happening. We appreciate Secretary Baker's efforts in that regard, and we certainly would like less-explosive volatility.

But the concept of bringing foreign currencies into close synchronization has not, in my opinion, advanced far enough; people still spend most of the time trying to push things back to the way they used to be. I do not think it will be that way. I do not think that the "broad band" concept, the "crawling peg" concept of Europe, has yet found a definition that is sensible. There is substantial mismatch between information about currencies and reality. I would like to see the currency discussion to be much more trade-weighted. Let's focus on what it really means when the dollar is down and the yen is up. We should put the trade relationships of the United States into perspective, where a third of the trade is Canada, Mexico, and maybe South America, rather than dwell only on the trade differences between the United States and Japan.

KIM SCHOENHOLTZ:
Salomon Brothers
Both speakers were quite diplomatic in reserving most of their criticism for their home country institutions. I was wondering if they might speak about the barriers they face in foreign countries — in the U.S. for Mr. Kusukawa, and Japan for Mr. Whittemore.

TORU KUSUKAWA:
As a bank, we have been in the U.S. for more than 25 years. Our activities in this country have kept pace with innovation here. Up to now, I don't think we have really had any difficulties in pursuing the banking business in the U.S. We believe in doing in Rome as the Romans do, and we are satisfied with our past and present situations and do not have much to complain about.

WHITTEMORE:
What a diplomatic graceful statement! Morgan Stanley has been in Japan

close to that amount of time, albeit in a very modest way. We have been pleased with the ability to grow in Tokyo, in a market sense. We have been allowed to join the Tokyo Stock Exchange recently, and not all our competitors have been allowed to do that. The rules require a great deal of disclosure, however. One of the reasons we went public in the United States is that we were already public to Japan's Ministry of Finance! They find out everything, so there was no privacy left. But we have been pleased at the speed with which we have been allowed to conduct the securities business in Japan; the breadth of it, I have to confess, leaves a touch to be desired. But I think we are a moving into that market a little bit faster than the orange grower or the beef manufacturer.

KUSUKAWA:
One more comment. The number of employees we have in the United States probably matches what you have in Tokyo. I have just made a comparison of Morgan Stanley and the Fuji Bank, and the number of employees are about equal, so probably our activities nearly balance.

WHITTEMORE:
You see, there is no privacy left!

STEFAN ROBOCK
Columbia University
Would Mr. Whittemore like to elaborate a bit on his forecast of interest rates, and would he confess something about his past record on forecasting?

WHITTEMORE:
Investment bankers are like economists. They conduct their business by keeping talking. So we keep forecasting all the time, and I've never met an economist who didn't start the first paragraph by saying, "As I said six months ago..." You never knew what he said six months ago.

I listen to and read all sorts of economist's forecasts, and I believe that our track record of trying to predict interest rates is as bad as everybody else's when one looks very far out into the future. Our mentality is that we must learn what our inventory should be today, and tomorrow, and maybe next week. We would say that short-term investment is as important as long-term investment, and so the worst way to get caught is to be wrong on a government-bond auction, or something of that nature. We have a shorter focus than most of you as investors, because we are middlemen.

Having said that, our track record as middlemen, as inventory owners of investment vehicles, is reasonably good. We certainly advise lots of people on interest rates, and all I can say is, I have been talking a long time, I've got a few clients, and they are still the same clients I used to have.

[COFFEE BREAK]

ROGER KUBARYCH:

Let me start by asking a question of Mr. Suzuki raised by Professor Edwards's paper: how important do you think federal deposit insurance is to the U.S. banking system? Do you think that it should be extended to other areas of the financial system, such as the Merrill Lynches, who do a deposit-like banking business? And if it is so good, would you recommend that Japan have a more explicit deposit-guarantee system?

YOSHIO SUZUKI:

It is a very good question. It is one of the difficult issues which we are now discussing in Japan. The essence of my answer is already included in my remarks. To recapitulate, too much widening of the deposit insurance system will surely increase moral hazard, and increasing moral hazard no doubt will increase the financial system's risks as a whole. So it should be limited to some extent. To what extent this strengthening of the insurance system should be is the main issue in Japan. We should insure the payments system, not deposits as a whole, so we are now discussing what the payment system is, and to what extent deposits or other accounts should be included in the payments system.

KUBARYCH:

I am very interested as to what Fred Whittemore would advise Morgan Stanley clients about buying or selling bank stocks if Professor Edwards's proposals were adopted. Would they be good buys in the market?

WHITTEMORE:

Well, I hesitate to tread where the warm intelligence of academia has gone, but I have to say that I find that fear somewhat overdone. There are some very good risk takers in the banking business. I think there is a role for deposit insurance. It is a subsidy which we don't share; it is one of the differences we have. I suggest that they keep their deposit insurance and we keep our freedom. They stay on their side of the table and we stay on ours. We will be happy to sell the stocks of those banks, and restructure those banks that need it, that find themselves in difficulty changing their risk/resource ratio. So Professor Edwards's statement is very thought-provoking, but the problem isn't quite at that level of seriousness yet.

MASARU YOSHITOMI

One question to Mr. Kusukawa and Mr. Whittemore. About the Glass-Steagall Act: opinions differ between the two of you, but I can't understand what the real issue is. From the banker's point of view, the Glass-Steagall Act is a barrier to your entry into other businesses, while to the security companies, it is a sort of protection against invasion of other businesses into their own turf. But what is the real issue in terms of the macroeconomic implications? What is the danger for economies which don't have a Glass-Steagall Act?

Do we really need it in our economies? What is the major difference in risk between having the Glass-Steagall Act, or not having it?

The other question, for Mr. Suzuki and Professor Edwards, is that we all talk about the enhancement of microefficiency and competition as Edwards clearly pointed out. And when we talk about macroeconomic conditions, we always discuss the systemic crises you mentioned. But somehow, without talking about microefficiency, without talking about the systemic crises, what are the macroeconomic policy implications of this financial innovation? That is, when we talk about financial innovations, we often talk about the difficulties imposed on monetary-aggregate control, as in the case of Mr. Suzuki; but are there any other important macroeconomic policy implications for the nation as a whole when we talk about financial innovations?

KUSUKAWA:

I'll try to answer that. The question is so wide-ranging, I really don't know whether I can make a proper answer. But my impression is that the Glass-Steagall Act is not an issue in macroeconomics, but is really a question of the management strategies of the banking industry. When we look back at what we have done in the past, we cannot help feeling that our traditional banking, such as lending and building up assets of good quality, was conducted with relative calm. But all these innovations we are having nowadays has changed this; for instance, treasurers of corporations are now getting into more sophisticated financial transactions, which are coming mainly from the securities industry. Now, with this sort of development, we are losing the business of our corporate customers. While the introduction of commercial paper in this country might have contributed to this trend toward securitization, we Japanese are nevertheless seriously discussing the possibility of introducing commercial paper in our country. Naturally, we bankers oppose this sort of securitization. However, this is one of the examples where the securities industry and the banking industry are coming closer together. Some of the traditional banking business is now also conducted by the securities companies. We cannot just stand there and watch our traditional activities going over to other industries. But as Mr. Whittemore just mentioned, the equity side of the business should remain with the investment bankers or with securities companies. I entirely agree with that, because banks have their limitations. We are something like a farmer, whereas the investment banker is something like a hunter. [Laughter]

But anyway, we will not be trespassing on the traditional field of the securities business, that is, the equity side of the business. But when it comes to corporate finance as a whole, the key point nowadays is not the size of lending, but it is how well you can serve as a consultant to corporations on their financial affairs. We have been traditionally concerned with the financial program for the corporations. So underwriting activities will be an inevitable consequence of such consultation with corporate customers. That is why we want to get rid of the restrictions of the Glass-Steagall Act. When we look back to the historical background, why you have this Glass-Steagall Act, we come across an interesting aspect. In the 1920s in Japan, when we wanted to maintain the principle of sound banking, we did not bother to push securities businesses out of universal banking but went into strengthening the discipline of collateralization; that is, not only bank lending but also debt issues should be, in principle, backed by specific collateral put up by the borrower. But in the U.S. case, I think probably you went to a rating system and disclosure principles to protect investors. The principle of sound banking is left with your commercial banks which were segregated from the securities business. But then all this securitization and innovation has made us feel that we would like to work in the way we used to work, that is, universal banking.

WHITTEMORE:

I will try to be brief, because I guess my comments have already been made. First, the Glass-Steagall Act, as far as I am concerned, is there because we are risking our money and commercial banks are risking somebody else's money. Fundamentally, banks take deposits and invest that money in a whole series of assets. We operate as a middleman, traditionally as an agent, and now as a principal more and more. As we operate as a principal, and as a combination of principal and agent, we are functioning and earning on the basis of our own assets within a set framework in this country of regulatory ratios far different than that appropriate for banks which are investing other people's money. So I think there is a fundamental difference in the position of trust. That doesn't mean that our markets don't compete actively; commercial paper obviously is a very significant part of that competition. I think it's clear that we need to have ways in which the securities markets and the banking system can function better together.

Another aspect of this which hasn't been mentioned, is that we have a lot of troubled loans in the banking system, particularly to the LDCs. I think it is interesting to note that in a case such as Mexico, for instance, there hasn't been any violation of the debt service of public loans. There may be lots of restructuring of bank loans. Securities issues potentially make available a breadth of capital that could be invested properly, and help in properly managing risk for various particular problems. However, securities markets have not effectively been called into play to help solve the Mexican political-economic equation, so that it all falls to a bank consortium. As an investment banker, I am glad that we don't have to do that because I am dealing with my money. But there are some real problems here, and some inefficiencies of the marketplace. Business schools teach that markets are efficient. I maintain that if markets were really efficient, investment bankers wouldn't be around. I don't think markets really are efficient at all. We are the middlemen that try and make them efficient, and the risk taking that implies is far different than the risk taking of a bank taking the collective deposits of various depositors and investing it in a particular loan asset. There is no question that the innovations and the substitution in terms of security-backed assets are certainly competitive factors of some significance. Basically, what the banking community and the investment banking community are doing is trying to preserve their turf and their profit-making ability, as we have discussed. We do it openly; there is no question that the banks would like to invade our business; there is no question, I suppose, that our firms have gotten into the interest-rate spread business.

KUBARYCH:
I think Mr. Yoshitomi is actually raising a broader question: would an economy with universal banking, without Glass-Steagall, over, say, a ten-year period, grow faster or slower, with more ups and downs, or fewer ups and downs, than an economy like the U.S. or Japan in which these markets are segmented? I don't really think we can know, but I know if you talk to our German friends, who have universal banking, they are very pleased with it, particularly because they don't have an awful lot of competition. Mr. Suzuki?

SUZUKI:
Your question concerns the macro-policy implications of financial innovation. As the economics textbooks say, financial innovation will enhance efficiency of resource allocation and fairness of income distribution. That's all right, but it might undermine the two main objectives of the central bank: stability of macroeconomic performance, and stability of the financial system. Stability of macroeconomic performance could be undermined by financial innovation mainly in two ways. The first one is that the demand-for-money functions will shift, and the central bank will lose its ability to judge the optimal quantities of money. The second and more fundamental possibility is that cash currency could disappear if you use IC cards, and electronic transfer systems. No one would use just currency. In that case, the base for effective monetary policy would disappear. We are discussing this possibility, and one of the major countermeasures against that is an enlargement of the reserve-requirement system as well as prohibition of the issuing of IC cards which can be perfect substitutes for cash. But anyway, it is a problem which we are going to discuss in the future.

Concerning the shifting demand-for-money functions, in the case of Japan we will never lose the ability to judge the quantity of money because our financial-innovation process has been and will continue to be slow and steady, thanks to the stability of macroeconomic performance. So I don't worry much about this danger. Concerning the possibility of systemic risk due to financial innovation, I have already talked about the deposit insurance system, but we have to have a wide safety net to keep the stability of the payments system. But no one measure can assure us of this stability, so we have a variety of measures to keep stability in the future. For instance, the stability of macroeconomic performance is a fundamental condition for the stability of the financial system. Also, we have to strengthen, to some extent, the deposit insurance system. The function of the central bank as lender of the last resort is also essential, and the surveillance by unified regulatory authorities is very important. With all these, we will try to keep the stability of payments system in the future.

EDWARDS:

First, I don't think there is any reason to have a Glass-Steagall Act. I don't think you can distinguish it from many other different regulations.

The thrust of my paper was not to impose the Glass-Steagall Act in the traditional form; the thrust of my paper is to get away from it. To get away from these constraints you've got to reform the present system. To reform the present system, you don't go back to the old system; the old system is Glass-Steagall. We have the Glass-Steagall Act because of what happened in the 1920s. It doesn't follow from what happened in the 1920s that similar conditions exist today.

I don't want to go back to that system. That is the last thing I want to do. Mr. Whittemore agrees with me when he says that he doesn't mind risk taking when he uses his own money but he doesn't want the banks taking such risks because they are using somebody else's money. That is my point: you don't behave the same way when you are using somebody else's money as you do when using your own. He doesn't like it; I don't like it. So I don't think there is a good reason; you can't defend the Glass-Steagall Act, other than by the argument that if you are going to give a bank a federal subsidy or guarantee then you have got to start constraining them in various ways, and that is what we have done for 50-60 years in this country.

How do we get away from it? We've got to think through how we are going to reform the present system to make the market system work again. It is not easy. Some of the proposals I made sound preposterous. That's true. And the reason is we have got to think through the end result; you just can't say "Let's reform the system" or "Let's impose risk-related insurance premiums." That is nonsense. You have got to think through where you go with this and when you do, you get to some very unhappy choices.

Partially, the thrust of my paper is that we may never do this, because it is too difficult. If we don't do it, then I'll tell you what we are going to do: we are going to go back to the old system. Something will happen that pushes Congress into resurrecting Glass-Steagall, resurrecting all the old things, pushing banks into a compartment, and that is not where I want to go.

Mr. Whittemore makes a good point when he says maybe I am overstating the case. That is true. Maybe I am. No one knows how much risk there is in the system. No one knows how much further we can go. No one ever knows that. I just refer you to a few speeches made in 1929, right before the Crash; everything looked terrific. In addition to that, those of us who are familiar with what is going on in Washington know that there are terms floating around like "zombie S&Ls." Zombie S&Ls are a real problem, because from 10-15 percent of savings institutions in this country are already bankrupt. They exist, and they are called, fondly enough, by the regulators "zombie S&Ls" because they are not alive. I don't know how many other zombie financial institutions we have now, and I don't know how many zombie financial institutions we will have in ten years. But the savings-institution problem is a direct result of the kind of thing I am talking about, and that is where we have to do something.

HUGH PATRICK
I think the problem of potentially excessive risk taking and moral hazard is very real, for the Japanese banking system as well as for the American banking system. I am not sure the collateralization approach solves the problem, since after all the market value of some real assets used as collateral have been known to drop sharply. Certainly, the American perception is that the Bank of Japan does guarantee Japanese banks against failure. Indeed, Moody's and other rating services give AAA ratings to Japanese banks, higher than to American banks, even though their stated primary capital ratios are much lower than American banks. Clearly there is an assumption that the Bank of Japan will act as the lender of last resort in a very strong way to prevent bank failure. Given that situation, how is the Bank of Japan going to deal with the moral hazard issue and the additional risk taking that is going on? I think the American problem that Professor Edwards described is also very much a Japanese problem, though described in a somewhat different way. I want to ask Mr. Suzuki what he intends to do about it.

KUBARYCH:
So the Japanese are giving implicit guarantees that are every bit as big as our explicit guarantees.

PATRICK:
That is right. The Japanese give Continental Illinois-type guarantees too.

SUZUKI:
The function of the Bank of Japan as a lender of last resort is stronger, I agree. But the background for this is that, as I have already stated, the Japanese financial institutions are small in number, less weak, and homogeneous. It is easy for us to provide our resources to many financial institutions. But, no doubt such wide functions of the lender of last resort will cause moral hazard to increase. So it must have a limit. In this case, as I have already stated, we always feel that the fundamental condition for the stability of the financial system is to keep stability of macroeconomic performance. We will continue to try this, and with that stability of macroeconomic performance we, the Bank of Japan, together with the Ministry of Finance, will strengthen the appropriate surveillance of the financial institutions to check their portfolios and liabilities. This, again, is easier for us because financial institutions are small in number, homogeneous, and less weak.

QUESTION:
Mr. Whittemore, you have presented a rather impartial opinion about the

banks versus securities houses, but because of your affiliation, I don't know whether the audience would accept that impartiality. I would like to provide you with the opportunity to be really impartial. That is this: my question is, now the issue in the United States, particularly in New York State, is the demarcation between the insurance industry and the commercial banks. What do you think about the attempt by banks to enter the insurance industry? If Mr. Kusukawa has any opinion about the Japanese situation, I would appreciate his comment as well.

WHITTEMORE:

I watch with interest as the banks reach into everyone else's good businesses. And there is no question that the insurance business, properly managed, is a good business. I am not here to protect the insurance industry necessarily, nor am I here to encourage the banks to get into that business. I frankly am not an expert on the risks of insurance regulation vis-à-vis bank regulation. We are not in the insurance business. If there is a way for the banks to get into it effectively, that provides an economic service that is profitable without adding to the risks of the banks' responsibility, I could be convinced that would be a reasonable thing to do. I must admit, though, that there is a thread that has gone through a number of the comments here which I must address. There ought to be someone who raises their arm for competition and its benefits. There are some real benefits to our financial system in my view, in that the economic functions of different institutions under different regulations attack some of the same problems. We know we have to assume some risk in making commercial paper available more cheaply, in effect trying to buy that economic function from the banks. There are some benefits to diversity in the marketplace. One of the things that I am concerned about is that I don't want to be the happy German with just universal banks, and I don't really want to be in a super-merged Japan. Surely banking institutions must change; they certainly shouldn't be zombies. Surely they require some regulatory change. But they ought to be able to function, survive, grow, and benefit the country. I think the United States has been a major beneficiary of the Securities Acts in the years since 1930, including the Glass-Steagall Act. We have been able to build a market which has been able to strengthen our economy and help bring about macroeconomic stability, and others have been able to share it. So diversity and competition are not all bad. If banks can get into the insurance business effectively, we wouldn't necessarily oppose it.

KUBARYCH:

Mr. Kusukawa, would you like to be in the insurance business?

KUSUKAWA:

No. I don't think so. In Japan, the demarcation between the insurance business and banking is very strictly watched by the regulatory authorities. It is not just because of the regulatory authorities' attitudes, but the commercial banks themselves feel that their field of activity does not overlap with that of the insurance companies. So we are happily living together in a mood of cooperation.

So far, I don't think any of the Japanese commercial banks has any intention of getting into the insurance business. Some big insurance companies are in one way or the other related to the commercial banks; some of the names like Yasuda, Sumitomo, or Mitsubishi are also used for insurance companies. On top of that, the life insurance companies in Japan are the biggest, largest shareholders of the commercial banks. We would naturally like to be nice to shareholders.

Let me just come back to Professor Patrick's question about the rating of Japanese banks. I can mention two things. One is that the Japanese commercial banks' rate of non-performing assets is lower than the U.S. equivalent. The other is about the primary capital ratio. If you just compare the figures in financial statements, probably you are right in saying that our capital ratio is terribly low. In the Fuji Bank's case, it would be somewhere around 3 percent. But in Japan we have a different sort of setup of our equity. That is, not only the stated equity account is considered, but also so-called hidden reserves in securities portfolio and also real-estate holdings are to be considered. Some newspaper people were very kind in calculating on our behalf just how big these hidden reserves were, and it came out to about two to three times of the stated equity account. Probably that would give you a fair ratio of the capital when you are assessing that.

On the question of the Bank of Japan as lender of last resort, I thought that the most prominent example of what they did in the past was not for the banks but for the securities companies. They went into rescue work. Well, now we have some troubled banks, but I don't think the Bank of Japan will really come directly to the rescue; they will just come up to the commercial banks saying, "Why don't you do it?" We may or may not do it.

Thoughts on Japanese Financial Liberalization

Yoshitoki Chino

Chairman, Daiwa Securities Company, Ltd.

I AM GREATLY HONORED to be invited to such a timely conference and to be given this opportunity to speak before such a distinguished group.

Today, I would like to express my personal impressions of the liberalization and internationalization of the Japanese financial and capital markets, which may be different from those of academics and policymakers.

Since I am not a scholar, I will not present a thesis which develops arguments leading to a logical conclusion. Instead, I would like to touch upon various episodes which I think describe the present state of the Japanese financial and capital markets, although not necessarily in logical order.

I would like to begin by noting that the Japanese market has been liberalized and internationalized more than you might think. As a person who has been involved in the securities business for some 40 years, I have been impressed myself by recent developments in the Japanese financial field.

For instance, one and a half years ago, the Japan Center for International Finance, a research institute specializing in international finance, conducted a survey in behalf of the Japanese Ministry of Finance, concerning the past and present situation and the future prospects for the Tokyo market as an international financial center. The survey was based on questionnaires addressed to branches and representative offices of all foreign banks and securities companies in Tokyo. It was done in such a way as to keep names of the respondents anonymous. Questionnaires were sent to 246 offices and 96 of them — 70 banks and 22 securities companies — returned their answers.

According to the survey results, the overall importance of the Tokyo market has substantially increased in the past ten years. Furthermore, based on the responses, it will continue to grow at a similar pace for the next ten years, and become comparable to New York and London in the not-too-distant future.

The most important market, next to London and New York, used to be Zurich or Frankfurt in Europe, and Hong Kong in Asia. However, based on the survey results, the relative evaluation for these markets seems to have declined substantially. Since there have been movements toward liberalization in these markets, results may be a little different if a different type of survey were conducted now.

In any case, I believe, with the survey result, that the Tokyo market is in the process of becoming one of the three most important international financial markets. Today, I think, many people share this view. This has been evidenced by the fact that increasingly, many foreign financial institutions have opened or expanded their offices in Tokyo. I personally welcome these movements, since the overall size of the Tokyo market is expanding.

As the market expands and internationalizes, the market arrangements and practices have come closer to those prevailing in other major markets in the world. In fact, I think there has been considerable progress in this regard. In the eyes of foreign investors and fundraisers, I believe, the market has become more understandable and accessible.

Reflecting successive easing of eligibility criteria and liberalization of issue rules, issues of yen-denominated foreign bonds (i.e., yen bonds issued by non-residents in the Japanese domestic market, commonly known as Samurai bonds) have steadily increased to reach more than 20 percent of the world total of foreign bond issues last year. It was smaller only than Swiss franc-denominated foreign bond issues.

In other developments related to the domestic bond-issuing market, issues of foreign currency-denominated bonds, which have come to be known as Shogun bonds, began last year in Tokyo. Denomination currencies used so far include the U.S. dollar, ECU, the Australian dollar, and the Canadian dollar.

Furthermore, Euroyen bond issues have increased considerably, reflecting the expansion of eligible issuers. The relative share of Euroyen bonds to total Eurobond issues rose to about 5 percent last year, compared to only 0.4 percent in 1983. Last year, the share was comparable to those of Euromark bonds, ECU bonds, and Eurosterling bonds. When Daiwa Securities initiated the Euroyen bond issue in 1977, Euroyen statistics were not even available, naturally.

Now I would like to bring up some harder realities pertaining to the internationalization of the Tokyo market. On the one hand, as I have just said, market arrangements and practices in Japan have come closer to those prevailing in other major markets. On the other hand, I think it is necessary for foreigners involved in the financial business in Japan to acquaint themselves with Japanese customs and manners. Customs and manners are different for different countries, like each person has a different face. When in Rome, do as the Romans do; or when in Tokyo, do as the Japanese do.

For example, how many foreigners can pass the examination qualifying them to conduct the securities business in Japan? These exams have to be taken in Japanese, of course. It is true that the number of foreign businessmen who can speak Japanese has increased, but it still seems insufficient, considering the recent rapid expansion of the Japanese market. I hope more people will get used to the Japanese language. I do not think Japanese is a difficult language for Americans who have language talent.

High expenses in Tokyo were pointed out by the survey mentioned earlier as one of the stumbling blocks for increased business. As one example, one of my friends, a European banker, is paying more than $10,000 per month for his apartment in Tokyo. His apartment is located in one of the most luxurious residential areas in the center of Tokyo. When he reported it to his headquarters in France, he was asked whether he made a mistake in adding one too many zeroes! He asked me to explain to headquarters how expensive apartment rent is in Tokyo. When he mentioned the same figure in his letter to his parents in France, they thought he was living in a palace and they wanted to see the place. As you know, the only family living in anything close to a palace in Tokyo is the Emperor and his family! This is not the end of the story. The chairman of his bank came to Tokyo recently. Apparently, he thought my friend was living in a large luxury apartment. When he saw the apartment, he was struck by its size, which was, of course, small by his standards and he suggested that my friend move into a larger apartment. Given the high progressive rate of income tax in Japan, however, persons who can pay more than $10,000 for monthly rent, would probably have to earn $2-3 million a year, with a tax rate of 78 percent, and an ordinary businessman certainly does not earn that much.

Foreign companies operate differently from Japanese companies in various ways. One is concerned with personnel management. Headhunting has recently become popular in Tokyo in connection with the growth of foreign corporations, especially in the field of finance. Actually, a number of employees of my company have transferred to foreign corporations. I am not in a position to encourage this, but I regard it as an increase in the number of graduates from Daiwa Business School. When they transfer, some of them are rumoured to be given as much as $300,000 per year. This is generally considered extremely high, but I do not necessarily agree with that view. In the case of my company, a typical employee who starts working at the age of 22 and retires at the age of 60 is supposed to earn about $3 million in his lifetime. This does not take into consideration expected general salary increases in the future and the various fringe benefits and pensions. Those who become executives can, of course, earn more than $3 million. I think the Japanese salary scale has improved more than is generally believed. In addition, employment with Japanese companies is still generally based on lifetime contract, although the recent Japanese labor market has tended to move in the direction of greater liquidity. Some of those who transferred to foreign corporations appear to have desired to return to previous Japanese companies. The choice between $3 million with a stable long-term contract, and $300,000 a year without it depends on his philosophy of life.

We now change the subject to a larger, less personal one. When we compare the composition of household financial assets between the United States and Japan, we find that about 35 percent of U.S. individual financial assets consist of bank deposits, while the corresponding ratio is about 60 percent for Japan. The difference is 25 percent. The magnitude corresponding to this 25 percent is estimated around Y130 trillion, which amounts to more than 40 percent of GNP of Japan. The ratio of holdings of other assets, such as stocks and bonds, is expected to increase as household savings increase. If the Japanese ratio moved toward its U.S. counterpart, it will create a revolutionary impact on the financial world. In my opinion, the essence of the so-called financial revolution is what will happen in the process.

In this regard, I'd like to touch upon corporate deposits. Japanese corporate deposits with banks match about 23 times their daily sales volumes. The corresponding figure for U.S. corporations amounts to only 7 times daily sales. Thus, in a sense, American companies are utilizing their funds more efficiently. If the ratio of Japanese corporate bank deposits can be reduced to match or come close to that of the U.S., the effect on the financial markets will also be revolutionary. Both individual and institutional investors are expected to move toward other domestic vehicles as well as international investment instruments.

For example, when 30-year U.S. government bonds totaling $9 billion were auctioned on May 8, 1986, Japanese institutions bid $6 billion, with Daiwa Securities accounting for $2 billion. This clearly shows that Japanese investors are still eager to accumulate U.S. dollar bonds and diversify their portfolio internationally, even with a strong yen. There is no other alternative international investment vehicle with such high returns and marketability in the eyes of Japanese investors. Personally, I was not one of those surprised at the auction results. I think international investments by Japanese investors will farther expand, if and when the falling exchange rates stabilize.

Now I'd like to point out that due to a modification of listing requirements, it has now become easier for foreign corporations to list their stocks on the Tokyo Stock Exchange. At present, 25 foreign stocks are listed. Furthermore, corporations including Chrysler, McDonald's, Kodak, American Can are scheduled for listing this year. Over 50 foreign stocks by early next year, and the number is expected to grow. By comparison, the New York Stock Exchange includes 54 listed foreign stocks; more than half of them are Canadian stocks. Internationalization of the Tokyo stock market is gathering steam in this respect.

For example, Procter & Gamble stock was listed on the Tokyo Stock Exchange last week. The listing was a success. On the first day of trading, May 28, more than 700,000 shares were traded compared with 350,000 traded on the previous day in New York. Furthermore, its closing share price in Tokyo renewed this year's record high in New York. After the initial welcome, volume dropped during the following days, but still remained significant. This incident, as well as a substantial increase in foreign stock listings seems to reflect wide recognition and expectations that the Japanese stock market is an easily accessible and stable source of long-term capital.

Although this might be unfamiliar to you, overseas investors occupy a more significant portion in the Tokyo stock market than in New York. When you compare the Tokyo market with New York, foreign investors account for approximately 7-8 percent of the market value, and 20 percent of the trading value for Tokyo compared with 5 percent and 15 percent respectively for New York. It would be right to say that these figures are indications of a fairly advanced internationalization of the Tokyo stock market.

Reflecting an increase in the number of listed overseas companies and increased overseas investment in Japanese shares, interest in membership on the Exchange by foreign securities houses has increased. In fact, six foreign securities companies obtained membership early this year. Three of them are American companies. The number of the Japanese securities companies which are members of the New York Stock Exchange also happens to be three. With increasing international capital flow, the number of foreign securities companies seeking membership on the Tokyo Stock Exchange is likely to increase.

In the Japanese bond market, foreigners' relative weight in terms of the value of bond holdings was about 6 percent at the end of 1985, and their weight in terms of turnover value was also about 6 percent in 1985. With such magnitude, their movement has had noticeable impact on the market. As Japanese investors continue to invest in U.S. dollar bonds, it is not surprising that their behavior has impact on the U.S. bond market. Net overseas securities investment by the Japanese amounted to $53.5 billion last year, with 98 percent in bonds. About three-quarters of overseas bond investments are concentrated in U.S. dollar bonds. Given the unchanged attitude of Japanese investors towards international diversification, their influence on the U.S. bond market will continue to increase.

A financial-futures market, now limited to long-term government bonds, was created within the Tokyo Stock Exchange in October 1985. With outstanding long-term government bonds reaching Y120 trillion, we expect this market to provide investors with an efficient means of hedging their investment risk. However, some have doubted its ability to function due to an insufficient number of speculators, compared with, for example, Chicago. Despite its short history, market transactions have been more active than was generally expected. Average trading value per day during the month of April was Y2.5 trillion, 64 percent of the average trading value in the futures market of U.S. Treasury bonds. Furthermore, the market has been functioning properly as a hedge market.

In Japan, we apply fixed-rate commissions on securities transactions. The United States, as you all know, liberalized commissioned rates on Mayday 1975. However, it resulted in higher commissions on small-lot transactions, and reduced commissions on larger ones. Currently, Japanese individual investors are able to trade at low rates. In the event that we liberalize commission rates to reflect costs incurred by each transaction, in my opinion, it would enable a reduction in commissions for large transactions, but might augment commissions for smaller ones, although others may think otherwise.

Individual stock investors, totaling 17 million, account for slightly less than 50 percent of total trading value in Japan, compared with 20 percent for the United States. After the disbandment of *zaibatsu*, post-war Japan continues to esteem "people's capitalism." We are treating the question of liberalizing the commission rates so as not to impair the protection of the individual stock investors, because we regard them as the grassroots of Japan's post-war capitalism. In this regard, it should be noted that the ratio of individual stock investors to total population is about 16 percent in Japan as well as in the United States, while the number of individual stock investors in the U.K. was only 1 million before the offering of British Telecom shares in 1984. The number in West Germany is not even available.

Instead of making concluding remarks, I'd like to say a few words which have some bearing on the recent rapid movement toward securitization. In connection with this, I am going to cite a passage from a book by Martin Mayer. I translated the book *Wall Street — Men and Money* a number of years ago and continued to read his books since then. In his recent work, entitled *The Money Bazaars* (p. 235), he wrote: "The misconduct of the U.S. banks of the 1920s that really pushed the Glass-Steagall Act through Congress in 1933, (prohibiting commercial banks from underwriting securities and selling them to the public), involved Latin American bonds that banks dumped out of their investment portfolios into the hands of their unsuspecting customers when the banks found out the paper was no good. It might be noted in passing that the international financial crisis of 1982–83 took the form it did, with the banks at risk, only because the public was protected by Glass-Steagall." This rather long quotation indicates that excessive securitization might endanger public interest.

In the same book, Mr. Mayer quoted from Gerald T. Dunne, editor of the *Banking and Law Journal*. Mr. Dunne "noted a competition between supervisor and the supervised alike to junk Glass-Steagall, a process the historically minded may well analogize to a peasants dance on the slope of Mt. Vesuvius in Pompeii." I will let you draw your own conclusions from this analogy.

Japan-U.S. Relations: Asymmetry of Institutional Features as a Source of Trade Frictions

Iwao Nakatani

Professor, Osaka University

THE BIGGEST ISSUE in Japan-U.S. economic relations over the last several years has been the large and growing current-account imbalance. To be sure, there are those who deny that this imbalance is a major problem. It has aspects, however, that cannot be ignored, such as the persistent and serious political issues that arise on the microeconomic level of individual industries and the possibility of investment decisions that are inefficient from the viewpoint of international resource allocation.

In this paper, I will discuss first that one of the most fundamental causes of international trade frictions lies in the fact that, under the free-trade system, goods, money, people, and firms are mobile across borders, whereas the state is fixed, and institutional features typically differ from one state to another.

Then, I will show, as an example of the above proposition, that the asymmetric features of tax systems between Japan and the United States may have been a major cause of recent external imbalances between the two countries. The paper concludes that it is essential to smooth out the institutional differences between Japan and the United States, in order to minimize distortions in the international movement of economic resources and external imbalances between the two nations. In particular, the paper demonstrates the importance of international coordination of tax policy as a policy issue for the future.[1]

1. *The Basic Issue*

Under the free-trade system, goods move across borders in search of markets where they can be sold. Capital also moves across borders even more easily and quickly, looking for a higher rate of return. People and corporations move to where their prospective incomes (measured in utility terms) are highest. The basic problem here is that, even if international markets for either goods or capital are perfectly competitive in the usual textbook sense of the word, there can be a distortion in the free movement of goods and capital, when institutional features such as tax systems differ significantly from one country to another. They tend to move toward where the institutional setting is more favorable, other things being equal. A visible increase in international economic transactions certainly accelerates this phenomenon, particularly when differences in institutional features which affect the profitability of economic activities are significant. A typical example is the $70-80 billion trade deficit, expected in 1986, of the United States with Japan and the associated massive capital outflow from Japan to the U.S.

Under the prevailing political system of "democracy," institutions of a particular country such as laws, taxes, rules, norms, principles, policy making procedures, and the like are determined and maintained in the light of its own domestic circumstances reflecting preferences and tastes of the people within the border. The state is a geopolitical unit which is not mobile and makes up a set of institutions that are a representation of the preference and attitude of its people. As long as people are different in preference and attitude from country to country, as they are, institutions will also be different.

On the other hand, as a result of the rapid internationalization of transactions, both of goods and money, national borders are losing some of their original meaning. Corporations and even people do not care much about the nation they belong to when it comes to profit seeking. Economic activities tend to be carried on freely across borders in a single international market, whereas political process is still confined largely to the domestic sphere.

Mobility of economic resources now limits the state's capacity to enforce its own law because economic agents can now choose the *exit* option rather than *voice* option.[2] Instead of relying on the cumbersome political process (*voice*) within the state, they can make an *exit* from it and achieve the intended objective (e.g., higher profits) much more easily.

For example, professional tennis players often choose the country where they pay their income tax according to the principle of income maximization (net of taxes). Multinational corporations have a clear tendency to adjust their corporate profits across nations so as to minimize their tax payments worldwide. Corporate stocks which are internationally known are traded at the stock-exchange where tax burden is slightest. Corporate bonds are issued where regulations for new issues are less stringent, and goods are exported to the country where demand is strong relative to the domestic market.

All of these examples seem to indicate that the existence of institutional differences among nations not only accelerates the cross-border mobility of economic resources but also produces external imbalances both in current and capital accounts. The basic issue here is, again, the fact that, while the world market is functioning as a single gigantic organ, there are more than 150 nation states on earth claiming their own sovereign power. As I pointed out earlier, the sovereign power of the state is waning slowly as a result of increasing mobility of goods, capital, people, and corporations. But the state pretends and behaves as if its monopolistic power were permanent and it could set its own rules solely in light of its own domestic circumstances, and enforce them effectively.

The point is that, after about 1971, the United States has shrunk in economic power relative to the world as a whole and lost its appetite for acting as the world's hegemonic power. To put it another way, the world has lost the powerful coordinating actor to take corrective actions when large external imbalances and other major problems emerge in the world scene. The international impact has been largely ignored by leading policy makers in the United States since around 1970.

The major tax reform by the Reagan Administration in 1981 is a typical example. It has created a major shift in direction of international mobility of goods, money, and corporations. Too-high interest rates attracted international money at an unprecedented pace. Too-strong domestic demand was a major driving force for promoting imports and slowing exports. The too-strong dollar forced American corporations to produce goods outside the U.S. In other words, the drastic change in economic policy in 1981 gave rise to a major shift in the relative position of the U.S. vis-à-vis the rest of the world.

2. Why are Effects of Market-Opening Policies Limited?

The above observation leads us to a more subtle question. When economic resources are as mobile as they are today, even the slightest differences in business rules and norms can be a major source of economic frictions among nations. Market mechanism is Pareto-efficient only if perfect competition prevails. But, because the state has, in principle, the sovereign power to set its own rules more or less independently of the rest of the world, institutional features of each state are generally different from each other, and these differences regulate the direction of movements of economic resources. Hence, strictly speaking, unless all the institutional settings are equalized over all the submarkets, Pareto-efficient allocation of resources will not obtain, even if all the other conditions for perfect competition are satisfied.

But, how can we equalize institutional settings among independent sovereign nations? We must admit readily that this is a very difficult task, particularly when we all believe that "nationalism" has some innate value in itself. That is, it is unclear whether such an attempt can be justified from the viewpoint of indigenous social values. Here we can see a clear conflict between "internationalization of economic activities" and "sovereignty of the state."

Let me proceed to a more specific example of Japan-U.S. frictions in this connection. Generally speaking, there is a strong sentiment in the U.S. that a major cause of the existing trade imbalance between Japan and the U.S. is the limited access of the Japanese markets. The key word is access, access to the markets, the opening of the markets and the same opportunities offered to American exporters and the investors that Americans offer to the Japanese.

Historically, Japan has liberalized its trade since the 1960s, and its tariff barriers are lower today on average than in most other GATT nations, including the United States. However, problems remain—especially in such areas as agriculture, forestry, oil and oil products, and capital markets. Their removal would not only increase our trade, but also improve the standard of living of the Japanese as well as the consumers of other nations.

Many experts also agree that non-tariff barriers in Japan, such as standards and certification procedures, are a serious obstacle to the free flow of trade among countries. Prime Minister Nakasone's "Action Program" announced on July 31, 1985 was a significant step forward, but the general perception has been pessimistic about its actual effect in reducing the trade imbalance between Japan and the United States.

There is no doubt that such action is important, since it is a step forward to eliminate the existing "institutional differences" by way of altering the Japanese systems to meet the "international standards." To the extent that such alteration is acceptable both to the Japanese and to the rest of the world, such action should be taken, perhaps more thoroughly and more quickly.

But, the problem is not that simple. What must be understood clearly is that actions that can be taken officially by the government are rather limited compared with all those actions needed. The reason is that what government can deal with are only *explicit* and *written* rules such as tariffs, quotas, standards, and certification procedures, and other regulations.

But, in reality, there are numerous *implicit* and *unwritten* rules which dominate people's thinking and behavior in economic and business transactions. *Explicit* and *written* rules may be altered in response to changes in the economic environment, domestic or international. They will be changed through an explicit legislative process as far as such action obtains sufficient support from the electorate.

Implicit and *unwritten* rules, on the other hand, are generally more difficult to change, and sometimes it is not even desirable to change them. They are constrained by cultural and social values of each society. They are recognized, often unconsciously, as fair and just inside its cultural border. Some of them may have their roots so deep that their removal and alteration might lead to the loss of cultural identity of the people.

Obviously, these *implicit* and *unwritten* rules cannot be changed by governmental or legislative action. What is possible at best will be "moral persuasion," but habits and customs are hard to change by moral persuasion alone. At any rate, we have to admit that, even if they can be changed, it takes time — time that may be too long for those waiting for a change.

As is well known, Japan is among the most homogeneous societies on earth. The United States is a nation of immigrants and perhaps the most heterogeneous society in the world. This difference alone makes communication between the two countries rather complex. In Japan, everyone inherently knows the rules (not only *explicit* and *written* rules, but also *implicit* and *unwritten* rules) and is comfortable with them. The American system is constantly being tested in a sometimes adversarial way. This means that it has to be transparent. But transparency is not always a virtue in the Japanese society, where people know what it means before it is completely exposed.

Some Americans talk about Japanese corporate groups called *keiretsu* as an obstacle to free entry to Japanese markets. That may be true, but the problem is that there is a solid economic rationality behind them. I myself did substantial research on the economic role of the financial corporate grouping in Japan and came to the conclusion that over time the formation of groups stabilizes corporate performance substantially.[3] We often see in Japan that member firms of a group help one another in times of serious business hardship. When a financial difficulty arises, for example, the member banks usually render assistance to the firm in trouble, financial or managerial, sometimes at a far greater cost and risk than normal business reciprocity requires. Likewise, in a buyer-seller relationship, the buyer will often accept a somewhat higher price if the seller is in the same group and is facing business difficulties. Of course, in the reverse case, when the buyer is in difficulty, the seller is willing to sell at a lower price, or take other measures such as extending usance on buyer's bills.

This sort of profit-sharing practice (or to say the same thing in a different way, risk-sharing) among group members can be interpreted as an implicit mutual-insurance scheme, in which member firms are insurers and insured at the same time. As a result of these implicit mutual-assistance programs, the firm in difficulties is able to recover relatively quickly from even the worst situation. To the extent that this sort of mutual-assistance mechanism is effective among group members, there will be fewer bankruptcies and lay-offs at a time of great external shocks. This may be one of the reasons why the unemployment rate has not risen enormously in Japan despite the two recent oil crises.

Price, quality, and delivery are important—but they do not, at least in the short run, entirely transcend this particular relationship among corporations. Foreigners obviously have an enormous hardship to overcome. But, this uniquely Japanese system has its own rationality and merit and, without trade frictions, there would be nothing there to condemn.

The attitude of those companies may be incompatible with short-run profit maximization, but is inherently long-run oriented. They are simply seeking for long-term stability and continued prosperity of their own companies at the sacrifice of short-term profits. While American corporations are also worried about long-term profits, their approach is clearly different. They rely more on markets, and less on long-term contracts.

These differences in business approach need not carry a suggestion of right and wrong, but they do raise the question of whether we can avoid serious trade conflicts when these nations are playing by different sets of rules.

Is there a solution to this problem? This is a difficult question, but for Japan, it should be made clear that "internationalization" immediately implies an acceptance of "heterogeneity." It is impossible to internationalize any society without accommodating foreigners and tolerating their customs and rules. As far as we take "internationalization" as an objective that is good and worth pursuing, we must be ready to change some, if not all, of our rules of the game (*explicit* or *implicit*). Among other things, the necessity for transparency in the Japanese system seems to be rapidly emerging at this time.

It is extremely important to note, however, that any culture, however strange it may appear, has its own rationality and *raison d'être*. It is essential for everyone to make special efforts to understand the value systems of others and to tolerate them as much as possible. Enhancement of cross-cultural communication is crucial for "internationalization," and ethnocentrism is the first thing to be avoided. What is required of internationally oriented business leaders today are not only specialized business techniques and professional knowledge, but also generosity and open-mindedness toward other cultures.

3. Difference in Tax Systems as a Major Source of External Imbalance

Probably the biggest item among the institutional differences that may affect the direction of movements of economic resources is the difference in tax structures among nations. Tax policy has traditionally been a domestic concern and taxes are set by each country in the light of its own domestic circumstances. But if economic transactions are carried on freely across borders in a single international market, economic resources are likely to move to where tax systems are favorable, other things being equal. To the extent that such movements are significant, differences in tax systems would become an important source of external imbalances.

This section develops, as a typical example, a detailed analysis of the difference in tax systems between Japan and the United States.[4] It will be shown that the asymmetric nature of the tax systems may be a major source of the massive movement of capital as well as the huge current-account imbalance between the two nations.

Taxes on Savings. The most prominent feature of the U.S. tax system with respect to savings and investment is an anti-savings and pro-invesment tendency as compared to the pro-savings and anti-investment tax system of Japan. The latter is known as one of the world's leaders in preferential tax treatment of savings. The *Maruyū* system provides tax exemption for interest on deposits up to 14 million yen per salaried person and the total saving under this system exceeds 250 trillion yen. The interest paid to this amount reaches 15 trillion yen annually which equals roughly five percent of the Japanese GNP.

In the United States, by contrast, there is virtually nothing that corresponds to Japan's *Maruyū*; all interest income is taxed together with other income. One of the few exceptions is the Individual Retirement Account which allows one to save tax-free up to 2,000 dollars per year on condition that he/she does not withdraw it before his/her retirement, but obviously it is by far more restrictive than *Maruyū*. As a result, marginal tax rates, particularly for those in upper-income brackets, are quite high. The way the U.S. system favors credit-financed consumption is also significant. In a lecture at George Washington University in Washington, D.C., on September 23, 1984, Peter G. Peterson, former U.S. Secretary of Commerce, contrasted the U.S. approach with Japan's pro-saving system, saying, "We have developed some of the world's strongest pro-consumption and pro-borrowing tendencies." A major factor behind these tendencies, he suggested, is that the United States, unlike many other countries, was not a battleground during World War II. When the war ended, Peterson said, "our plants and factories were intact; what we needed was strong consumer demand to keep them producing up to capacity. The keys to long-term prosperity for Americans seemed to be saving less, borrowing more, and spending heavily on domestically produced consumer goods."

This pro-consumption, pro-borrowing posture produced a fundamental difference in direction between the Japanese and U.S. economies that is evident in the following figures cited by Peterson: "In 1982, for example, installment plus mortgage debt amounted to 5.5 percent of Japan's GNP. In the U.S. such borrowing for consumption and housing was almost ten times higher as a per-cent of our GNP (48.2 percent)." That is, if the interest rate for borrowing is 10 percent, almost five percent of the U.S. GNP is deductible from taxable income.

It is clear from the above discussion that Japan's tax system for savings is diametrically opposed to America's pro-borrowing and pro-consumption policy, and that almost the same percentage of GNP is favored — just in opposite directions.

It is a purely empirical problem how well such differences in tax systems for savings explain the difference in personal savings rates between the two na-tions. As is well known, recent personal savings rates in Japan and the U.S. range around 17 percent and 5 percent respectively.

Many observers deny that tax rates affect savings rates, but this conclusion is, I must say, surprising. To be sure, econometric methods may reveal no significant effect on the savings rate from a change in the tax rate, or they may lead to the conclusion that the degree of responsiveness is extremely slight. But because the tax system is not changed annually, tax-rate data for use in econometric analysis tend to be insufficient. And even when the system is changed, not all people react immediately. This is because decisions about saving are made from a lifetime perspective. It is natural that people do not change their saving behavior in response to changes in the interest rate itself because changes in interest rates are often short-term cyclical phenomena. However, people may alter their saving behavior in case of large-scale permanent tax re-form. Suppose that the tax systems for savings of two nations, Japan and U.S., are completely replaced permanently. Can we insist that savings rates in both countries will not change at all even after such a large-scale tax reform? The answer would be evidently "no."

It is sufficient, however, if the responsiveness of the savings rate to the tax rate is concluded to be slight (in other words, a level that is statistically significant but that shows low elasticity of saving to taxation). By making great enough changes in the tax system, it will still be possible to effect the change in the savings rate that is needed to achieve policy goals.

Taxes on Investment. Figure 1 compares the changes in corporate tax rates in Japan and the United States. The figures are derived by dividing corporate tax payments by corporate income as it appears in national income accounts. Though they cannot show the effects of specific tax measures or the distortions caused by inflation, they do provide a rough view of trends.

From Figure 1 we can observe that the Japanese corporate tax rate was al-most uniformly lower than the American rate throughout Japan's post-war rapid-growth era (the only exceptions being 1951, 1964, and 1965). We also see that the difference was a significant one, generally on the order of 10 percentage

FIGURE 1

CORPORATE TAX RATES IN JAPAN AND THE UNITED STATES

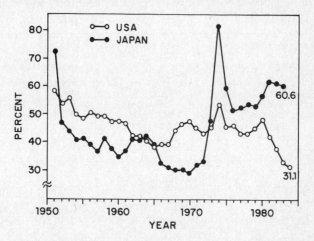

NOTE: CORPORATE TAX RATE = CORPORATE TAXES PAID ÷ CORPORATE INCOME

SOURCES: ECONOMIC REPORT OF THE PRESIDENT. FEBRUARY 1985: KOKUMIN KEIZAI
KEISAN NENPŌ (ANNUAL REPORT ON NATIONAL ACCOUNTS) ECONOMIC
PLANNING AGENCY, 1983 AND 1985: KOKUMIN SHOTOKU TŌKEI NENPŌ
(NATIONAL INCOME STATISTICAL ANNUAL). ECONOMIC PLANNING
AGENCY, 1966.

points; in 1970, in particular, the gap widened to 18 points, with the U.S. rate at 47.9 percent and Japan's at 29.5 percent.

When the oil crunch hit in 1973, however, the relationship between the two countries' tax rates was reversed. Since the Reagan Administration took office in 1981, U.S. corporate tax rates have shown a pronounced drop. In Japan, where a campaign to pare the budget deficit is under way, corporate taxation has been made more stringent, and rates have risen significantly. As a result of these opposite trends, U.S. rates (estimated at 31.3 percent in 1984) are now only about half Japan's (60.6 percent in 1983).

However, corporate investment decisions will not be so heavily affected by the average corporate tax rate as by the marginal corporate tax rate (which we shall call *the effective tax rate* from now on) and the cost of capital. Table 1 is the effective tax rates for investment in Japan and the U.S. based upon an investment-decision model by Hall-Jorgenson.[5] According to this table, rates in both machinery and equipment and buildings are higher in Japan. The difference in effective tax rates for machinery and equipment is remarkable, particularly after the massive tax reform in the U.S. in 1981. The huge difference after 1981 was created by the introduction of an accelerated cost recovery system (ACRS) and an investment tax credit up to 10 percent. The effective tax rates

TABLE 1

*Effective Tax Rates for Investment
in Japan and the United States (in percentages)*

	Machinery and equipment		Buildings	
	Japan	USA	Japan	USA
1975	96.3	30.6	92.6	42.7
1976	81.2	31.9	70.5	43.7
1977	54.9	32.8	48.5	44.6
1978	54.9	42.7	48.5	50.2
1979	97.8	42.0	95.5	49.3
1980	57.6	36.1	50.3	44.4
1981	50.8	−9.6	46.7	38.1
1982	48.4	−16.0	45.2	36.6
1983	49.6	−33.5	45.9	35.8

for machinery and equipment in the U.S. have been negative since 1981. This is simply due to the fact that the increase in cash flow by accelerated cost recovery system and investment tax credit was larger than corporate tax payments.

On the other hand, the difference in the cost of capital (Figure 2) is not as large as the effective tax rate. The cost of capital in Japan is sometimes less than that of U.S. (1975, 1976 and 1979). The cost of capital is computed from the formula;[6]

$$\text{cost of capital} = \frac{\text{average cost of fund}}{1 - \text{effective tax rate}} + \text{rate of depreciation}$$

This would mean that the cost of capital depends not only on the effective tax rate but also on the average cost of funds.

The average cost of funds tends to be lower for Japan because Japanese interest rates have been generally lower than American rates, and the debt-equity ratio of Japanese corporations is higher than that of their American counterparts.[7] Therefore, the average cost of the Japanese corporate funds becomes relatively low. Japanese corporations are facing higher effective tax rates and lower average cost of funds. As a result, the difference in the cost of capital becomes small. However, since 1981, the cost of capital for machinery and equipment has become considerably lower in the U.S. due to the ACRS.

External Imbalances Due to Differences in Tax Systems. As we have seen, the tax structures of Japan and the United States are diametrically opposed in regard to savings and investment. The Japanese system favors saving and penalizes investment, while the U.S. system penalizes saving and rewards investment. My speculation is that this structural difference is one of the most important factors behind the long-term evolution of Japan's saving surplus and America's investment surplus.

In a closed system (or in one where current-account imbalances are instantly corrected by exchange-rate adjustments), as long as interest rates are flexible, savings and investment should balance domestically, regardless of tax-system

FIGURE 2

COST OF CAPITAL IN JAPAN
AND THE UNITED STATES
(MACHINERY AND EQUIPMENT)

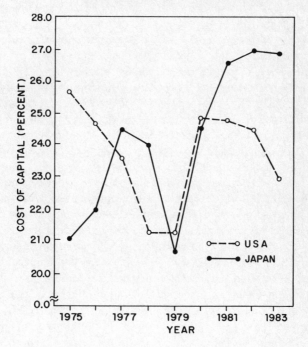

distortions favoring saving and penalizing investment or vice versa. This domestic balancing function is effected by adjustment of the after-tax real rate of return on savings and investment.

In an open system, by contrast, people can invest their savings in foreign securities. Since U.S. tax policy is anti-saving and pro-investment, real interest rates tend to be pushed up, while in Japan, whose tax system is pro-saving and anti-investment, they tend to be lower relative to those in U.S. Japanese people attracted by these high rates are able to invest their savings in American securities.

The result is a massive capital outflow of an expected $70 billion or more in 1986 from Japan to the U.S. The movement of capital has raised the value of the dollar significantly to produce a large trade deficit. In view of the above argument, it seems necessary to smooth out the existing differences in tax structures of both nations, if present external imbalances are regarded as intolerable. Such measures would also serve for promoting efficiency in the world market by eliminating distortions in the movements of economic resources enhanced by the asymmetric nature of the tax systems.

4. Conclusion

In this paper, I have shown that institutional differences among nations are not compatible with efficiency of international allocation of resources and may be a major source of external imbalances. After the historical experiment over the last 16 years, we have learned that the flexible exchange-rate system is imperfect and limited in its capacity to adjust current-account imbalances between nations. As was evidenced in the Tokyo economic summit meetings in May 1986, macroeconomic policy coordination has become one of the most urgent economic issues in world politics, and this is certainly a reflection of the fact that the flexible exchange-rate regime is not functioning perfectly.

However, as Charles Kindleberger of MIT rightly pointed out in his presidential address delivered at the ninety-eighth meeting of the American Economic Association in 1985,[8] macroeconomic coordination is probably among the most difficult policy goals to be pursued. First of all, macroeconomic coordination, such as coordination in monetary and fiscal policies, usually requires reasonably quick action, because these policies are typically counter-cyclical Keynesian policies. But negotiation among nations, each of them having vested interests of its own, is almost always time consuming, and even if the world should ultimately agree on some kind of policy coordination, the macroeconomic situation may have changed completely by that time. Second, the accumulation of knowledge about the effects of macroeconomic coordination on the world economy in general and on the external imbalance in particular is far from sufficient.[9] Views are very diverse, and policy makers would have a hard time committing themselves to a particular set of policies.

Coordination of tax policies and other institutional aspects is more "structural" and "long-term" in nature. Even if the quantitative effects of such coordination were not precisely known beforehand, it would still seem possible to agree that too huge a difference in tax structure, as in the case of savings-investment tax systems of Japan and the United States, and extraordinary unevenness of institutional features among nations are undesirable in that they distort direction of movements of goods, money, and corporations across borders. It does not seem too difficult for Japan and the United States and for other OECD countries to agree that differences in various institutions, including tax systems, should be smoothed out in order to reduce the trade imbalance among themselves.

Needless to say, there remains the intrinsic problem of conflict between "international coordination" and "the sovereignty of the state." In political science, the right to levy and collect taxes is regarded as among the most important sources of the power of the state, and for some it may be hard to accept the idea that tax policy is subject to international consultation. However, as long as we admit that "internationalization" of economic activities benefits us, and as long as we take "internationalization" as an objective worth pursuing, we must recognize that there is a real trade-off between "internationalization of economic activities" and the "preservation of the autonomy of the state."

NOTES

1. See Nakatani, 1985a, for a more detailed analysis.
2. See Hirschman, 1972, for a very stimulating discussion. While Hirschman's analysis is largely for the relationship between workers and the firm or between consumers and the firm, the situation is readily applicable to the situation here. In the present context, workers and consumers correspond to economic agents (the firm and the individual) seeking for a higher rate of return, whereas the firm corresponds to the state.
3. See Nakatani, 1982; 1984.
4. See Nakatani, 1985b.
5. For more discussion on Table 1, see Nakatani, et al., 1986. For the Hall-Jorgenson model, see Hall and Jorgenson, 1960.
6. See Inoue, 1985.
7. If corporations finance their investment through debt, the interest paid against it is deductible from taxable income. Therefore, *ceteris paribus*, the higher the debt-equity ratio, the lower the average cost of funds.
8. See Kindleberger, 1986.
9. Recently, however, a number of interesting papers have appeared in this connection. See for example, McKibbin and Sachs, 1986, and Ishii, McKibbin and Sachs, 1986, for empirical analyses of the effects of macro-policy coordination in the OECD.

REFERENCES

Hall, R., and D.W. Jorgenson. 1960. "Tax Policy and Investment Behavior." *American Economic Review*, pp. 388–401.
Hirschman, Albert. 1972. *Exit, Voice and Loyalty*. Cambridge, Massachusetts: Harvard University Press.
Inoue, T. 1985. "Shihon kosuto kettei no ni sokumen — zeisei yōin to kinyū yōin" [Two Aspects of the Determination of the Cost of Capital — The Tax Factor and the Financial Factor]. October. Mimeo.
Ishii, N., W. McKibbin, and J. Sachs. 1986. "The Economic Policy Mix, Policy Cooperation, and Protectionism: Some Aspects of Macroeconomic Interdependence Among the United States, Japan, and Other OECD Countries." *Journal of Policy Modeling* 7(4).
Kindleberger, C. 1986. "International Public Goods Without International Government." *American Economic Review*, March. pp. 1–3.
McKibbin, W., and J. Sachs. 1986. "Coordination of Monetary and Fiscal Policies in the OECD." Working Paper No. 1800. National Bureau of Economic Research.
Nakatani, Iwao. 1982. "The Role of Intermarket *Keiretsu* Business Groups in Japan." *Pacific Economic Papers* No. 97. Australia-Japan Research Centre, Australian National University. December.
Nakatani, Iwao. 1984. "The Economic Role of Financial Corporate Grouping." In M. Aoki, ed., *The Economic Analysis of the Japanese Firm*. Amsterdam: North Holland.
Nakatani, Iwao. 1985a. "Proposal for a Tax Summit." *Japan Echo* 12(3):31–37.
Nakatani, Iwao. 1985b. "Curing Trade Friction by Coordinating Taxes." *Economic Eye* 6(3):4–6.
Nakatani, Iwao, T. Inoue, Y. Iwamoto, and M. Fukushige. 1986. *Wagakuni kigyō zeisei no hyōka to kadai* [Evaluation and Policy Issues in Corporate Income Tax in Japan]. Business Policy Forum. January.

Trade, Yen, and Politics:
Comments on the Political Implications of U.S.-Japan Economic Relations

Gerald L. Curtis
Professor and Director, Toyota Research Program, Columbia University

I HAVE BEEN ASKED to comment this afternoon on the implications for the political relationship between the United States and Japan of what we have been hearing these past two days about the economic relationships between these two countries. My comments come at the end of what I think has been a very fruitful and extraordinarily interesting conference. It is also the end of a very long day. Many of you look very tired; some of you look as though you might be asleep.

It is not my purpose in what I am going to say to wake you up, at least not in the literal sense. But it does seem to me that we all should be awakened to the fact that if American and Japanese policies proceed along the course that was outlined in the remarks made yesterday and this morning, the political relationship between these two countries will get considerably worse, and fairly soon. This impression only reinforces a feeling of uneasiness that I brought back from Japan last week after a three-week visit there.

Americans and Japanese are quite at loggerheads, at a standoff, as to what each country—or rather what the other country—should do to deal with the problems that we face. The tendency in both countries is to focus on what they think the other country's obligations are to resolve these problems, rather than what their own obligations are. This applies equally to the United States and to Japan. Japanese rightly complain that Americans often make Japan a scapegoat for their own problems. But now a similar phenomenon is beginning to occur in Japan as Japanese blame Americans for problems that Japan itself must play a more central role in resolving.

Now, we have had serious political problems in U.S.-Japan political relations for at least the past 20 years, and we have muddled through. Indeed, we might well muddle through again. There are many countervailing factors that inhibit a full-blown protectionist drive in the United States. There are also pressures pushing Japan to readjust its macroeconomic policy mix despite the Ministry of Finance's (MOF) desire to stick to the current course. These countervailing forces may be just strong enough to contain our mutual dissatisfaction and enable us to muddle through.

But I do not think that we can take it for granted that that will indeed be the case. In particular, I believe that the risks inherent in current Japanese policy — a policy that sets the goal of fiscal consolidation as the priority objective of government budgeting policy and relies almost exclusively on exchange-rate changes to restore a degree of equilibrium to Japan's balance of payments — are quite large and that they are not fully appreciated.

There are three basic points I want to stress in my remarks this afternoon. The first one is directed mainly at Americans who fail to understand why it is politically so difficult for the Japanese government to adopt fiscal policies that would contribute in a substantial way to stimulating greater domestic demand. The second is directed mainly at Japanese who have come to believe that the U.S. Congress is something of a paper tiger when it comes to protectionist threats. The third is directed to the professional economists and economic bureaucrats in both countries who do not seem to recognize the potential political costs involved in relying on exchange-rate adjustments to restore some degree of equilibrium to American and Japanese current-account balances.

But on balance my remarks are directed mainly at our Japanese colleagues. This is not because I do not believe that the U.S. needs to do a great deal more to put its own economic house in order nor because I do not recognize that America's trade deficit globally, and bilaterally with Japan, is primarily an American problem. It is because I believe that Japan's continuing enormous current-account surpluses are alienating all of its trading partners at a rapidly increasing rate, and that a failure by Japan to act in a way that conveys a real determination to reduce these surpluses and contribute to world economic growth will make it increasingly difficult for Japan to manage its political relationships with the U.S., Western Europe, Southeast Asia, and other countries and regions.

Japanese speakers at this conference have explained in quite lucid terms why it is not in Japan's interest to increase government spending as a way to stimulate greater domestic economic growth. We have also heard from virtually all the American speakers who touched on the subject of Japanese fiscal policy the view that the Japanese should increase their spending on public works, housing, and other areas to raise the Japanese standard of living, stimulate increased domestic demand and, to use a term that is not now in fashion but seems to sum up the position of these American observers, make Japan a "locomotive" of world economic growth.

I do not believe that the Japanese government, whether under Nakasone or some other prime minister, will follow this prescription unless and until Japan's economic circumstances become considerably worse than they are now. The Ministry of Finance representatives at this conference have left no doubt where they stand on this issue. The priority concern for Japan is what Japanese call fiscal consolidation or fiscal restructuring (zaisei saiken) and that precludes spending that would raise the level of government debt.

But there are also powerful political pressures pushing in the same direction and reinforcing MOF's position. For one thing fiscal conservatism is politically popular in today's Japan. The Nakasone government's campaign for administrative reform, privatization, and deregulation has convinced the Japanese public that a smaller government and a more vigorous private sector are the only hope Japan has for avoiding catching the "British disease" (or what some people now refer to as the "American disease"). In Japan, as in the United States and many European countries as well, big spenders are seen as mouthpieces for insidious "special interests." The government has asked the public to tighten its belt, and to exhibit those traditional values of frugality, thrift, and perseverance that brought Japan to its present level of well-being. Such a basic policy thrust cannot be easily or quickly turned around.

Nor can the Liberal Democratic Party (LDP) change its policies of "zero ceiling" and "minus ceiling" budgets, that is a general budget freeze, in a "rational" manner. It has been suggested by American speakers at this conference that the Japanese government increase government spending and target it at particular specific projects and sectors. But such a proposal denies the role of politics in determining how government money is spent. The LDP has been able to hold back interest-group pressures to spend more on their favorite projects by arguing that its budget freeze distributes sacrifices equitably across the society. This is a powerful argument in Japan where a great deal of value is attached to norms of equity, fair play, and balance.

It is in some ways more risky politically for the LDP to spend more than to keep to its current, tight fiscal policies. Of course there would be no problem if the party could spend enormous amounts of money, as it did during the high growth years of the 1960s. But nobody expects that kind of increase in government spending. Increasing government spending would set LDP politicians and factions against each other in the fight for shares of this scarce resource. Invariably this would mean that money would be parceled out in small sums to satisfy a large number of political demands and that it would not go to areas most in need of support and most capable of contributing to effective domestic demand — urban housing for example — but to rural areas in the form of subsidies for farmers and windfalls for provincial real-estate and construction industries.

Some knowledge of recent history is not irrelevant to understanding Japanese reluctance to shift its policy priorities. In 1977, Prime Minister Fukuda did respond to the Carter Administration's pressures that Japan become a locomotive of world growth. He increased public works spending by more than 35 percent over the previous year's budget, the single largest year-to-year increase in public-works spending in Japanese history. The goal was to raise the growth rate to 7 percent. But the only thing that this enormous influx of government funds into public works increased was the political influence of the construction industry; the growth rate came in one tenth of a percentage point lower than it had been the previous year. This was a bitter experience, and it has made Japanese leaders extremely cautious about treating public-works spending as a kind of miracle cure for economic sluggishness.

There are other political factors that make the kinds of policies blithely suggested by foreign observers difficult to implement. Someone said yesterday that Japan should change the housing code to allow taller residential buildings in Tokyo, as though all that was needed was some bureaucratic decision to do so. But this is an intensely political issue, one that involves the public's so-called "right to sunshine" and the reluctance of land owners to sell their small land holdings, given their asset value and the disincentives to sell that are built into the Japanese tax code.

It is not my point to go on with a catalog of reasons why the Japanese government and the Liberal Democratic Party are not eager to jump onto the American bandwagon advocating greater government spending by countries like Japan and West Germany. I merely want to stress that one important reason the Japanese government does not spend more is because it is politically easier to stick to current policy than to formulate a different one. In Japan, as elsewhere, politics is domestic. LDP politicians have their attention focused on the domestic political impact of their actions much more than on their impact on Japan's external relations. In domestic political terms holding to a budget freeze policy is an easy way out.

Again, the only thing that will bring about a basic shift in Japanese priorities is a new national consensus that such a shift is needed. What troubles me is that it is hard to see how such a consensus can be formed without a marked deterioration in Japan's economic circumstances, meaning zero or minus growth over several quarters and a rise in unemployment rates. What is desired, of course, are policy changes before such economic troubles arise. The Japanese political system is not structured to make these kinds of timely adjustments.

Rather, what we are likely to see are the kinds of half-way measures that have characterized much of Japan's economic policy making relevant to its international economic relationships. The government is likely to allow local governments to borrow more, front load public works, issue new construction bonds — all while maintaining a posture of fiscal consolidation and zero-ceiling budgets.

This is exactly the reverse of what is needed in terms of managing the political relationship with the United States. What is needed is for Japan to make the most of what it does, not the least. Its policies should be designed and pronounced in such a way as to show that it accepts the responsibilities its pivotal role in the world economy imposes on it, and that it is determined to shift policy priorities where necessary. Substance of course is important, but so, too, is the rhetoric, even if the actual policies fall short of reaching the goals implied by it. To some extent the Japanese problem is one of buying time to allow long-term economic trends to work to ameliorate political tensions. But rather than buy time, the current course of Japanese policy is likely only to further irritate American Congressmen and encourage the protectionist thrust that already is all too strong in this country.

This brings me to my next point which involves Congress and the American reaction to our enormous bilateral trade deficit with Japan. At the heart of the problem is a perception that Japan is unwilling to pay a price for its economic success and for refusing to adopt policies to shift the economy away from export-led growth, which in the past few years has been export-to-the-United States-led growth.

Yesterday, Mr. Gyooten stated that "Even if Japan pursues current fiscal policy and the U.S. moves to greater fiscal consolidation there will be no conflict in our national interest." I beg to disagree. Perhaps yen revaluation will work its magic in time to prevent conflicts from becoming exacerbated, but the Japanese resistance to move away from its fiscal consolidation policies and the U.S. determination (through Gramm-Rudman) to adopt such policies are already causing conflicts in our national interests to surface. They have helped create the most severe protectionist pressures this country has experienced since the 1930s. Increasingly, they have pushed the Reagan Administration to adopt a kind of creeping protectionist policy in order to stop Congress from doing something worse.

Congress has relentlessly escalated its rhetoric about trade and about Japan. It passes with near unanimous votes resolutions demanding that Japan reduce its trade surplus or increase its defense spending, and threatens the most dire consequences if the Japanese do not do as told. This, naturally enough, has a strong backlash effect in Japan where people are no more prepared to be told by foreigners how to run their country than Americans would be if the Diet passed a resolution demanding that the U.S reduce its budget deficit and cut military spending.

Congressmen appear to believe that their actions send important "signals" to Japan. But the signal that has been read by many Japanese is that the Congress's bark is stronger than its bite. The Japanese mass media continues to pay close attention to every Congressional threat against Japan — indeed almost every Congressional utterance about Japan finds its way into the Japanese papers — but many people in industry and government have come to discount these Congressional threats.

The Omnibus Trade Bill that recently passed the House is a good example. It got a lot of media attention, but Japanese in responsible positions know that the chances of the House and Senate agreeing on a bill are slight, that the President will veto the bill if it is passed, and that Congress does not have the votes for an override.

The danger of Congressional "signal" sending is that it lures the targets of the signals into a false sense of security that nothing really is going to happen after all. After hearing Congress cry wolf so many times, it is little wonder that people refuse to believe that the wolf is really at the door. This forces Congress to escalate its rhetoric and the level of threat. After awhile people can no longer distinguish between tactics and the substance of their complaints. The result is a dangerous thrust toward protectionism and an ill-temper in the dialogue that is totally out of place in a relationship as close, important, and mutually beneficial as the one between the U.S. and Japan.

I would like to add one more point about protectionist sentiments in Congress. Many people in Japan, and in the United States as well, exaggerate the extent to which protectionism is a partisan issue. There is a feeling widespread in Japan that as long as the Republicans are in control, protectionism will be contained, and that the Democrats are using it as a political issue against the Republicans. There is no doubt that the Democrats think they can score political points by attacking what they characterize as President Reagan's hands-off policy on matters of foreign trade. But there is also a lot of wishful thinking in this assessment.

In fact, protectionism cuts across party lines. The trade bill being considered by the Senate Finance Committee where the Republicans are the majority is not fundamentally different from the Democrat-sponsored Omnibus Trade Bill that got through the House. There is a general protectionist thrust in Congress for the reason that our global current-account deficit is so large, and that sentiment gets focused on Japan for the reason that our bilateral trade deficit is so huge. As long as these trends continue, protectionist feelings will continue to grow stronger among both Republican and Democratic Congressmen; if they are reversed, support for free trade will win out in both parties.

Many speakers here over the past two days have made the point that, if Japan does not use other measures to deal with its current-account surplus, the exchange rate will deal with it, maybe not completely but enough to bring the Japanese surplus down to within a more normal range. I suspect that this is an attractive prospect for economists because they can see in it the workings of impersonal market forces bringing the system into better equilibrium. Professor Komiya stated yesterday that contrary to the popular Japanese view that yen appreciation is a threat to the Japanese economy, academic economists and economic bureaucrats tend to welcome the yen's rise as the appropriate way to deal with balance of payment problems. I fully agree with his assessment of professional economist opinion. Anyone who favors a monochromatic view of Japanese opinion, who believes that Japanese differ little in their perceptions, would be rudely shocked to realize how divided Japanese elite and mass opinion is on the issue of yen appreciation.

The Japanese public is alarmed by the rapid shift in the exchange rate and this reaction is politically important and troubling. It would be wrong to dismiss the public view as somehow irrelevant. The public reaction to the recently concluded Tokyo Economic Summit is instructive in this regard. The reaction was more than disappointment that the U.S. did not do anything to try to stop the rise of the yen; it came close to a feeling of betrayal. "We gave Reagan what he wanted in referring to Libya by name in the terrorist statement," many Japanese were saying, "and he gave us nothing back in trying to control the appreciation of the yen." The feeling that Reagan somehow owed it to Japan to do something about the yen, that yen appreciation was yet another example of Japan being victimized by stronger powers, and that the U.S. would respond to the Japanese expectation that it would help protect was very strong. Also

very much a part of the Japanese mood was the conviction that yen appreciation was being used to punish Japanese for working hard, for being productive, and for making high-quality products that Americans want to buy.
Economists have talked about the importance of taking advantage of the "merits"
of yen appreciation, but one does not hear many LDP politicians making this
case. The intense emotional reaction to yen appreciation, and the almost complete absence in the public discussion of it of Japan's responsibilities both for
making it necessary and for dealing with its consequences is troubling. The
public mood in Japan about this issue is, in its own way, as adverse to the smooth
management of the bilateral relationship as is the protectionist and intolerant
mood that is growing in the U.S. Congress.

What I have heard at this conference does not give me confidence that either
side is prepared for the time being to blink first and make policy shifts that
would alleviate some of these pressures. I believe that what we have heard here
accurately reflects the views of decision makers in both countries. But I wonder
whether this is a prudent policy, particularly for Japan. Every policy option
has its downside and its risks. But a policy of sitting tight and waiting until
the storm blows over is perhaps the most risky of all.

Discussion: Session IV

HUGH PATRICK

Professor Nakatani has some comments on some current macroeconomic policy issues in Japan, in light of our discussions these two days.

IWAO NAKATANI:

I am a member of the Forum for Policy Innovation, which is a group of economists and political scientists in Japan. We get together and discuss policy issues fairly frequently. Recently, we announced several policy proposals, which I would like to discuss briefly.

What sort of policies should Japan be pursuing in the short run, given the present situation? In our recommendations, fiscal expansion was declared to be very urgent and necessary for the immediate future for the following reasons. One of the characteristics of the Japanese economy is that while the export sector is fairly competitive, facing fierce worldwide competition, day to day, the import sector in Japan is much less competitive, and more monopolistic in nature. The export sector is now being affected quite severely by the very rapid appreciation of the yen, up to 40 percent. However in the importing sector, because of its monopolistic and price-rigid character, lower import prices due to the appreciation of the yen and the sharp drop in oil prices are not as yet being passed through to the pockets of the consumer. That takes some time. Profits accruing from lower import prices are being kept within the importing institutions, including various governmental agencies and distribution channels, and their propensity to spend is quite low. It means that the benefit of the stronger yen is not yet passed through to the consumer, and consequently purchasing power has not increased as was expected.

What does this all mean? It means that while export industries are hit now, domestic demand is not increasing substantially. So for the immediate future, the Japanese economy will face a situation in which both export and domestic demand do not increase substantially. In this connection the OECD estimate of real growth of domestic demand, which Yoshitomi presented to us yesterday, is apparently a little too optimistic. It says that through 1986 real total domestic demand would grow at a 4¼ percent pace. But the predictions made by various research organizations in Japan are much more pessimistic. Most of their estimates of the growth rate of the Japanese economy for 1986 are in the neighborhood of 2 percent, while the OECD estimate is 3¼ percent. The EPA official, and perhaps wishful, estimate is 4 percent a year.

If the 2 percent growth prediction is more realistic, as I believe, it would mean that the Japanese economy is experiencing the lowest growth rate of the last 12 years. This is certainly below the growth potential of the Japanese economy, and is a bad time for fiscal consolidation as well as for the current-account imbalances between Japan and the United States. By saying this I do not mean that the policy objective of fiscal consolidation should be abandoned altogether. Rather, I take the view that fiscal consolidation is necessary, at least in the long run.

The expansionary measures I have talked about should be taken only for one or two years, because domestic demand will eventually pick up with the consumer demand and sufficient decline in wholesale prices. This scenario is now accepted widely not only by economists but also by many business leaders and political leaders in Japan. Indeed it is most likely that what will happen in the six months to come will follow along the lines of this scenario.

ROBERT DUNCAN:
U.S. Department of State
I would like to make a comment underlining an extremely important point that Professor Curtis made.

I would certainly argee that many of the Congressmen who voted in favor of some of the current protectionist legislation are doing so because they anticipated that the President would veto it. I also agree that most observers feel that there is a lot of partisanship in the recent House action. However, I think Professor Curtis is completely correct; one of the most dangerous things that could happen would be to feel that this is all a Congressional charade and political partisanship, and that if we just wait for the next elections, it will all blow over.

I would give an example which I think illustrates this. Earlier this year, when Paul Wolfowitz, the former Assistant Secretary of State for Far Eastern Affairs, was up for his Senate hearings to go as Ambassador to Indonesia, and the present Assistant Secretary for East Asian Affairs, Gaston Sigur was up at the same time, the atmosphere in the Foreign Relations Committee was very friendly. It was right after the developments in the Philippines, and there were good feelings. After the rather rapid hearings and the positive reaction toward confirmation, Senator Thomas Eagleton turned to Gaston Sigur and said, "Gaston, you know as well as I do that a year from now the figures are going to be far, far worse than they are now. At that time, we will have nothing to do but take drastic action in the form of imposition of quotas or surcharges." Senator Eagleton, in this context, was reflecting the views of Senator Danforth. I highlight the atmosphere in which this was said; I highlight the nature of the individuals, who are not given to public polemics in that context. I think the only rational way to take that is that these Senators sincerely believe what they are saying.

KAZUO UEDA:
I would like to ask two questions, which are fairly naive in political terms, but with important economic significance.

The first question is for Professor Nakatani. He suggested that the Japanese government should expand its fiscal policy for the next couple of years. I wonder what the purpose of the fiscal expansion is? Do we need that to offset the deflationary impact of the yen appreciation, or do we need that to decrease the current-account surplus? Let me then make the question much larger. That is, I think we all learned yesterday that the current-account imbalance problem, especially if you look at the U.S. current-account deficit, is an American problem, not a Japanese problem. That is to say, in order to decrease the size of the U.S. deficit, what has to happen is a decrease in the U.S. budget deficit, or an increase in savings and a decrease in investment in the United States. Any Japanese action would have a very minor impact on the U.S. current account. Then the next question is, why would Americans want the Japanese to expand domestic demand when it has a very small impact on the U.S. current-account deficit? That is my first question.

The second question is a lot more naive. I can't resist the temptation to ask what is wrong with the $100 billion or $150 billion deficit in the U.S. current account? I haven't heard any economic analysis about the sustainability of the U.S. current-account deficit. Is it really unsustainable? Or is it possible for the United States to run that large a deficit for the next two years, or even for five or six years?

NAKATANI:

The purpose of expansionary fiscal policy is primarily due to my recognition that the projected 2 percent growth rate of the Japanese economy is far from its potential. Up to the point where lower import prices are passed on to the consumer, some kind of stimulus seems to be necessary. Also, in the past, when growth rates were higher in Japan, relative to America or Europe, the current-account imbalances tended to be smaller. But when the growth rate of Japan is lower that the United States and Europe, the current-account imbalances tend to be larger. So the gap in the growth rates is a fairly important determinant in current-account imbalances between these nations.

PATRICK:

On your second question: I suppose it was implicit in yesterday morning's discussion, what I might call the conventional view, or at least the Bergsten conventional view, which is that in the long run the rest of the world will not be willing to lend to the United States at the rate of $150 billion a year. Therefore, at some point there will be a loss of confidence in the dollar, and a sharp fall, a hard landing, high interest rates and a recession in the United States. So acting now to avoid a potential crisis in the future is one argument.

I don't think that is what is really pushing Congress at all. Rather, I believe Congress is responding to the fact that there is a lot of unemployment in manufacturing in important states and Congress responds to those interest-group activities. The high dollar value has affected the industrial structure of the United States, tending to shift employment from manufacturing into services. There is some political and perhaps some economic perception that, in the long run, that is not the desirable course for the American economy. Clearly, there is a mixture of political and economic arguments.

I think there has been a general consensus at this conference that a large trade deficit is not sustainable, and not desirable within the American context, and a recognition that it is predominantly an American issue. I think where there has been a clear difference of emotion between Americans and Japanese at this conference, the American perception is that while the U.S. trade deficit is predominantly an American issue, it is also an issue for other countries. The Japanese perception, as Professor Ueda said very clearly, is that it is solely an American issue, and only for the United States to absorb. I think there is an underlying tension in the U.S. that other countries are not helping to resolve the problem of the trade deficit in a constructive way. That is one of the themes that has underlain differences in points of view at this conference.

MINORU MAKIHARA:
Mitsubishi International Corporation

As one who spends half of his time in Washington, D.C., and having returned there after almost 10 years, I wish to say that what Professor Curtis said is exactly what I feel now in Washington. The situation there compared with a few years ago, I think, is worse than one perceives in Japan, worse than one perceives in New York. I feel very pessimistic about it.

I felt even more pessimistic after hearing Professor Curtis's statement, because I thought he might offer some kind of solution. But Professor Curtis recognizes that in Japan there are political circumstances which make it difficult to float the domestic economy. I wondered whether, and this follows Professor Patrick's statement, there is a movement now to move manufacturing facilities into the United States. I was wondering if some sort of orchestrated effort to move manufacturing facilities, or to increase direct Japanese investment (as opposed to portfolio) would make sense?

CURTIS:

I am not entirely certain how a managed Japanese direct investment into the United States is brought about in political terms. I think, obviously there will be greatly increasing Japanese direct investment in the U.S., partly as a function of the appreciation of the yen. This is very desirable in every sense, I believe. One sees American state governors and state representatives in Tokyo competing furiously with each other to try to get Japanese companies to come to their state rather than to go somewhere else. As a general trend, this is highly desirable. There are some risks, I think, of a new kind of *masatsu* or trade frictions; there are risks of frictions over the way in which Japanese or foreign companies may invest, because of the concentration: if it is too concentrated time-wise, or region-wise, or in other ways, it can create some problems. As a general trend, it is very important.

I don't think it is a direct counter to the concerns that Congress expresses about Japanese fiscal policies. As Professor Patrick just said so well, there is a feeling that Japan should do something more to deal with these problems which are, to a much greater extent, American problems. I don't think direct investment counters that; there is no direct trade-off.

So over the long run, direct investment is desirable; in terms of short- to medium-run in the management of political relationships, I don't see that it has that kind of consequence.

PATRICK:
It depends very much on the way in which it is done. If this is perceived as a market response to market forces and market opportunities, it will be welcomed. If this is perceived as a government policy of Japanese investment in the United States, I suspect it will have very adverse political effects because it will be seen as "Japan buying the United States." I would hope, if it is to be encouraged, it will be encouraged privately and delicately, the way things are often done in Japan.

ROBERT INGERSOLL
Consultant
If the Maekawa Report proposals were to be implemented rather quickly, would this have a positive reaction in the United States in terms of solving some of these tensions?

NAKATANI:
I perceive the basic problem in the Japanese economy to be that all sorts of systems, including tax systems, have been discouraging expenditures. So the stimulus to the demand side and the supply side may have to be reversed, and if it is done, particularly through the process of tax reform which has been going on in Japan, I think the situation will improve. But I don't think it is a very easy step politically.

CURTIS:
The answer to your question is a simple "yes;" that is, if it were implemented, it would relieve a lot of the tensions in the relationship.

It seems to me the problem with something like the Maekawa Report, and, in a sense, the problem with the whole series of market-opening packages that have preceded it over the past eight or nine years, is that they build up expectations in the U.S. which are then disappointed. That raises the level of irritation rather than anything else. The Maekawa Report is probably the best-known report written by a Japanese government advisory group, written by any foreign-government advisory group in postwar American history. Why should the Maekawa Report get such attention? Because people thought it would make a difference in Japanese policy. Now when they see that it is not making much of a difference in Japanese policy, it is not unnatural for them to feel as though they were led down the garden path. So there is a problem, I think, with over-selling things to which there is not any follow-through, and underselling things that the Japanese government actually does. I don't know how one changes this balance, but obviously the Japanese government has done a great number of things to try to deal with problems that it has not been very successful in getting Americans to understand. It has gotten Americans to think that they understood something that in fact it wasn't going to do. This is part of the problem.

Concluding Comments

Hugh T. Patrick
Professor and Director, Center on Japanese Economy and Business,
Columbia University

I do not intend to summarize the discussion of this conference; there simply were too many important matters considered. I do not intend even to say many of the things I would like to say. I do want to highlight a few broad concerns.

Clearly one key macroeconomic issue has been the huge and sustained trade imbalances, particularly the immense U.S. global trade and current-account deficits. There was general agreement that these were neither desirable nor sustainable — Mr. Wojnilower was the main dissenter — and that the United States has the main responsibility for solving its balance-of-payments problems. There is a real difference of opinion as to how much Japan can or should do to improve the U.S. balance of payments — to what extent responsibility for solutions rests with Japan and other major countries in addition to the United States.

We have discussed the very large Japanese global trade surplus at some length. I find it interesting that many Americans have moved from saying earlier "deficit countries should be the ones to adjust" to saying "surplus countries should be the ones to adjust." We did not really define very clearly how much of the Japanese surplus is structural; certainly this is an important policy issue. As an aside, my guess is that if the United States had not run a large and increasing trade deficit over the past several years, if the U.S. had a current-account balance of zero, and if Japan, because of its surplus of savings over domestic investment, had been running a current-account surplus of $30 or $40 or $50 billion, then we would all be applauding because those monies would be going to finance the deficits of developing countries, a very desirable outcome. I think much of the American perception that Japan's surpluses are bad is a reflection of our own problems.

Another key issue is that of world growth. This has lain behind our discussion of U.S. growth, Japanese growth, German growth — who should be expanding, who should be taking more leadership. Americans tend to pose these issues in stark terms: either the world economy expands or the United States unilaterally imposes protectionist policies, with all their severe implications for the world-trading system. In reality, we will probably muddle through somewhere in between. Nonetheless, we all — and especially the American participants — expressed real concern that if the rest of the world does not grow

210 | HUGH T. PATRICK

reasonably well in a period in which the U.S. locomotive will be slowing down in terms of its stimulus to the world economy, then serious difficulties may emerge.

I was surprised there was relatively little discussion of the U.S. growth rate. Obviously, considerable concern has been expressed about Japan's prospective growth rate over the next year or two. I sense a great deal of private-sector skepticism, both American and Japanese, about the growth-rate projections by the OECD and particularly by the Japan Economic Planning Agency. The question is: will Japan grow as fast as is projected over the next six months to a year? This has important domestic political implications in Japan, as Professor Curtis pointed out. If the economy should grow through private domestic demand as rapidly as is officially projected, then growth problems and pressures are not serious — at least for a while. If growth slows somewhat but not enough to overcome the domestic political costs of fiscal expansion, then the difficulties may intensify; this is the worst scenario. However, if growth performance is very bad, then it probably will force a major change in domestic fiscal and monetary policy. The Curtis scenario — somewhat slower growth, and a decision to expand domestic demand but probably not in such overt ways as an increase in the central-government budget deficit, the decision being made mainly for domestic-growth rather than balance-of-payments reasons — seems a reasonable projection, and probably will bring about desirable changes.

We have considered U.S., as well as Japanese, macro and fiscal policies at some length. There appears to be general agreement that not only is reduction in the U.S. budget deficit desirable, but that it will occur through Gramm-Rudman and other forces at work. On monetary policy, we had a lovely Alphonse-Gaston dance between the Bank of Japan and the Federal Reserve Board. I suppose the next few weeks or next few months will tell us whether it is a lovely waltz, or a disco, or God-knows-what kind of dance!

The discussion this morning on U.S. and Japanese financial markets was fascinating. There is increasing integration between the U.S. and Japanese financial markets, and that is driving a great deal of change; and provides pressure for further deregulation. At the same time, deregulation itself raises a number of issues of broader social concern. Risk-taking has fundamentally changed. Institutions are able to take on new kinds of risk and greater amounts of risk; new mechanisms of risk-sharing are being developed; perhaps society as a whole is taking on new and increased risks. What is the appropriate regulatory system in such a situation? I think there is a serious moral-hazard issue when banks and others take on excessive risk in the expectation that their government will bail them out; this has not yet been resolved in either country. In Japan, apparently the monetary authorities already perceive this as a potential problem, even though deregulation has proceeded less rapidly. I am not at all confident that in the United States we have the same desire to try to anticipate what may become an important problem and to plan how to deal with it.

The implications for U.S.–Japan economic relations of our respective macroeconomic performances and policies, the exchange rate, and financial-market interactions are broad-ranging and profound. We have considered, in one context or another and to one degree or another, the direct and indirect implications of both macro and financial issues and what might be termed harmonization issues — harmonization of macroeconomic policies, of microeconomic policies, and of institutions. We did not have time to develop these themes fully; after all, it was not the central purpose of the conference.

Obviously the macro and financial side of the relationship is directly important, as our discussion of growth rates, balance of payments, exchange rates, and capital flows have emphasized. It also has important effects on the trade side — on flows of trade in goods and services, bilaterally and globally; on export competitiveness; on import demand; and on the evolution of comparative advantage.

The issue of macroeconomic coordination or surveillance is important. Many expressed the view that such macro-policy harmonization is necessary and desirable — the IMF view. On the other hand Mr. Wojnilower suggested it can be the road to hell if it has a deflationary bias, hell being defined as zero growth. We would have benefited from further discussion of the macro coordination issue. My guess is that most of us feel it is premature to consider seriously; the May 1986 Tokyo Summit may have been a step forward but there is a long way to go. Indeed most of our discussion has been on the harmonization of interest rates, and particularly on the degree to which central bank discount rate changes should be, and will be, coordinated between countries, particularly the U.S. and Japan. Given the immediate financial-market importance of such changes, or even of hints of such changes, our interest in what policymakers and policy influencers have had to say here is not surprising. We raised, without getting clear answers (to no one's surprise), such questions as: to what extent should there be discount-rate leadership, and if so who should take it? Should Japan take the leadership now in an interest-rate reduction? Is it willing to do so? Should the U.S. take that initiative? Unilaterally? Is it willing to?

Clearly market forces are pushing for greater interaction and harmonization between U.S. and Japanese financial markets and associated institutional arrangements. Japan, which remains behind the U.S. in the deregulation process, is well aware of these pressures and has been pursuing policies to promote financial-system harmonization. As Professor Nakatani has stressed, it is more difficult but also very important to seek greater harmonization of the tax systems.

The management of the U.S.—Japan economic relationship is essentially a matter of policy and politics. Complete and sole reliance on the economics of pure, free-market forces in certain major sectors is not politically acceptable in either country. As a representative of the U.S. Office of the Special Trade Representative said last December, in the American perspective the issues of the U.S.—Japan economic relationship are essentially political not economic, and essentially domestic not international. That is also true to a considerable extent in Japan. In the very near term, with the Diet double election being held a month from now, in July 1986 and perhaps for some time thereafter it will be difficult to ascertain what Japanese policymakers are really thinking. We are in an interregnum period. Even so we must look beyond the immediate short run to longer-run prospects and problems for the relationship.

I am somewhat more optimistic than the doom-and-gloom tone which has surfaced here. It is hard to know what the key variables are in increasing or reducing U.S—Japan bilateral tensions; often they are cumulative and interactive. Some are immediate, others are less direct. U.S. domestic economic performance has always been an important variable; when things are going badly we blame Japan, when things are going well, friction subsides considerably. Politically if not economically, the rapidly rising and now immense bilateral trade deficit has been of overwhelming Congressional concern. In my judgment, the bilateral-trade issue will turn around within a year; the numbers are going to go down not up. That will reduce Congressional pressure; the real question is whether the turnaround will occur quickly enough.

Japanese export growth to the U.S. is a significant factor — in terms both of the overall numbers and of the superior competitive performance of Japanese firms in specific major products in the American market. In volume terms, Japanese exports to the U.S. will not increase; indeed they will decline, perhaps substantially. That source of pressure will decrease, and Japanese global export volume will level off and indeed probably decline.

Another policy concern is American access to Japanese markets. The yen appreciation makes American products much more price competitive. However market-access issues may become more severe because the import barriers which impede exporters from the U.S., or Southeast Asia or wherever, will become more obvious and important. Inevitably, since no country pursues completely free-trade policies, market-access issues will always be with us. There will always be problems of barriers to trade in specific goods and services in both countries, but they alone are not the major issue at present and probably can be handled without undermining the overall relationship.

On the other hand the yen-dollar exchange rate is going to become a new source of tension, and one emanating from Japan. This is new because almost all of the tension in the management of the relationship until now has emanated in the United States, in response to Japanese action (and inaction). I anticipate Japanese criticism of U.S. unwillingness to support the yen-dollar exchange rate at a "reasonable" level, i.e., somewhere between 160 and 180 yen to the dollar. I can hear the Japanese message: "Hey, we don't like the way you're doing things, and you're hurting us." This will be new for us, since Americans are so used to telling the Japanese: "Hey, we don't like the way *you're* doing things, and you're hurting *us*." Such messages may not improve the relationship, at least in the short run, because Americans do not respond to criticism very well. While it may temporarily make matters worse, it will change the nature of the forum.

Japan will face continuing foreign pressure to exercise greater leadership as a major economic power. The emphasis on access to the Japanese market will continue, as will emphasis on further expansion of Japan's foreign-aid program.

Probably there will be pressure on Japan to expand its direct role in the financing of developing countries and the management of Third World debt problems. It is likely that Japan's growth performance will become a front-burner issue in the months ahead.

Finally, I thank you for your participation in this conference. We have had a very instructive two days. I personally want to thank all those persons in Japan and the United States who worked so hard behind the scenes to make this conference so substantive and insightful, and to go so well. We were fortunate in assembling a distinguished group of speakers and panelists, and we have maintained a high level of conversation throughout. I thank you for that too.

Conference Speakers and Moderators

C. Fred Bergsten
Director, Institute for International Economics
C. Fred Bergsten is Director of the Institute for International Economics, the only major research institution in the U.S. devoted to international economic issues, monetary and trade topics.

From 1977–81, Bergsten was Assistant Secretary of the Treasury for International Affairs. He was a Senior Fellow at the Brookings Institution from 1972 to 1976 and served as Assistant for International Economic Affairs to Henry Kissinger on the senior staff of the National Security Council, 1969–71. Bergsten has received the Exceptional Service Award of the Treasury Department and the Meritorious Honor Award of the Department of State.

A graduate of Fletcher School of Law and Diplomacy, where he received his M.A., M.A.L.D. and Ph.D. degrees, Bergsten is the author of 15 books and a number of articles on international issues.

Yoshitoki Chino
Chairman, Daiwa Securities
Yoshitoki Chino has been Chairman of Daiwa Securities Co., Ltd. since 1982. In 1946, after receiving his law degree from Keio University, Tokyo, Chino started work for Daiwa. He was named General Manager of the Sales Department and Foreign Department in 1959, Managing Director in 1966, Executive Vice President in 1972 and Vice Chairman in 1980. Chino is also Chairman of the Board of Governors for the Tokyo Stock Exchange and Director of The Securities Dealers Association of Japan. In 1982 he served as Executive Director of the Federation of Economic Organizations.

Richard N. Cooper (Moderator, Session I)
Boas Professor of International Economics, Harvard University
Richard N. Cooper is Boas Professor of International Economics at Harvard University. Cooper is the Chairman of the Executive Panel to Chief of Naval Operations, and is a member of the Trilateral Commission of the Council of Foreign Relations and the Committee for Economic Development.

From 1977–81, Cooper was Under-Secretary for Economic Affairs at the Department of State. Prior to that, he was Altschul Professor of International Economics at Yale University, 1966–77, and the Provost of Yale between 1972 and 1974. During the Kennedy administration, Cooper was a senior staff economist for the Council of Economic Advisors.

Cooper received his A.B. from Oberlin College in 1956, his M.Sc. from the London School of Economics in 1958, and his Ph.D. from Harvard University in 1962.

Gerald L. Curtis
Professor and Director, Toyota Research Program, Columbia University
Gerald L. Curtis is Professor of Political Science and Director of the Toyota Research Program at Columbia University. He was Director of Columbia's East Asian Institute

(1973–81), Director of the U.S.-Japan Parliamentary Exchange Program (1968–78), a Visiting Professor of Political Science at Keio University and a Fellow of The Royal Institute of International Affairs, London.

Curtis received his B.A. from the University of New Mexico in 1962, his M.A. and Ph.D. from Columbia University in 1964 and 1968. He has written extensively on Japanese politics and U.S.-Japan relations and writes a monthly column for the *Chunichi* and *Tokyo Shinbun*.

Rimmer de Vries
Senior Vice President, Morgan Guaranty Trust Company

Rimmer de Vries is Senior Vice President, International Economics of Morgan Guaranty Trust Company, and editor of the Bank's publication, *World Financial Markets*. He joined Morgan Guaranty in 1961, after five years with the Federal Reserve Bank of New York.

De Vries served on President Reagan's Commission on Industrial Competitiveness, 1983–84. He is also a member of the Economic Advisory Board of the U.S. Department of Commerce, a member of the *Time* Board of Economists, the Council on Foreign Relations, and the Advisory Committee of the Institute for International Economics, among others.

De Vries received a B.S. from the Netherlands School of Economics and M.A. and Ph.D. degrees from Ohio State University.

Franklin R. Edwards
Professor and Director of the Center for the Study of Futures Markets,
Graduate School of Business, Columbia University

Franklin R. Edwards is Professor and Director of the Center for the Study of Futures Markets at Columbia University's Graduate School of Business.

Edwards has published over 50 articles on economic and legal aspects of regulation and financial markets. He is associate editor of the *Journal of Futures Markets*.

Edwards received his Ph.D. from Harvard University and his J.D. from New York University.

Toyoo Gyooten
Director General, International Finance Bureau, Japan Ministry of Finance

Toyoo Gyooten joined Japan's Ministry of Finance in 1955 and became Director General of the International Finance Bureau in 1984.

He has held a number of government appointments over the years including Assistant Vice Minister for International Affairs (1979–80). He served from 1964–66 at the Japan Desk of the International Monetary Fund.

Gyooten received his B.A. in Economics from the University of Tokyo, and studied at Princeton University on a Fulbright Scholarship.

Manuel H. Johnson
Member, Board of Governors, Federal Reserve System of the United States

Manuel H. Johnson was sworn in February 1986 to a 14-year term as a Member of the Federal Reserve Board, and was designated as Vice Chairman in May.

Johnson served as Assistant Secretary of the Treasury for Economic Policy from 1982 until 1986, and as Deputy Assistant Secretary, 1981–82. He has served as a consultant to a wide variety of organizations, including the U.S. Congress, trade associations, corporations, law firms, research firms, universities, and policy institutes and foundations.

From 1977 to 1981 Johnson was an Associate Professor of Economics at George Mason University, Fairfax, Virginia. From 1973 to 1977 he was an instructor at Florida State University, where he received an M.S. in Economics in 1974 and a Ph.D. in Economics in 1977. He is author and co-author of four books and has published over fifty articles in academic journals and professional publications.

Toru Kusukawa
Deputy President, Fuji Bank Ltd.

Toru Kusukawa has been Deputy President of Fuji Bank since 1981. He began his career in Fuji Bank's International Division in 1950, and served as chief manager of Fuji's Dusseldorf office from 1966–72, and as chief manager of one of the bank's largest Tokyo branches.

Kusukawa became Deputy President of Fuji Bank in 1981. He served as a member of the Japan Committee for Economic Development and the Committee on Anti-Trust Law of the Tokyo Chamber of Commerce.

He is a graduate in Law from the University of Tokyo.

Ryutaro Komiya
Professor, University of Tokyo

Ryutaro Komiya is Professor of Economics at the University of Tokyo and President of The Japan Association of Theoretical Economics and Econometrics. He has served as Dean of the Faculty of Economics (1979–80), and Deputy President of the University of Tokyo (1981–83).

Komiya was a Research Associate at Harvard and has been Visiting Professor at Stanford. He has written 11 books and many articles in both Japanese and English on the Japanese economy, and issues in international economics and finance.

He received his Ph.D. from the University of Tokyo in 1955.

Roger M. Kubarych (Moderator, Session III)
Senior Vice President and Chief Economist, New York Stock Exchange, Inc.

Roger Kubarych is Senior Vice President and Chief Economist of the New York Stock Exchange. Prior to that, he had a thirteen-year career with the Federal Reserve Bank of New York, where he managed the Bank's foreign exchange operations and later served as Senior Vice President and Deputy Director of Research.

In 1978–79, Kubarych served as Special Assistant to the U.S. Treasury's Under Secretary for Monetary Affairs. More recently, he served as Vice President and Chief Economist of the Conference Board. He is a member of the Council on Foreign Relations.

Kubarych is a graduate of Williams College, Oxford University and Harvard University.

Frederic S. Mishkin
Professor, Graduate School of Business, Columbia University

Frederic S. Mishkin joined the faculty of Columbia's Graduate School of Business in 1983. His research focuses on monetary policy and its impact on financial markets and the aggregate economy. He has published widely in leading economic journals, and is author of *A Rational Expectations Approach to Macroeconometrics* (University of Chicago Press, 1983).

He has taught at the University of Chicago and Northwestern University. He has been associated with the Carnegie-Rochester Conference on Public Policy and the Brookings Panel on Economic Activity, and has been a visiting scholar at the Federal Reserve Board.

He received his Ph.D. from the Massachusetts Institute of Technology.

Iwao Nakatani
Professor, Osaka University

Iwao Nakatani has taught economics at Osaka University since 1974, and was made a full professor in 1984. His research interests are in economic theory and macroeconomics, and he is author of six books and numerous articles on the subject.

A 1965 graduate of Hitotsubashi University, he received both his M.A. and Ph.D. from Harvard University.

Hugh T. Patrick (Moderator, Session IV)
R.D. Calkins Professor of International Business and Director, Center on Japanese Economy and Business, Graduate School of Business, Columbia University

Hugh T. Patrick joined the faculty at Columbia in 1984 as R.D. Calkins Professor of International Business, and was named Director of the Center on Japanese Economy and Business.

Patrick has published numerous books and articles on the Japanese economy. He was a member of the Japan–U.S. Economic Relations Group established by President Carter and Prime Minister Ohira, 1979–81. Among other activities, he is chairman of the Pacific Trade and Development (PAFTAD) conference series, and chairman of the Social Research Council.

Patrick was Professor of Economics at Yale University, 1968–84.

He received his B.A. from Yale, and his M.A. and Ph.D. from the University of Michigan.

Yoshio Suzuki
Director, Institute for Monetary and Economic Studies, Bank of Japan

Yoshio Suzuki became Director of the Institute for Monetary and Economic Studies in 1984. Prior to this, he held several positions with the Bank of Japan, which he joined in 1955. He was Visiting Lecturer at the University of Tokyo and Lecturer at Shinshu University.

The author of books in English and Japanese on monetary policy and banking, Suzuki was awarded the Economist's Prize from the Mainichi Newspaper Company in 1975 and the Nikkei Cultural Prize for economic literature in 1967.

Suzuki received both his B.A. and his Ph.D. in Economics from the University of Tokyo.

Ryuichiro Tachi
President, Institute of Fiscal and Monetary Policy, Japan Ministry of Finance

Ryuichiro Tachi is President of the Institute of Fiscal and Monetary Policy at the Japan Ministry of Finance. He is also Professor of International Politics and Economics, Aoyama Gakuin University, and Professor Emeritus of the University of Tokyo.

Tachi taught economics at the University of Tokyo from 1961 to 1982, serving as Dean of the Faculty of Economics in 1972, and Vice President of the University of Tokyo, 1979–81.

He received his B.A. in Economics from the University of Tokyo.

James Tobin (Moderator, Session III)
Sterling Professor of Economics, Yale University

James Tobin is Sterling Professor of Economics at Yale, where he has been on the faculty since 1950. He has served as a Member of President Kennedy's Council of Economic Advisors, and as consultant to the Federal Reserve System, the U.S. Treasury, and other government agencies.

In 1981 he received the Nobel Prize in Economic Science.

Tobin is author or editor of eleven books and more than two hundred articles. His research interests include macroeconomics, monetary theory and policy, fiscal policy and public finance, consumption and saving, unemployment and inflation, portfolio theory and asset markets, and econometrics.

Since 1955 he has been a member of the research staff of the Cowles Foundation for Research in Economics at Yale and has served as the Foundation's director.

Tobin received his B.A. and Ph.D. from Harvard University.

Kazuo Ueda
Senior Economist, Institute of Fiscal and Monetary Policy, Japan Ministry of Finance

Kazuo Ueda became Senior Economist for the Institute of Fiscal and Monetary Policy, Japan Ministry of Finance in 1985, on leave from Osaka University where he has been an Associate Professor of Economics since 1982. He was an Assistant Professor at the University of British Columbia (1980–82).

Ueda has published papers in English on monetary economics, macroeconomics and international finance.

A 1974 graduate of the University of Tokyo, Ueda received his Ph.D. in Economics from the Massachusetts Institute of Technology in 1980.

Frederick B. Whittemore
Managing Director, Morgan Stanley & Co., Inc.

Frederick B. Whittemore is a Managing Director of Morgan Stanley.

He has served as Vice Chairman of the American Stock Exchange.

He also served as International President of the Pacific Basin Economic Council in 1984, and is a member of the Council on Foreign Relations. He is on the board of several educational institutions.

He has an A.B. and an M.B.A. from Dartmouth College.

Albert M. Wojnilower
Managing Director, The First Boston Corporation

Albert M. Wojnilower has been with The First Boston Corporation since 1964, and was appointed Managing Director and Chief Economist of this international banking firm in 1978. He has specialized in foreign countries, U.S. business conditions, monetary economics, and Federal Reserve open-market operations.

Prior to joining First Boston, Wojnilower was an economist for First National City

Bank (1963–64) and for the Federal Reserve Bank of New York (1951–53), where he became Chief of the Financial Statistics and Domestic Research Divisions.

Wojnilower received his Ph.D. from Columbia University.

Masaru Yoshitomi
Director, Economics and Statistics Department, Organization for Economic Cooperation and Development

Masaru Yoshitomi is Director of the Economics and Statistics Department of the Organization for Economic Cooperation and Development (OECD). Previously, he was Deputy-Director General and Chief Economist of the Economic Research Institute at the Japanese Economic Planning Agency, and Lecturer at the University of Tokyo.

Yoshitomi has published on topics relating to the U.S., Japanese and Pacific Basin economies.

He received his B.A. and Ph.D. from the University of Tokyo.

Conference Participants

Senji Adachi
Director, Dai-ichi Kangyo Bank, Ltd.
Tokyo, Japan

Fanueil Adams
Executive-in-Residence, Graduate School of Business, Columbia University
New York, New York

Michael Adler
Professor, Graduate School of Business, Columbia University
New York, New York

Youichi Aoki
Manager, American Honda Motor Co., Inc.
New York, New York

Robert E. Armstrong
Vice President and Executive Director, The Henry Luce Foundation
New York, New York

Haresh Balani
W.I. Carr (America), Ltd.
New York, New York

Dimitri Balatsos
Director, Global Investment Strategy, Kidder, Peabody & Company
New York, New York

John Baldwin
Jardine Fleming (Securities) Ltd., Tokyo Branch
Tokyo, Japan

Wayne Barnstone
Investment Officer, Asia and Pacific Region, American International Group
New York, New York

C. Fred Bergsten
Director, Institute for International Economics
Washington, D.C.

Lawrence Bruser
Assistant General Manager, Mitsui and Company, U.S.A., Inc.
New York, New York

John C. Burton
Dean and Arthur Young Professor of Accounting and Finance,
Graduate School of Business, Columbia University
New York, New York

Owen Butler
Vice Chairman, Committee for Economic Development
New York, New York

Tom Caddigan
Director of Treasury Operations, IBM World Trade Far East/Americas
North Tarrytown, New York

Steven Chen
Associate Attorney, Simpson Thacher & Bartlett
New York, New York

Yoshitoki Chino
Chairman, Daiwa Securities Company, Ltd.
Tokyo, Japan

Robert Cohen
Assistant Vice President, Drexel Burnham and Lambert
New York, New York

Kay Ellen Consolver
International Treasurer, Marketing and Refining, Mobil Oil Corporation
New York, New York

Richard Cooper
Professor, Department of Economics, Harvard University
Cambridge, Massachusetts

Patrick Corcoran
Vice President, Economics, Prudential Insurance Company
Newark, New Jersey

Ben Crain
Staff Director, Subcommittee on International Finance, House Banking
Committee, U.S. House of Representatives
Washington, D.C.

Gerald Curtis
Professor, Department of Political Science, Columbia University
New York, New York

Masako Darrough
Assistant Professor, Graduate School of Business, Columbia University
New York, New York

Catherine Davidson
Managing Editor, Graduate School of Business, Columbia University
New York, New York

Lisa Skoog de Lamas
Policy Analyst, International Corporate Affairs, American Express
New York, New York

Rimmer de Vries
Senior Vice President, Morgan Guaranty Trust Company
New York, New York

Elisabeta DiCagno
Associate Director, Publications, Graduate School of Business, Columbia University
New York

Robert Dillon
Associate Director, Development, Corporate Affairs, Graduate School of Business, Columbia University
New York, New York

Robert Duncan
Director, Office of Economic Policy, Bureau of East Asian and Pacific Affairs, U.S. Department of State
Washington, D.C.

Franklin R. Edwards
Professor and Director, Center for the Study of Futures Markets, Graduate School of Business, Columbia University
New York, New York

Mort Epstein
Director, Multinational Programs, Northern Telecom, Inc.
New York, New York

Jeffrey Frankel
Professor, Department of Economics, University of California at Berkeley
Berkeley, California

Jacob Frenkel
Professor, Department of Economics, University of Chicago
Chicago, Illinois

Yooichi Funabashi
Staff Writer, Asahi Shimbun
Washington, D.C.

Mariko Fujii
Senior Economist, Institute of Fiscal and Monetary Policy,
Ministry of Finance
Tokyo, Japan

Kimitake Fujino
Executive Director, International Monetary Fund
Washington, D.C.

Toshihiko Fujita
Deputy Consul, Consulate General of Japan
New York, New York

John W. Georgas
Senior Vice President, The Coca-Cola Company
Atlanta, Georgia

Toyoo Gyooten
Director General, International Finance Bureau, Ministry of Finance
Tokyo, Japan

Jeffrey Hanna
Economist and Senior Vice President, Salomon Brothers, Inc.
New York, New York

Kazuaki Harada
Director, The Sanwa Bank Ltd.
Tokyo, Japan

Yoshio Higuchi
Visiting Professor, Department of Economics, Columbia University
New York, New York

Kouji Hirao
General Manager, New York Branch, The Long-Term Credit Bank
of Japan, Ltd.
New York, New York

Robert Hirst
Capital Markets/Swaps Group, Bear, Stearns and Company
New York, New York

Makoto Hosomi
Consul, Consulate General of Japan
New York, New York

Minoru Imai
Director and General Manager, New York Agency, The Fuji Bank, Ltd.
New York, New York

Robert Ingersoll
Consultant
Chicago, Illinois

Takuro Isoda
Chairman, Daiwa Securities America, Inc.,
New York, New York

Jeri Jensen
Economic Advisor, Office of the Chairwoman, International Trade Commission
Washington, D.C.

Manuel H. Johnson
Vice-Chairman Designate, Board of Governors, Federal Reserve System of the United States
Washington, D.C.

Takashi Kagawa
Chairman and President, The Tokio Marine Management
New York, New York

Hiroyuki Kasai
Chief Economist, New York Agency, The Bank of Tokyo, Ltd.
New York, New York

Tetsuo Kasuya
General Manager, Corporate Planning Division,
Sumitomo Corporation of America
New York, New York

Kenichi Kato
General Manager, United States Office, Toyota Motor Corporation
New York, New York

Yasuo Kazahaya
Treasurer, Suntory International
New York, New York

David Klock
Deputy Director, Office of Industrial Nations and Global Analysis,
U.S. Department of the Treasury
Washington, D.C.

Ryutaro Komiya
Professor, Faculty of Economics, University of Tokyo
Tokyo, Japan

Takehiko Kondo
Assistant Vice Minister of Finance for International Affairs,
Ministry of Finance
Tokyo, Japan

Douglas Kruse
Vice President, International Strategy and Marketing, Merrill Lynch & Co.
New York, New York

Roger Kubarych
Senior Vice President and Chief Economist, The New York Stock Exchange
New York, New York

Masatoshi Kuratani
Deputy Consul General, Consulate General of Japan
New York, New York

Motoo Kusakabe
Chief Economist, Institute of Fiscal and Monetary Policy, Ministry of
Finance
Tokyo, Japan

Toru Kusukawa
Deputy President, The Fuji Bank, Ltd.
Tokyo, Japan

Patricia Kuwayama
Assistant Vice President, Foreign Exchange, Federal Reserve Bank
of New York
New York, New York

John D. Langlois
Vice President, Asia Division, Morgan Guaranty Trust Company
New York, New York

Lawrence J. Lanza
Assistant Director, Treasurer Asia Pacific, Westinghouse Electric
Corporation
Pittsburgh, Pennsylvania

Melanie Lau
Vice President, Economics Group, The Chase Manhattan Bank, N.A.
New York, New York

Noah Levy
Economic Analyst, Mitsui and Company, U.S.A., Inc.
New York, New York

Robert Liberatore
Director, Federal Policy and Legislative Affairs, The Chrysler Corporation
Washington, D.C.

Edward Lincoln
Senior Economist, The Brookings Institution
Washington, D.C.

Kevin Logan
Vice President, Citicorp Investment Bank
New York, New York

Bonnie E. Loopesko
Division of International Finance, Federal Reserve Board
Washington, D.C.

David MacEachron
President, The Japan Society, Inc.
New York, New York

Minoru Makihara
Executive Vice President, Mitsubishi International Corporation
New York, New York

Shigetaka Matoba
General Manager, Nippon Credit Bank
New York, New York

Hiroshi Matsuzaki
Audit Manager, Arthur Andersen and Company
New York, New York

Claudette Mayer
*Vice President and Manager, Foreign Financial Institutions Division,
The Mellon Bank*
New York, New York

Charles G. Meyer
*Business Planner, Public Policy Issues, Corporate Strategies Staff,
The Ford Motor Company*
Dearborn, Michigan

Ken H. Militzer
Chief Economist, AT&T
New Brunswick, New Jersey

Richard Miller
Partner, Simpson Thacher & Bartlett
New York, New York

Tsutomu Mishina
Manager, Planning Department, NEC Corporation
Tokyo, Japan

Frederic Mishkin
Professor, Graduate School of Business, Columbia University
New York, New York

Hideki Mitani
Vice President, International Investment Banking, Goldman, Sachs & Company
New York, New York

Koichi Mizuno
President, Dentsu, Inc.
New York, New York

Toshihide Mizuno
Manager and Economist, New York Branch, The Sanwa Bank, Ltd.
New York, New York

Akihiko Morita
Economic Correspondent, Mainichi Shimbun
Washington, D.C.

Hiromi Murai
Consul, Consulate General of Japan
New York, New York

Thomas Murray
Assistant Staff Coordinator, Affiliate Analysis, Texaco Corporation
White Plains, New York

Yuichiro Nagatomi
Councilor, Minister's Secretariat, Ministry of Finance
Tokyo, Japan

Takeshi Naito
Managing Director, Yamaichi International America, Inc.
New York, New York

Sam I. Nakagama
Planning Manager, Managing Director and Chief Economist, Nakagama and Wallace, Inc.
New York, New York

Masato Nakamura
Foundation for Advanced Information and Research, Japan
Tokyo, Japan

Toru Nakamura
Nakagama and Wallace, Inc.
New York, New York

Yoshikatsu Nakashima
Assistant Manager, New York Branch, The Daiwa Bank, Ltd.
New York, New York

Iwao Nakatani
Professor, Faculty of Economics, Osaka University
Osaka, Japan

Akira Nambara
Chief Representative, New York Representative Office, Bank of Japan
New York, New York

Katsuyoshi Narumiya
Economist, New York Branch, The Tokai Bank, Ltd.
New York, New York

Hiroshi Nishiki
General Manager, New York Branch, The Mitsui Trust and Banking Company, Ltd.
New York, New York

Hidefumi Nishizato
Associate, Smith Barney, Harris Upham International, Smith Barney, Harris Upham and Co.
New York, New York

Kozo Nogami
General Manager, New York Representative Office, Nippon Life Insurance Company
New York, New York

Jim O'Neill
Economist, Capital Markets Group, Marine Midland Bank, N.A.
New York, New York

Toshiharu Okubo
General Manager, New York Branch, The Bank of Yokohama, Ltd.
New York, New York

Toshio Osu
Minister, Embassy of Japan
Washington, D.C.

Robert Pachlofer
Associate Market Planner, AT & T Technologies
Jamesburg, New Jersey

Patrick Paradiso
Merrill Lynch Capital Markets
New York, New York

Hugh T. Patrick
Professor and Director, Center on Japanese Economy and Business,
Graduate School of Business, Columbia University
New York, New York

Richard L. Perman
International Treasurer, Estee Lauder, Inc.
New York, New York

Richard Petree
President, United States-Japan Foundation
New York, New York

Gerald Pollack
Coordinator, Financial Economics, Exxon Corporation
New York, New York

Clyde Prestowitz
Fellow, Woodrow Wilson Center
Washington, D.C.

Alicia Ralske
Staff, Center on Japanese Economy and Business, Graduate School of
Business, Columbia University
New York, New York

David Ressler
Chief Economist, Nomura Securities International, Inc.
New York, New York

Yul J. Rhee
Vice President, Equitable Life Assurance Society
New York, New York

Mary Ann Richardson
Policy Analyst, House Banking Committee, U.S. House of Representatives
Washington, D.C.

Stefan Robock
R.D. Calkins Professor Emeritus of International Business,
Graduate School of Business, Columbia University
New York, New York

Hobart Rowan
Associate Editor, Economics, The Washington Post
Washington, D.C.

Leonard Santos
Staff, Senate Finance Committee
Washington, D.C.

Nick Sargeant
Salomon Brothers
New York, New York

Dale Sarro
Associate Attorney, Simpson Thacher & Bartlett
New York, New York

Kazuo Sato
*Professor, East Asian Institute, School of International and Public Affairs,
Columbia University*
New York, New York

Yoshiyasu Sato
Minister, Embassy of Japan
Washington, D.C.

Tim Schilt
Research, Japanese Investment Division, Morgan Stanley and Company
New York, New York

Kim Schoenholtz
Salomon Brothers
New York, New York

Michihiro Sekiya
*General Manager, New York Branch,
The Mitsubishi Trust & Banking Corporation*
New York, New York

Jean-Pierre Sevos
First Vice President, Paine Webber International, Inc.
New York, New York

Joanna Shelton
*Professional Staff, Committee on Trade, Committee on Ways and Means,
U.S. House of Representatives*
Washington, D.C.

Kanji Shibata
Bureau Chief, New York, Mainichi Shimbun
Washington, D.C.

Naoyuki Shinohara
Representative, Japan Center for International Finance
Washington, D.C.

Shinichi Shirai
Executive Vice President, Nissho Iwai American Corporation
New York, New York

W. Edward Singletary
Assistant Director, Center for Telecommunications & Information Studies,
Graduate School of Business, Columbia University
New York, New York

Lindley Sloan
President, Japan-U.S. Friendship Commission
Washington, D.C.

Gary Smeal
Vice President, Chemical Bank
New York, New York

Laurie Strachan
Staff, Center on Japanese Economy and Business, Graduate School of
Business, Columbia University
New York, New York

Katsuhiko Sugimura
President and Chief Executive Officer, The Yasuda Fire and Marine
Insurance Company of America
New York, New York

Osamu Suguro
Vice President and Treasurer, Toray Industries America, Inc.
New York, New York

Eiji Sumino
Vice President, Sumitomo Bank
New York, New York

Lawrence Summers
Professor, Department of Economics, Harvard University
Cambridge, Massachusetts

Peter Sura
Senior Vice President, Manufacturers Hanover Trust
New York, New York

Masatoshi Suzuki
Nihon Keizai Shimbun
New York, New York

Takashi Suzuki
General Manager, New York Representative Office,
The Nikko Research Center, Ltd.
New York, New York

Yoshio Suzuki
Director, Institute for Monetary and Economic Studies, The Bank of Japan
Tokyo, Japan

Ryuichiro Tachi
President, Institute of Fiscal and Monetary Policy, Ministry of Finance
Tokyo, Japan

Masaru Takagi
Senior Economist, New York Agency, The Fuji Bank, Ltd.
New York, New York

Akitoshi Takatsuki
Economist, New York Branch, The Mitsui Bank, Ltd.
New York, New York

Rudy Tanaka
Vice President, Asia-Pacific Division, American Express International
New York, New York

Yoshio Tanikawa
Assistant General Manager, Raw Materials, Nippon Steel, USA
New York, New York

Sadao Taura
President, Sumitomo Corporation of America
New York, New York

Teizo Taya
Assistant General Manager, Economic Research Department,
Daiwa Securities Research Institute
Tokyo, Japan

James Tobin
Sterling Professor of Economics, Yale University
New Haven, Connecticut

Thomas Trebat
Vice President, Bankers Trust Company
New York, New York

Edwin Truman
Director, Division of International Finance, Federal Reserve Board
Washington, D.C.

Kazuo Ueda
Senior Economist, Institute of Fiscal and Monetary Policy,
Ministry of Finance
Tokyo, Japan

Masayasu Ueno
Senior Deputy Manager, New York Branch, The Sumitomo Bank, Ltd.
New York, New York

Hidetoshi Ukawa
Ambassador, Consulate General of Japan
New York, New York

Robert Uriu
*Conference Coordinator, Center on Japanese Economy and Business,
Graduate School of Business, Columbia University*
New York, New York

Haruhiko Wakatsuki
*Deputy General Manager, New York Branch, The Industrial Bank of
Japan, Ltd.*
New York, New York

John Wheeler
Vice President, The Japan Society, Inc.
New York, New York

Frederick Whittemore
Managing Director, Morgan Stanley & Company
New York, New York

Maurice Wilkinson
Professor, Graduate School of Business, Columbia University
New York, New York

John Oliver Wilson
Senior Vice President, Economics Department, Bank of America
San Francisco, California

Albert Wojnilower
Chief Economist and Managing Director, The First Boston Corporation
New York, New York

Takehiko Yamamoto
Director, NEC America, Inc.
New York, New York

Hiroshi Yamashita
Vice President, Information Systems International, Honeywell, Inc.
Minneapolis, Minnesota

Ken Yanaihara
Vice President, The Mellon Bank
New York, New York

Shiro Yasuno
President, Suntory International Corp.
New York, New York

Shunroku Yokosuka
General Manager, New York Branch, The Toyo Trust and Banking Company, Ltd.
New York, New York

Haruo Yoshida
Vice President Japanese Financial Institutions, Continental Bank International
New York, New York

Minoru Yoshida
Representative, New York Office, Dai-ichi Mutual Life Insurance Company
New York, New York

Taroichi Yoshida
President, Foundation for Advanced Information Research, Japan
Tokyo, Japan

Masaru Yoshitomi
Director, Department of Economics and Statistics, Organization for Economic Cooperation and Development
Paris, France

332.042
J271

120952